Michigan

A Field Guide to State History

Michigan

A Field Guide to State History

JAN LEIBOVITZ ALLOY

PRC

Produced in 2005 by
PRC Publishing
The Chrysalis Building
Bramley Road, London W10 6SP
An imprint of **Chrysalis** Books Group plc

ISBN 1 85648 730 X

Printed and bound in Malaysia

Contents

Introduction

Chief Tecumseh helped the British capture Detroit in the War of 1812. He was killed in battle in 1813.

With its 58,527 square miles of land, Michigan is the 23rd largest U.S. state. If you were to include its 97,102 square miles of **Great Lakes** it would be the 10th largest. According to the 2000 census, the 9,938,444 **Michiganders** make this the eighth most populated state. **Lansing** is the capital city.

Located in the north central portion of the United States, Michigan is bordered by Canada, Wisconsin, Indiana, and Ohio and surrounded by four of the five Great Lakes: Erie, Huron, Michigan, and Superior. Michigan is easily recognized on a map because its shape resembles a right-hand **mitten**.

Michigan has the distinction of being the only continental state divided into two big land portions. One runs 300 miles north to south; the other runs 300 miles east to west. The **Upper Peninsula** in the northern part of the state runs eastward from northern Wisconsin between Lake Superior and Lake Michigan. The Lower Peninsula, in the southern part of the state, reaches north from Indiana and Ohio.

Michigan enjoys the longest freshwater shoreline in the world—3,288 miles to be exact. Naturally separated by the Straits of Mackinac, the narrow passage that joins Lake Michigan and Lake Huron, the peninsulas were connected in 1957 by Big Mac, the five-mile long **Mackinac Bridge** spanning the Straits of Mackinac. Lake Huron and Lake Erie separate the Lower Peninsula from Canada.

In the western part of the Upper Peninsula is the Superior Upland, a rugged area filled with hills and forests. Volcanic activity and erosion produced the Porcupine and Huron mountain

Calumet Hecla and Red Jacket, Michigan, shown in an illustration from 1881. The population at this time was 7,500.

ranges, the only mountain ranges between the Allegheny Mountains and the Rocky Mountains. There are 19.3 million acres of forest in Michigan. In other words, nearly 50 percent of the land in the state is covered with trees. Two-thirds of those trees are birch, aspen, and oak, though the official **state tree** is the white pine. Michigan has the fifth largest timberland acreage in the United States. Today, the lumber industry contributes more than $12 billion annually to the state's economy.

Water abounds in the state. Regardless of where a person stands in Michigan, he or she is not more than six miles from a lake or river, and not more than 85 miles from one of the

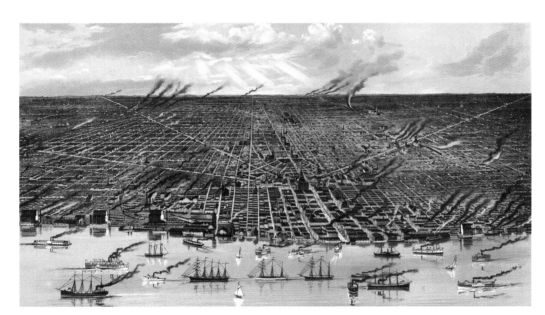

*A bird's eye view of Detroit
from 1889*

*Arch Rock, Mackinac Island,
Michigan*

Great Lakes. Not only are there 40,000 square miles of Great Lakes inside Michigan's borders, but there are 11,000 inland lakes and 36,350 miles of river. Additionally, there are more than 150 waterfalls just in the Upper Peninsula. **Pictured Rocks National Lakeshore**, sandstone cliffs created by glaciers, is also in this region.

With so much water, it comes as no surprise how Michigan got its name. Michigan is derived from the Chippewa word *michi-gama*, which roughly translated means "great waters."

The Early Days

Variously nicknamed the Great Lakes State, Water Wonderland, and Winter Wonderland, Michigan was formed by the glaciers' demise at the end of the Ice Age. As temperatures rose and the ice melted, hunters crossed the Bering Straits between Asia and North America and began hunting the mastodons and wooly mammoths that roamed the area. Early inhabitants fished and ate the berries and wild rice

that grew all around. Some believe people inhabited the region as long ago as 1000 BC and may have mined copper to make the first metal tools and weapons.

By 500 BC, more people found their way to this land of water and forests. The **Native Americans** who settled here, particularly the Hopewell, found the lush and fertile Michigan land perfect for hunting and dwelling. Although a variety of groups of Native

Michigan's fertile lands and abundant resources enticed Native Americans to settle in the region. This picture was taken on Mackinac Island in 1903.

The Upper Peninsula, rich in natural resources, is more than 90 percent forested.

Americans lived in the area, Michigan became home to three main tribes known as the People of the Fires: Ojibwe (Chippewa), Ottawa, and Potawatomi. These natives hunted, fished, trapped, and grew corn, beans, and squash. The Huron (Wyandot) and Miami tribes also inhabited the state.

These tribes lived here more than 2,000 years ago, long before the first Europeans made their way to the Michigan shores. There are a number of myths and legends about Michigan rooted in Native American folklore, such as the tale of how **Sleeping Bear Dunes National Lakeshore** was formed. According to the legend, a mother bear and her two cubs swam across Lake Michigan to flee a forest fire. She made it to shore, but her cubs did not. While she waited at the top of a hill for her cubs to appear, she was covered with sand and turned into a dune. The cubs became the North and South Manitou Islands.

Explorations

French **explorers** were the first Europeans to come to Michigan. In 1618, Samuel de Champlain, governor of New France, as Canada was called then, sent explorer **Étienne Brûlé** to find the much-talked-about Northwest Passage, the trade route to China or India. Brûlé and his companion, Grenoble, landed in the eastern part of the Upper Peninsula. They are credited with being the first white men to see Lake Superior.

Brûlé is believed to have lived among the Algonquin Indians for a year to learn their language. He then became a self-appointed interpreter between the French and various tribes, including the Hurons. Although the details of his death are unsubstantiated, several accounts maintain he was killed and eaten by the Hurons, the tribe that adopted him. Huron lore forever more proclaimed a lingering curse related to his untimely murder.

Soon after Brûlé's unsuccessful attempts to find the elusive passage, Gov. Champlain sent another French explorer to the area. **Jean Nicolet** sailed through the Straits of Mackinac, putting him in Lake Michigan. He landed near Green Bay, Wisconsin. Neither Brûlé nor Nicolet were able to discover a route to China, but they were elated to discover animals such as beaver, mink, and fox. These animals had fur skins that were greatly desired for making hats and clothing.

Wildlife has always thrived in this area. An abundance of big game, small game, fish, and fowl continues to populate Michigan. Among the large animals are white-tailed deer and black bears, moose, timber wolves, bobcats, and red foxes. Smaller Michigan denizens include rabbits, squirrels, opossums, mink, otters, muskrats, skunks, and porcupines. In addition, the Great Lakes State boasts 351 species of birds, including game fowl partridge, ring-neck peasant, and sharptail goose, as well as many ducks, geese, and loons. Then there are nongame birds such as the Jackpine, Kirkland warbler, and the legislatively recognized **state bird**, the red-breasted robin.

If there is a heaven on earth for fishermen, it must be Michigan. With all its lakes and streams, it is not surprising to know there are 149 types of native fish in those waters. Of that number, 25 species are game fish. Whitefish and lake trout were caught and eaten by the Native Americans. While the brook trout is the recognized **state fish**, some of the most popular today are rainbow and brown trout, coho and Chinook salmon.

In the 1660s, the quest for pelts led to the establishment of trading posts up and down the Great Lakes. This in turn prompted missionary priests to go forth and preach Christianity to the Native Americans. The missionaries traveled with *voyageurs*, French-Canadian trappers and hunters. In 1660, René Ménard established a Jesuit mission at Keweenaw Bay on the Upper Peninsula.

But it was another Jesuit missionary, **Father Jacques Marquette**, who founded the state's

Indian peoples inhabited Michigan for 2,000 years before the arrival of European explorers. This picture depicts George Armstrong Custer during the Wilderness and Shenandoah campaigns.

first permanent settlement, Sault Ste. Marie, in 1668. Just three years later, in 1671, he also founded **St. Ignace Mission** on the north shore of the Straits of Mackinac. It was Marquette and Canadian adventurer **Louis Jolliet** who explored the upper Mississippi River and recorded the first accurate data about the river's course. One of the most interesting historic stories recounts Marquette and Jolliet's perilous journey through this section of the New World.

In the 1700s, the French explored and claimed much of the Michigan territory, establishing forts, trading posts, and missions. Convinced Michigan would make a perfect place to settle, and to protect the fur trade, French nobleman **Antoine de la Mothe Cadillac** and his lieutenant, Alphonse de Tonty, founded a trading post on the **Detroit River** in 1701. Called Fort Pontchartrain and later La Ville d'Etroit, it was renamed **Detroit** in 1751. A second French post at the Straits of Mackinac, **Fort Michilimackinac**, was established in 1715.

Both forts became valuable military strongholds for the French.

Enterprising British explorers saw the possible profits in fur trapping and trading and wanted their fair share. During the 1700s and the beginning of the 1800s, the British, French, and Native Americans competed vigorously for trading rights and control of the forts. This animosity eventually erupted into the French and Indian War (1754–1763). Forced to choose sides, the Native Americans joined the French, but it was not enough to overcome the British. By 1763, the British had successfully gained control of North America east of the Mississippi River, which included Michigan.

But the Native Americans were unhappy about being driven out of their lands by the British. Ottawa Chief **Pontiac** galvanized the tribes to join forces and attack three major forts: Machilimackinac, in the north; St. Joseph, in the west; and Detroit, in the southeast. Despite holding Detroit under siege for 135 days and killing many British soldiers, Pontiac's

Rebellion was not successful and Britain regained control of all the forts and, inevitably, the **fur trading** business. Britain maintained its rule over the forts in Michigan, even after the American Revolution, until 1796, when the United States army finally forced the British out of Michigan.

Approaching Statehood

After the Revolutionary War, the upper Midwestern states of Michigan, Ohio, Indiana, Illinois, Wisconsin, and parts of eastern Minnesota were lumped together and called the Northwest Territory. Michigan was included in the Northwest Territory in 1787. The territory's governor was unable to prevent the Indian attacks, so President George Washington assigned Gen. Anthony ("Mad Anthony") Wayne the task of quelling the uprisings. Finally, following the battle of Fallen Timbers, peace was achieved between the Native Americans and the settlers. Because of Wayne's success, and to honor him, the Michigan portion of the Northwest Territory was named Wayne County.

For a short period of time, beginning in 1803, Michigan was declared a part of the Indiana Territory by the United States Congress. Then, in 1805, Congress established the Michigan Territory, once again shifting boundaries and including the Lower Peninsula and eastern segments of the Upper Peninsula. Detroit was selected as the seat of government and later destroyed by fire. Also at this time, **William Hull** was appointed as governor.

Further problems ensued when another conflict arose between the United States and Great Britain in the **War of 1812**. United States troops surrendered Detroit and **Fort Mackinac** in a bloody battle; however, Americans reclaimed Detroit the following year.

As more settlers streamed into Michigan, they forced the Native Americans out of their living space. A series of treaties was signed with the Native Americans in 1819. In these

formal agreements, the United States promised money in exchange for some of the land. Additionally, the Indians maintained their rights to hunt and fish on the land. Americans often broke the treaties and took land that belonged to the Indians. By the mid-1800s, the majority of the Native Americans who had first populated Michigan were living on reservations.

Michigan experienced a surge in population when the **Erie Canal** opened in New York in 1825. The canal connected the Great Lakes and the Atlantic Ocean and made travel between the eastern and western states much faster. According to the **Northwest Ordinance**, regions within the Northwest Territory with at least 60,000 could apply for statehood. The increased number of residents gave Michigan the right to apply. In 1835, the first **constitutional convention** was held and it was decided to make Detroit the state capital. The Michigan territory also enacted its first constitution that same year.

But there was an obstacle in the way of gaining the much-desired statehood: clearly established borders. Imprecise land surveys conducted in the early 1800s showed the southern tip of Lake Michigan in two different locations. A boundary set by Ohio delegates showed a line that fell south of the Maumee River mouth. Ultimately, the disagreement concerned a strip of land at the mouth of the Maumee River called the Toledo Strip. A dispute known as the **Toledo War** ended when Congress gave Toledo to Ohio and the Upper Peninsula to Michigan. Michigan gained another nickname, the Wolverine State, because of this war. Angry Ohioans likened Michiganders to the ugly wild creatures, and the name stuck.

The resolution of the Toledo War allowed Michigan to pursue statehood. On January 26, 1837, President Andrew Jackson signed the bill that officially admitted Michigan to the United States as the 26th state in the union.

Once statehood was achieved, Michigan's growth increased at a rapid rate. When the

Carlton's map of Michigan, showing the Toledo, Ann Arbor & North Michigan Railway

Toledo War was resolved, no one realized the wealth of the resources in the Upper Peninsula. In 1841, Michigan geologist **Douglass Houghton** discovered copper on Keweenaw Peninsula.

Houghton County, organized in 1848, was named after Houghton, who confirmed the existence of copper in the Keweenaw Peninsula. Houghton, a graduate of Rensselaer (Polytechnic Institute), was a geologist, chemist, and medical doctor. Named Michigan's first state geologist, he discovered the Saginaw Valley salt beds and, more important, copper. While working on a complete survey of

Michigan's wild lands, approved by Congress, he drowned in a storm on Lake Superior.

Houghton's report to the state legislature about the copper led to a mining rush, but the area also offered iron ore and timber. Copper was valuable because in the 1800s, items such as pots, pans, coins, roof material, ship bottoms, and gun metal were made from the metal. With **Thomas Edison**'s invention of the light bulb, copper's value increased even more, since copper conducts electricity. Fifty percent of the copper mined in Michigan in the 1870s was used in the electrical industry.

Mining was profitable for the state, but getting the iron ore to iron and steel centers located along the Great Lakes presented a problem. The St. Mary's River, the only waterway used for shipping, could not accommodate boats. To help ships easily go up and down the river, the State Lock, a passageway that raised and lowered water levels, was built in 1835. This method was so successful that the United States built and operated the **Soo Locks**.

The seat of state government was moved from Detroit to **Lansing** in 1847, mainly because Lansing was located more closely to the center of Michigan. Michigan was a prosperous state, and business grew in all areas as better roads were built and railroad lines were laid. The first railroad in Michigan, the Erie and **Kalamazoo**, was built between Toledo and Adrian in 1836. Despite the growth and prosperity the state was enjoying, as in the rest of the country, the slavery issue posed problems for everyone. Michigan was a free state and strongly opposed to slavery.

The War Years

Many settlers in Michigan were abolitionists. Prior to the war, many citizens helped to free slaves and advocated changing laws that made slavery legal in other states. Michiganders also helped slaves to escape through the **Underground Railroad**, which ran through Michigan to Canada. During the day, fleeing slaves were hidden in buildings or cellars. At night, they traveled north to freedom. North Berrien was a stop along the way and Vandalia was a city with several homes that offered safe haven to the runaways. The Underground Railroad operated between 1830 and 1861.

Among the well-known antislavery proponents were **Laura Haviland** and **Sojourner Truth**. Considered a **Civil War** heroine, Truth, born into slavery, traveled throughout the country and spoke out against slavery. She also fought for women's right to vote.

As a strong antislavery state, Michigan remained loyal to the United States when the southern states threatened to secede and form their own country. During the Civil War, Michigan fought on the side of the Union.

More than 90,000 Michigan men, representing nearly one-fourth of the male population, fought in the Civil War. Nearly 15,000 of those soldiers died. Michigan whites, blacks, and Native Americans fought in almost every major battle. John Lincoln Clem, known as Johnny Clem, was the youngest soldier to serve in the war. He joined the 22nd Michigan Infantry as its drummer when he was nine years old. Meanwhile, **Sarah Edmonds** disguised herself as a man and served with the

General George Armstrong Custer, of the Michigan Cavalry Brigade

Second Michigan Volunteer Infantry for two years as a nurse and spy.

Gen. **George Armstrong Custer** led the well-known Michigan Cavalry Brigade, made up of the First, Fifth, Sixth, and Seventh Michigan cavalries, into battle during the Wilderness and Shenandoah campaigns. It was Custer who accepted Gen. Robert E. Lee's flag of truce when the Confederates surrendered.

Initially, the fur trade had attracted Europeans to Michigan, but as demand for fur skins declined, outsiders looked to the other resources the state offered. Michigan's fertile farm lands, timber-laden forests, and rich veins of copper, iron ore, and salt promised riches to anyone willing to journey to America. European **immigrants** from Germany, Ireland, the Netherlands, Poland, Finland, and Italy poured into Michigan during the late 1800s. Today, Michigan still boasts a culturally diverse population.

One of the first commercial breakfast foods was a bran and molasses mixture developed by **Charles William Post**. **William Keith Kellogg** developed the first cornflakes. The Post and Kellogg corporations still exist in Michigan.

Agriculture was a driving economic force throughout the 1800s, but at the start of the 20th century the Industrial Revolution brought the tractor, telephone, and other mechanized conveniences. It also brought horseless carriages.

The Motor City

Ransom E. Olds in Lansing and **Henry Ford** in Detroit developed automobiles in the 1880s. After developing gasoline-driven cars such as the Olds Runabout, Olds began Olds Motor Works in 1897. Ford founded the Ford Motor Company in 1903 and five years later introduced the Model T, a car that dominated the industry until 1927. **Walter Chrysler** founded the Chrysler Corporation in 1925. Chrysler was the final member of what became known as the Big Three automobile companies.

Olds developed the assembly line, but Ford improved the concept. In 1913, he started

The seven Fisher brothers, made rich by their company's manufacture of enclosed automobile bodies, built the Fisher building as their contribution to the city of Detroit.

to use standardized interchangeable parts and assembly-line methods to produce automobiles. This revolutionized the production of automobiles and made Michigan the country's center of automobile manufacturing.

When the United States entered World War I in 1917, Michiganders again answered the call. More than 135,000 men from the state joined the armed forces. Michigan's industrial might provided an equally important contribution. Already set up for manufacturing, the state's factories were easily adapted to produce guns, tanks, truck engines, and other needed military supplies while still producing autos.

Detroit's **automobile industry** thrived after the war; the construction industry exploded. Some of the city's most famous buildings, including the Penobscot Building, New Union Trust Building, Cadillac Tower, David Stott Building and **Fisher Building**, were erected in 1927–28.

The economy was strong in the beginning of 1929 and economists were predicting continued prosperity for Americans. But on Thursday, October 24, 1929, the stock market crashed. Panic ensued as investors rapidly

Immigrants in an English class given by the training services department of labor at Ford Motor—circa 1920.

dumped their stocks. Five days later, on Black Tuesday, the New York Stock Exchange was reeling from the loss. President Herbert Hoover declared the downturn a depression.

A state that relied heavily on industry, Michigan suffered acutely during the Great Depression. The automobile factories laid off most of their workers, and Michigan experienced higher unemployment rates than the rest of the nation.

The harsh conditions of the Great Depression changed the political climate in Michigan, where the **Republican Party** had dominated for a long time. But in 1932, Michiganders voted Democratic, handing over the state's electoral votes to presidential candidate Franklin D. Roosevelt. They also voted Democrats into most of the state offices.

In the midst of this turmoil, workers who remained at the automobile factories were unhappy. Workers at the factories worked long hours, received little pay, had no say in factory operations, and could be fired at any time for any reason. Angered by those conditions, workers joined labor unions. The **United Auto Workers** was formed in Michigan in 1935; the same year Congress passed the National Labor Relations Act, which guaranteed workers the

right to organize unions. Still, factory owners did not want to recognize the UAW. In protest, workers held a series of sit-down strikes to get factory owners to recognize the unions. Ford Motor Company was the last to recognize the union and allow collective bargaining, but finally agreed in 1941.

World War II transformed Michigan's economy almost overnight. Factories that formerly produced automobiles now made B-24 bombers, tanks, guns, artillery, torpedoes and ammunition. Ford Motor Company's **Willow Run Plant** made airplanes; Chrysler Motor Company's Warren Tank Plant made Tanks and Detroit's Gibson Refrigerator Company, made airplane engines. Michigan earned the nickname the Arsenal of Democracy. Jobs were plentiful, and numerous workers from other states came to work in the plant. While the men were fighting overseas, the women worked at the factory jobs.

By the 1950s, Michigan's economy again burgeoned as automobile factories toiled to keep up with the demand for cars, trucks, tractors, and buses. Michigan's economy was centered primarily on the auto industry. The suburbs around Detroit grew as the population increased by 23 percent over the next ten years.

Peninsular Stove was among the manufacturers that earned Detroit the nickname Stove Capital of the World.

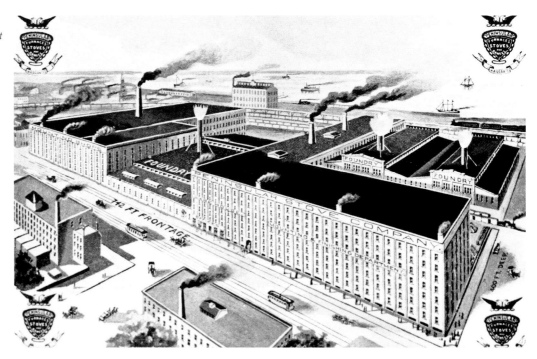

A 1942 poster announcing employment opportunities for farm and industrial laborers in Michigan

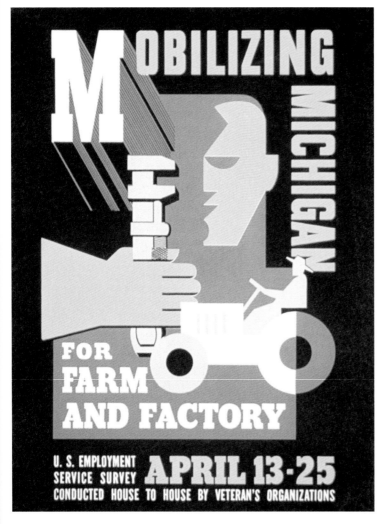

Fall and Rise

The 1960s were tumultuous years nationwide. Michigan college campuses exploded with demonstrations protesting the Vietnam War. Factory jobs attracted many African Americans from the south. Racial tensions between African Americans and whites existed in cities across the country and were particularly tense in Detroit. The city's real estate agents refused to sell houses or rent apartments in certain neighborhoods to African Americans. Banks refused to lend African Americans money, forcing them to live in low-income areas. Dissatisfied over unfair treatment, some African Americans became angry and started riots. In July 1967, Detroit endured riots that killed 43 people.

Gasoline shortages, as a result of a Middle Eastern oil embargo in the 1970s, negatively affected the automobile industry because people preferred to purchase smaller, more economical European cars. Tourism, the second largest industry, also suffered from the gas shortage. In addition, recovery from the Detroit riots was slow. Some of the auto plants and their suppliers moved to other states, increasing the unemployment rate.

For a while in the 1980s, Michigan's economy slumped as car sales dropped again. **Agriculture**, the third top industry in the state, also saw a decline. Unemployment in the state reached a level unseen since the Depression. Through the rest of the 1980s, Michigan diversified its industry and improved its products and services. That set the stage for the Michigan business community to expand manufacturing and encourage high-tech companies to move to the state.

High unemployment rates and an unstable economy again plagued the state during the 1990s. While there was a decline in the number of low-skilled, high-paying manufacturing jobs, there seemed to be countless opportunities for jobs in information technology such as software development, Web page design, and database administration. When the auto industry recovered and the state prepared for the 21st century, the economy was once again on solid footing.

Michigan's strategic location has played a major role in its economic strength. The state's abundant natural resources, acres of forests, breathtaking scenery, and thousands of miles of lakes and streams have contributed to

Michigan's commercial strength. There is little mystery surrounding the **state motto**: *Si Quaeris Peninsulam Amoenam Circumspice*, which translates as, "If you seek a pleasant peninsula, look about you."

The Science Center, Detroit, is also home to a domed IMAX movie theater.

Detroit was Michigan's capital from 1835 until 1847, when Lansing became the capital.

A

Abbott's Magic

The largest magic company in the world, its walls are covered with photos of the famous magicians who have shopped there. Thousands of magicians attend the company's Magic Get-Together every August. The shop, at 124 St. Joseph Street, Colon, is open 9 a.m. to 5 p.m., Monday through Friday; and 9 a.m. to 4 p.m., Saturday.

Abrams, Talbert (1895–1990)

The Tekonsha native, nicknamed "The Father of Aerial Photography," developed his own aerial photography cameras and manufactured the first aircraft designed solely for aerial photography. He was the first person inducted into the Michigan Aviation Hall of Fame. With his wife, Leota, he created the Abrams Foundation, which funds engineering scholarships.

Agriculture

When settlers first came to Michigan the **logging** industry and **fur trade** were more lucrative occupations than farming. However, agriculture became a more viable industry when the **Erie Canal**, which was completed in 1825, created an easier route to the state. Additional lands were opened up following the 1830s federal Indian policies that removed most **Native Americans** from Michigan.

Below: Migrant workers on a Michigan farm

Below right: Michigan is among the most agriculturally diverse states in the country.

Most farming is done in the southern half of the Lower Peninsula. About 500,000 Michigan residents are employed in production agriculture and food processing. In the mid- to late-19th century European **immigrants** began farming in portions of southern Michigan. Dutch farmers, for

example, introduced the modern type of celery to the area, and today the area around Grand Rapids remains a producer of celery and other truck crops.

Michigan has many microclimates that support the growth of more than 125 food and fiber products, making Michigan the second most diverse agricultural state in the nation.

Specialization has been the key to Michigan's more recent agricultural success. Using the state's diverse soil, topography and climate, Michigan farmers produce a dizzying array of foods: potatoes in the north, navy beans in the Saginaw Valley, sugar beets in the thumb area, fruit along the Lake Michigan shore, peppermint and spearmint in the midlands, and soybeans in the southeastern counties.

Michigan is one of the country's major fruit-growing states, ideally suited in large part because of the lake-effect climate near the Lake Michigan shoreline. The lake waters serve as a buffer against weather extremes in the spring and fall. Sandy loam soils found in the rolling hills of these western Michigan counties have resulted in substantial acres being devoted to fruit production. Michigan leads the nation in tart cherry production and is typically ranked second or third in the United States in apple production. In 1995, Michigan's record apple production was 1.2 billion pounds. Peach, plum, and pear orchards, plus the grape vineyards that produce fine Michigan wines, are also found in southwestern and western counties. The state's blueberry region is mainly near Lake Michigan from north of Benton Harbor to near Muskegon.

Harvest season is an excellent time to visit these areas. Apple lovers flock to the state's orchards, to pick and purchase from the state's many varieties. A trip wouldn't be complete without a sip of cider from one of the mills.

Sugar beet workers, photographed in 1917

A

Throughout the year Michigan communities proudly celebrate their local food products through a variety of festivals. Some of the most notable: Maple Syrup Festival, Vermontville, late April; Blossomtime, St. Joseph and Benton Harbor, late April; National Morel Mushroom Festival, Boyne City, mid May; National Asparagus Festival, Shelby, early June; World's Longest Breakfast Table, Battle Creek, mid June; National Cherry Festival, Traverse City, early July; National Baby Food Festival, Fremont, late July; National Blueberry Festival, South Haven, mid August; Mint Festival, St. Johns, mid August; Wine and Harvest Festival, Paw Paw, mid September.

Air Zoo

Once a local museum, Air Zoo is now among the largest nongovernmental aviation museums in the nation. The museum honors everything about flight, down to the innards of the airplane, and has a collection of 80 vintage aircraft. Air Zoo, at 6151 Portage Road, **Kalamazoo**, opens at 9 every morning. Closing times vary.

Alden B. Dow House and Studio (*see* **Dow House and Studio, Alden B.**)

Alfred P. Sloan Museum (*see* **Sloan Museum, Alfred P.**)

Air Zoo features restorations of planes from America's wars. This image shows an American Moth plane from 1927–28.

All-American Girls Professional Baseball League

In May 1943, after female softball players heard of a women's league being formed in the Midwest, by chewing gum mogul Philip K. Wrigley and a group of investors, nearly 300 potential players showed up for spring training. Wrigley and the group had recommended establishing the league with the thought that men's major league baseball would suffer when players were called up in World War II.

The first year, players were signed to one of four teams: Kenosha (Wisconsin) Comets, Racine (Wisconsin) Belles, Rockford (Illinois) Peaches, and South Bend (Indiana) Blue Sox. Michigan joined the League in its third year when the Milwaukee Chicks relocated and became the Grand Rapids Chicks. The Racine Bells moved to Battle Creek in 1951 and then to Muskegon in 1953 for one final year of play. The Muskegon Lassies, who joined the league as an expansion franchise in 1946, relocated to Kalamazoo in 1950. Additional teams were formed throughout the Midwest.

On and off the field, the players were expected to act like ladies. They had to be properly made up and were not permitted to wear slacks in public or cut their hair in "boyish bobs." Social engagements required a chaperone's approval. After daily practice, they were required to attend charm school.

Televised major league baseball and mounting financial troubles led to the League's demise in 1954. In all, more than 600 women played in the league.

Allen, John (n.d.)

The Virginia native co-founded Ann Arbor in 1824. He purchased 480 acres of land north of Huron Street and developed Ann, Catherine, and Lawrence Streets. He served as first village president in 1834.

Ambassador Bridge

At its completion in 1929, the bridge connecting Detroit and Windsor, Ontario, was the world's longest suspension bridge. It runs 7,500 feet end to end, with a suspension span of 1,850 feet. The roadway hangs 152 feet above the **Detroit River**.

More than 1.6 million vehicles were recorded crossing the bridge in 1930, the first full year it was open. That same year, the **Detroit-Windsor Tunnel** opened, and travel across the bridge slowed.

Seventy-five years later, however, the bridge remains the busiest international border crossing in North America. More than 25 percent of merchandise trade between the two countries crosses the bridge.

American Car and Foundry Company

Detroit was famous for manufacturing train cars. American Car and Foundry incorporated 13 companies. It was a consolidation of a number of railroad car companies, including the Michigan-Peninsular Car Company, itself a combination of two giants. Its Detroit plant was the first to move cars from work station to work station with each station performing a single operation—the beginnings of the assembly line.

American Museum of Magic

The only museum of its kind in the world, it opened in 1978 in a restored 1868 building in Marshall. Houdini's famous milk can escape apparatus is there, as are artifacts of all the other great magicians since the 19th century. Also included are nearly a million items of memorabilia.

America's First Shopping Mall

The advent of freeways that cut directly across **Detroit** brought with it new shopping opportunities. Northland Mall in Southfield was the first shopping center in the country to gather a number of smaller shops with a major department store. It opened with 65 stores on March 22, 1954, an event covered by national publications. *The Detroit Free Press* warned shoppers not to lose their cars in the 60-acre expanse of parking lots. By its 50-year anniversary, the mall averaged nine million shoppers a year. During its heyday in the 1980s, it pulled in 18 million shoppers to what the *The Detroit Free Press* had called the "new shopping paradise."

Top right: The Ambassador Bridge offers travelers a magnificent view of the Detroit River.

Above right: Railroad enthusiasts still avidly study American Car and Foundry trains.

Above left: Detroit was famous for manufacturing train cars. American Car and Foundry incorporated 13 companies.

A.M. Todd Company (*see* Todd Company, A.M.)

Amway Corporation

Founded in 1959 by Richard M. DeVos and Jay Van Andel, Ada-based Amway markets personal care, health and fitness, and home care products. With $5 billion in annual sales, it's the largest direct-selling organization in the world.

Anderson, Cora Reynolds (1883–1950)

Educator, legislator. She was the first woman elected to the Michigan House and served one term. She was known for her support of **Prohibition** and her efforts in improving public health. Before serving in the legislature, she organized the first public health service in Baraga.

Anderson, George "Sparky" (1934–)

Baseball manager. He managed the American League **Detroit Tigers** from 1979 to 1995, leading them to a World Series in 1984. While with the National League Cincinnati Reds, he won two Series, the only manager ever to win in both leagues. He was inducted into the Baseball Hall of Fame in 2000.

Ann Arbor

In 1824, two easterners seeking their fortune in land speculation decided to settle in Michigan near the Huron River. The river could provide water and transportation. The forested lands meant abundant lumber. The open grasslands invited farming. **John Allen** bought 480 acres and Elisha Rumsey bought 160 acres. They created a plan for a village they called Annarbour, later Americanized to Ann Arbor, in honor of their wives, Ann Allen and Mary Ann Rumsey.

Within a few years, Ann Arbor was a thriving farming center with a population above 2,000. A railroad was under way. There was a grist mill and a tannery and a general store. More easterners came, as did German and Irish **immigrants**. In 1827, Gov. **Stevens Mason** named Ann Arbor the county seat of Washtenaw County. John Allen became village president in 1834. The village was incorporated as a city in 1851.

In 1837, as the state legislature planned to reorganize the **University of Michigan**, founded in **Detroit**, Ann Arbor made a bid for the university and won. Ten years later, the town

Panoramic view of the city of Ann Arbor, from 1880

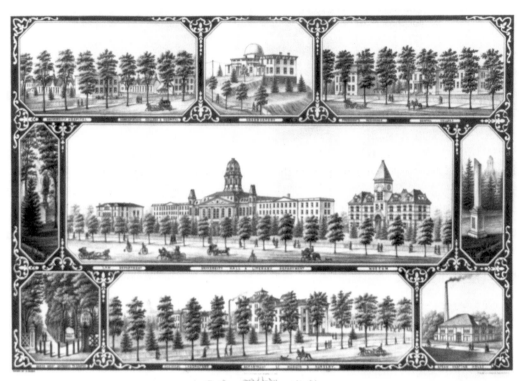

U N I V E R S I T Y   O F   M I C H I G A N
ANN ARBOR

tried for the state capital. Although it eventually lost the competition to become capital of the state, it quickly became the education capital of the Midwest.

The University of Michigan Ann Arbor campus opened in 1841 with two professors to teach a student body of seven. The city never looked back. Ann Arbor steadily grew and now, with a population of 110,000, is the seventh largest city in Michigan. In addition to U of M, Ann Arbor is home to three postsecondary schools: Cleary College, Concordia College, and Eastern Michigan University. *U.S. News & World Report* ranks the **University of Michigan Medical Center** among the best hospitals in the country.

Companies that call Ann Arbor home include NSK Corporation, an international producer of ball and roller bearings, and **Borders Booksellers**. **Domino's Pizza**, which began in 1960 with a single store, now has more than 7,000 stores throughout the world. The company's headquarters are still in Ann Arbor.

The city has a small-town feel. And it has its traditions. Every spring film buffs flock to the **Ann Arbor Film Festival**, the oldest showcase of independent film and video in the country. And every summer Ann Arbor hosts one of the nation's premier art festivals, encompassing four juried art fairs.

Some of the traditions are a bit wackier. Since 1986, U of M's graduating seniors have dashed across campus in the altogether on the evening of the final day of classes. Once tolerant of the Naked Mile, in the past several years the university and police have looked less kindly on the event and participants have begun to strip down only to their skivvies. And then there's the famous rivalry between the UofM and Ohio State University football teams. It's been hot and heavy for more than 100 years.

Ann Arbor Ark

The nonprofit Ark, one of the Midwest's premier venues for acoustic music, has been a landmark in **Ann Arbor** since 1965. Performers over the years have included David Bromberg, Malvina Reynolds, Kate McGarrigle, and Ramblin' Jack Elliott. The Ark presents a folk festival the last Saturday of every January.

Ann Arbor Art Fair

The four-day Ann Arbor Art Fair, one of the premier art fairs in the country, has happened every July since 1959. Although thought of as a single giant event, it is actually four separate fairs, each with its own sponsor. With displays by more than 1,200 artists, the fairs feature a variety of outdoor entertainment and related events as well as arts and crafts.

Ann Arbor Blues and Jazz Festival

The Ann Arbor Blues and Jazz Festival was organized in 1972 by poet-activist-MC5 guru John Sinclair, promoter Peter Andres, and Rick Dykstra. Each year the legendary festival provides the community with a spirited program of truly American music. B.B. King closed the first show. Other past performers include Lightnin' Hopkins, Buddy Guy, Etta James, Bonnie Raitt, and Taj Mahal.

Ann Arbor Film Festival

Founded by George Manupelli in 1963, it is the oldest festival in the country that honors experimental and independent films. More than 1,000 films a year are entered in the festival. Ken Burns, Gus Van Sant, George Lucas, and Andy Warhol all entered films early in their careers.

Auden, Wystan Hugh (W.H.) (1907–1973)

Poet, playwright, literary critic. The British Auden taught at the **University of Michigan** from 1941 to 1942 and became an American citizen in the former Huron Street courthouse. He won a Pulitzer Prize for *The Age of Anxiety*. His other works include *The Ascent of F6*, which he co-authored with Christopher Isherwood, and *The Dance of Death*.

Au Sable River International Canoe Race

When the cannon fires in late July, 50 teams grab canoes and run to the Au Sable River in Grayling. What follows is a grueling 14-hour, 120-mile race across the northeastern Lower Peninsula. The race ends in Oscoda. A parade

The expansion of the auto industry resulted in the opening of the Detroit–Windsor auto tunnel. This photograph of the toll gate was taken in 1930.

Au Sable is home to the world's longest canoe marathon.

and bicycle race and a **Native American** pow-wow also are held during the event.

Auto Industry

Today's environmentalists tout electric cars as the wave of the future. But electric-powered automobiles were gliding over streets in the United States and Europe long before **Henry Ford** started selling the Model T.

Borrowing from the technology that ran trolley cars, inventors started producing battery-powered vehicles in the mid 1880s. The novelty of the horseless carriage intrigued the public, but the technology had its limits. The considerable weight of the batteries slowed down the slight vehicles. The cars couldn't stray too far from a power source before they had to be recharged. What's more, the batteries wore out after a few years and were expensive to replace.

Still, America was quickly hooked on the relative speed and comfort of the automobile compared to the horse and buggy. The introduction of the internal combustion engine, powered by gasoline, was the first of many improvements that cemented the automobile in the hearts of the American public and turned Michigan's largest metropolis, **Detroit**, into the Motor City.

The Big Three U.S. automakers—General Motors, Ford, and Chrysler—are all that's left of the hundreds of companies that began the auto revolution. They survived the Great Depression and bloody battles with the **United Auto Workers**.

Henry Ford may remain the most recognizable name, but **Ransom E. Olds** was the United States' first mass producer of cars. The native of **Lansing** built the first Oldsmobile in the mid-1890s. The Olds Motor Works factory opened in Detroit in 1900. A fire in 1901 forced Olds to rebuild, and he did so in **Lansing**. That city, Michigan's state capital, is the current site of the **R.E. Olds Transportation Museum**.

A Like most early automobile inventors, Olds teamed up with other entrepreneurs so he could meet the demand for his new product. Olds bought transmissions from two brothers named Dodge. The machine shop of **Horace** and **John Dodge** also produced parts for Henry Ford. Meanwhile, another machinist, **Henry Leland**, was building engines that were installed in Oldsmobiles and Fords. Leland's ego must have been smaller than those of his contemporaries. When Leland developed a more sophisticated engine, he insisted the car in which it was installed be named after **Antoine de la Mothe Cadillac**, Detroit's

founder. The Cadillac company was eventually bought by General Motors. Leland also developed the Lincoln, which he sold to Ford.

General Motors had been established by **William Durant**, who collaborated over the years with **David Buick**, **Charles Nash**, and **Louis Chevrolet**, all of whom loaned their

names to automobiles. **Alfred P. Sloan** was appointed president of GM in 1923 and later became its chief executive officer. His innovative management strategies helped GM in overtaking Ford as the best selling brand in the nation.

William and **James Packard** established their automobile company in Detroit just after 1900. Their factory, designed by famed architect **Albert Kahn**, still stands on East Grand Boulevard, though the company stopped making cars in the 1950s.

Walter Chrysler, like Nash, was a Durant protégé who went on to establish his own brand of auto. Nash at one point teamed with the Hudson Company and created American Motors. Chrysler acquired American Motors in 1987 and merged with the German manufacturer Daimler-Benz in 1998.

While other auto barons were making and breaking professional partnerships, Henry Ford remained at the helm of the company he had founded in 1903. His assembly lines produced Model Ts quickly and inexpensively.

Ford became a hero to his workers when, in 1914, he doubled their daily salary to $5. Building cars is a tedious, physically demanding and even dangerous task. Ford figured the pay raise would engender loyalty as well as put his workers in a position to afford to buy the cars they were building.

Twenty years later, Ford's relations with his employees reached an all-time low. The United Auto Workers union had formed in Detroit in 1935, but Ford was the last of the major automakers to recognize the union. General Motors, which by the 1930s had a major plant in **Flint**, had little choice but to enter collective bargaining. Workers staged a 44-day sit-down strike, refusing to work or to leave the facility. The tactic worked, and after GM recognized the UAW, Chrysler and others followed suit. Not Ford. It took a bloody battle and some bad publicity to convince Ford to capitulate.

Walter Reuther was a major figure in organizing the UAW and taking it to Ford's

The invention of the automobile set the world on its ear. General Motors had a major plant in Flint, hence the name "Vehicle City" as shown in this old photo.

A

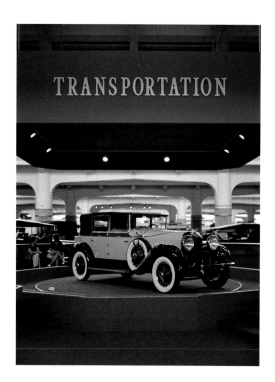

The R.E. Olds Transportation Museum focuses on Lansing's part in the development of the auto industry.

plants. On May 26, 1937, Reuther and three others planned to hand out union literature outside the massive **Ford Rouge River** plant in Dearborn. Overt union organizing at the plant was unheard of.

Ford had hired security officers to intimidate organizers and break up union meetings. Workers had even been fired for union activities. Reuther knew his mission was uncertain. He had the foresight to invite witnesses, including the press, to view his recruiting efforts. It didn't take long for Ford's men to confront Reuther's.

The altercation began on a footbridge that led to the plant, so the incident became known as the **Battle of the Overpass**. The union organizers were severely beaten, and the violence was captured by news photographers. Shocking images of the bloodied men garnered public support for unions. The historic overpass confrontation eventually led to the UAW's successful organizing of Ford workers.

The automotive industry remained viable during **World War II** despite the fact that no cars were produced. Instead, the massive factories were used to build equipment for the military.

Post-war America was prosperous, and the availability of automobiles gave people the freedom to conveniently commute from the burgeoning suburbs to jobs in urban areas. Automakers continued to design new models every year in an effort to create demand among the public, and more and more people were members of two-car families.

In 1973, the Organization of Petroleum Exporting Countries slapped the United States with an oil embargo. Suddenly Americans were waiting in line to buy gasoline and were limited in how much they could purchase once they reached the pump.

The oil crisis renewed efforts, begun in the 1960s, to produce more fuel-efficient compact cars. It also brought a wave of foreign competition into the U.S. auto market. The German Volkswagen Beetle had gained popularity in the 1960s, and the 1970s saw increased sales of Japanese imports.

In the 1990s, the United States entered the North America Free Trade Agreement. The plan called for the removal of trade barriers between the United States, Mexico, and Canada. Some say the pact encouraged automakers to move jobs out of the United States to its new trade partners. GM, which some had long referred to as Generous Motors because its workers made such a comfortable living, was slowly eliminating jobs in Flint. Filmmaker **Michael Moore** directed a 1989 documentary, *Roger and Me,* that chronicled the effect of plant closings on the city.

The automobile industry may be returning to its "electric" roots, thanks to concerns about oil importation from the Middle East. Toyota produced the first hybrid vehicle in 1997. Its Prius has both a gasoline engine and an electric motor. Just after the new millennium, Toyota and Nissan started a joint venture to develop hybrid cars. In 2004, Ford entered an agreement with Toyota to use the hybrid technology.

B

Mine disasters, such as the one at Barnes-Hecker, are now rare in the United States, thanks to today's technology.

Barnes-Hecker Mine Disaster

Fifty-one men died on November 3, 1926, in the second worst mining disaster in American history. Only seven bodies were found. After attempts to reclaim the mine resulted in a second cave-in, the mine was sealed. The cause of the collapse was never determined.

Battle Creek

Battle Creek has achieved fame as the Cereal City, thanks to its serving as the home for the world headquarters of the Kellogg Company, the Post Division of Kraft Foods, and Ralston Purina—the companies that produce many of the breakfast cereals consumed by the nation.

Battle Creek is located in southern Michigan at the confluence of the **Kalamazoo** and Battle Creek rivers. The city, which is about 70 miles east of Lake Michigan, is midway between **Detroit** and Chicago. It's Michigan's third-largest city in land area, with 44 square miles, and has a population of 53,000. A nearby 1830s skirmish between a government land surveyor and two Indians provided the city with its name. In its early years Battle Creek was a market and mill center for prairie farmers, later developing into an industrial center that produced a variety of goods, including farming implements, violin strings, and newspaper printing presses.

Before the **Civil War** the city was an abolitionist stronghold. Quaker pioneers operated a station on the **Underground Railroad**. **Sojourner Truth**, a former slave and a famed speaker for abolition and women's rights, moved to Battle Creek in 1858. Her grave is in Oak Hill Cemetery, on the east side of the city.

In the mid-1800s Battle Creek became known for its tolerance and openness to new ideas. A small group of Seventh-day Adventists invited Sister Ellen White and her husband to settle in the city and make it their headquarters. Dr. **John Harvey Kellogg**, the director of the famous **Battle Creek Sanitarium**, soon began to incorporate health and dietary principles based on White's teachings. Dr. Kellogg's brother, **William K. Kellogg**, developed new food products for the patients, breakfast cereals among them. In 1891, **Charles W. Post**, a patient at the "San," became interested in the business potential of the new health foods. Soon he created Grape Nuts cereal, and an industry

Late 19th-century engraving showing the mills and manufacturers of Battle Creek

B

was born. By 1906 William Kellogg had decided to form his own company. Kellogg's of Battle Creek would become an industry giant.

Battle Creek contains many physical reminders of its rich history, including the Victorian Kimball House Museum, stately mansions on Capital Avenue, cereal worker housing in the Post Addition, and the Sanitarium building, now used as the Federal Center.

Each year, on the second Saturday in June, the city hosts the World's Longest Breakfast Table. The city's three cereal companies dish up a free breakfast to some 60,000 diners at tables covering a four-block area. Kellogg's Cereal City celebrates William Kellogg's accidental creation of the cereal industry.

More than 750,000 spectators come to Battle Creek every July for the International Hot Air Balloon Championship. The city is also home to the **Battle Creek Symphony Orchestra**. Scenic Linear Park, with 17 miles of landscaped walkways, boardwalks, and bridges, extends across much of the city. The Binder Park Zoo features exotic animals in a natural park setting.

Battle Creek Sanitarium

The world-famous health treatment center, known locally as the San, was founded in **Battle Creek** in the 1860s by Seventh-day Adventists and became renowned for its water and fresh-air treatments, exercise regimens, and diet reforms. During its 65 years of operation, the San served thousands of patients, among them presidents, movie stars, and captains of industry. The sanitarium's long-time director was Dr. **John Harvey Kellogg**, whose brother, **William K. Kellogg**, first developed ready-to-eat breakfast cereals there.

The San was immortalized in T. Coraghessan Boyle's novel *The Road to Wellville* and the 1994 movie of the same name.

Battle Creek Symphony Orchestra

The orchestra, founded in 1899, is Michigan's oldest and one of the oldest in the country. In

1941, the orchestra moved into its current home, the W.K. Kellogg Auditorium, known for its superb acoustics and classic décor.

Battle of Bloody Run

In the fiercest battle of **Pontiac**'s Uprising, Indians attacked a British unit at Parent's Creek, in what is now **Detroit**, in July 1763, killing Captain James Dalyell and 60 of his troops. Thereafter, the creek was known as Bloody Run. A Michigan Historical Marker at 3321 East Jefferson shows the spot.

Battle of the Overpass

On May 26, 1937, several activists, including **United Auto Workers** president **Walter Reuther** and **Richard T. Frankensteen**, prepared to hand out leaflets outside the **Ford River Rouge** complex. They were attacked, beaten, and thrown off an overpass by Ford Motor Company security officers. The incident, caught on film, proved the brutal methods automakers were willing to use to keep the unions out and turned public opinion in favor of unionization. The incident cemented Reuther's reputation as an organizer and began a four-year push that culminated in acceptance of the UAW by Ford, the final holdout among the Big Three automakers.

Baum, L. Frank (1856–1919)

Author Baum and illustrator William Wallace Denslow produced the children's books *Father Goose, His Story* and *The Wonderful Wizard of Oz*. Baum wrote several *Oz* sequels and continued to publish books for children under his own and several pen names. The last of the *Oz* books was published posthumously. Baum spent summers on Lake Michigan.

Bay View Association

Opened in 1875 as a Methodist camp meeting resort, the Emmet County community was adapted to include the education ideals of the Chautauqua, New York, Methodist resort. While participating in religious study, reading circles, and recreational activities, summer residents took classes in art, music, cooking, and dramatic readings.

Bay View was designed as a garden-like romantic landscape, its cottages on narrow, fenceless lots evoking its tight-knit community. Nearby rail and steamboat access brought visitors from throughout the Midwest.

The community, including 437 privately owned Victorian cottages and two hotels, continues as a religious summer resort. It is owned and governed by the Bay View Association, which promotes scientific and intellectual development. Bay View is listed on the state and national registers of historic places and is a National Historic Landmark.

Beaumont, William (1785–1853)

As physician, he served in the **War of 1812,** then was assigned to **Fort Mackinac.** There he treated a 19-year-old trapper, Alexis St. Martin, who had accidentally been shot point blank in the abdomen. Substantial bits of membrane and muscle had been blown off, and St. Martin's left lung and stomach had been perforated. The injuries were so severe St. Martin was not expected to live, but he did. The wound, however, never completely healed but allowed interior access to his stomach, which

otherwise functioned normally. St. Martin became known as "the man with a window in his stomach."

St. Martin consented to let Beaumont experiment on him. For the next eight years, Beaumont fed St. Martin different kinds of foods and observed how they were digested. He discovered that vegetables are not as digestible as some other foods. Studying the relationship between digestion and weather, he noted that dry weather increases the temperature in the stomach, while damp weather lowers it. He noticed the positive effects of exercise on the production and release of gastric juices. He learned from St. Martin's periodic annoyance at the arrangement that mood has an effect on digestion.

Beaumont published several reports of his findings, including one of the classic works of medical research, *Experiments and Observations on the Gastric Juice and the Physiology of Digestion.*

During the course of his work with Beaumont, St. Martin married and had children. He lived into his 80s.

Belle Isle

About a half mile offshore in the **Detroit River,** the island has had a variety of names and incarnations. **Native Americans** called it Swan Island, for its flocks of migratory swans, or Rattlesnake Island, for its snakes. French settlers who tried to make the island habitable released wild hogs to destroy the rattlesnakes, and the island became known as Ile au Cochon, "Isle of the Pigs."

Legend has it that Belle Isle, the name that stuck, was coined by Barnabas Campau, who owned the island at the time, in honor of Isabelle Cass, daughter of former Michigan territorial governor **Lewis Cass.**

The French used the island as grazing land. The English who followed bought it from the Chippewa and Ottawa tribes, and the island changed hands several times before Campau bought it and placed a fishery there.

William Beaumont's famous patient was commonly known as "the man with a window in his stomach."

B

The city of Detroit paid $200,000 for Belle Isle in 1879. This picture shows the Belle Isle Casino in 1910.

By the time the city of **Detroit** bought Belle Isle from Campau's heirs, it was already considered public property, a favorite place for picnics and duels. It was also used to quarantine troops during the cholera epidemic of 1832.

The city hired landscape architect Frederick Law Olmsted, famed for his designs of Central Park and the U.S. Capitol grounds, to create a development plan for the island. Today the island is a year-round playground. It has about 20 picnic shelters, a 36-acre athletic

complex, swimming and fishing areas, and miles of roads ideal for walking and skating. Belle Isle Aquarium is the oldest continuously operating public aquarium in North America. Other attractions include a conservatory, and a casino, both designed by **Albert Kahn,** and the **Nancy Brown** Peace Carillon Tower.

Belle Isle Conservatory

Located on the historic island of **Belle Isle** in the **Detroit River,** the conservatory opened in 1904. It was designed by **Albert Kahn** and patterned after Thomas Jefferson's Monticello. In 1953, it was renamed in honor of Anna Scripps Whitcomb, who left her 600-plant orchid collection to the city of Detroit. The conservatory features permanent displays of rare flora as well as hundreds of cacti, succulents, ferns, palms, tropical plants, and one of the largest orchid displays in the country.

Benzonia College

Central to the educational Christian community for which it was named, Benzonia College offered teacher training, then a wider college curriculum. With several name changes, it lasted from 1883 to 1918. It was home to **Civil War** historian **Bruce Catton,** whose father taught

The Belle Isle Conservatory has one of the largest collections of orchids in America.

Benzonia College was home to Civil War historian Bruce Catton.

there. Mills Cottage, one of the dorms, is now the Benzonia Public Library.

Bergen, Edgar (1903–1978)

Entertainer. As a boy gaining proficiency in ventriloquism, the Decatur native asked a local artisan to create a dummy for him; Bergen named the dummy Charlie McCarthy. After attending Northwestern University, Bergen made his radio debut in 1936. By 1937, he had his own show, which remained one of radio's highest rated programs until 1956. As television made inroads into radio's popularity, Bergen appeared on television specials and *Do You Trust Your Wife?* In 1976, he returned to live performing. He died in Las Vegas, just hours after completing the second night of an engagement. The *Edgar Bergen/Charlie McCarthy Show* was inducted into the Radio Hall of Fame in 1990.

Bertha Hansbury School (*see* Hansbury School, Bertha)

Bibb, Henry Walton (1814–1854)

Born into slavery in Kentucky, Bibb escaped to Michigan in 1842 and published *Narrative of the Life and Adventures of Henry Bibb, An American*

Slave in 1847. In 1850, he moved to Ontario, where he published *The Voice of the Fugitive,* Canada's first black newspaper.

Bingham, Kinsley (1808–1861)

Within three years of arriving in Michigan, the native New Yorker was elected to the state legislature, where he served five terms before election to the U.S. Congress. He broke from the Democratic Party over slavery and helped

Kinsley Bingham was the nation's first Republican governor.

Bissell offered early customers an inexpensive sweeper and a gift.

The Bissell Sweeper

The handy, useful, every-day labor-saving convenience of the home.

It is not enough to take up carpets once a year, or to clean them with compressed air process, for after this comes the daily necessity for a good carpet sweeper. Dust accumulates fast, and unless you have a good carpet sweeper always at your command, your house is bound to get very dirty.

The corn broom simply scatters the fine grit and dust, whereas the Bissell sweeper gathers it completely, depositing it in the pan receptacles.

Then consider how it lessens the labor of sweeping 95 per cent., raises no dust; making sweeping a positive pleasure instead of a drudgery.

It's a great economy, too, as a Bissell will last longer than fifty corn brooms.

For sale by all the best trade. Price $2.50 to $5.50.

Buy now, send us the purchase slip, and receive a neat, useful present *free.*

**Bissell Carpet Sweeper Co.
Grand Rapids, Mich.
Dept. 64.**
(Largest Sweeper Makers in the World.)

Harry Blackstone Jr.'s magic trick kits have inspired many young magicians.

form the **Republican Party**. He was the nation's first Republican governor.

Bissell

In 1876 Melville Bissell patented a carpet sweeper he'd designed to help his wife clean their crockery shop. The Bissell manufacturing plant opened in **Grand Rapids** in 1883. After Melville Bissell's death, **Anna Bissell** took over the company and made it a successful international empire.

Bissell, Anna (1846–1934)

Anna Bissell became the first American woman CEO. Anna's husband, Melville, invented the carpet sweeper. In 1876, the sweeper was patented and Anna went on the road selling the sweepers. She also handled the manufacturing end of the business.

On her husband's death in 1889, Anna ably stepped into his shoes as CEO. She remained CEO until 1919 and chaired the board from 1919 to 1934. During her tenure, she promoted the company internationally and instituted many fair labor practices, well in advance of their general acceptance in the business community. She was the mother of a large family and respected as a philanthropist in the **Grand Rapids**.

Blackstone, Harry, Jr. (1934–1997)

Magician, educator, author. As an infant, the Colon native served as a prop in his father's shows. Later, he presented the longest-running magic show in the history of New York theater. He was twice named Magician of the Year by the Academy of Magical Arts.

He was well known as a television personality and had a recurring role using magic tricks to teach math on PBS's Square One TV. The magic trick kits he designed are the standard for beginning magicians.

His books included *The Blackstone Book of Magic and Illusion* and *Blackstone's Modern Card Tricks and Secrets of Magic.*

Harry Blackstone Sr., the celebrated illusionist.

Blackstone, Harry, Sr. (1885–1965)

Magician, author. Born Harry Bouton, he was second only to Houdini as an innovator, creating such well-known routines as the Buzzsaw Illusion and the Dancing Handkerchief. In perhaps his greatest illusion, at the Lincoln Theater in Decatur, Illinois, he announced a routine so elaborate the audience had to adjourn row by row to the street to see it. Outside, the trick was revealed: The building was on fire, and Blackstone had effected an orderly evacuation.

Blackstone summered in Colon, where he developed and rehearsed his shows. He toured with the USO during the 1940s. He wrote *Blackstone's Secrets of Magic*.

Blair, Austin (1818–1894)

Governor. Born in New York, Blair moved to Jackson to practice law. He began a long and illustrious political career with his election as Eaton County Clerk in 1842; he also served in Michigan's Senate and House of Representatives and in the U.S. House of

B

Austin Blair was a leading Civil War governor and civil rights radical.

The British built three block-houses on Bob-Lo Island in the 1830s, after an uprising by Canadians. This timber fort was built in 1837.

Representatives. He helped establish the **Republican Party** and was a delegate to the 1860 Republican National Convention that nominated Abraham Lincoln for president.

Blair was Michigan's governor from 1861 to 1864. Deemed a leading **Civil War** governor and a **civil rights** radical, Blair opposed slavery, secession, and capital punishment. He favored women's suffrage and equal rights.

Bob-Lo Island

From 1898 until 1993, Detroiters could board a boat and get ferried down the **Detroit River** to a Canadian island that became known as Bob-Lo. In the early 1900s, visitors enjoyed picnic areas, a huge dance hall, baseball diamonds, and tennis courts.

Amusement park rides were added after **World War II**, and soon a jaunt to Bob-Lo was

synonymous with a day of roller coasters and other tummy-tickling rides. The amusement park closed in 1993 and has since been replaced by pricey residential development.

Boeing, William (1881–1956)

Aviation pioneer. William Boeing was the founder and first president of Boeing Airplane Company. He was born in Michigan, the son of a wealthy timber baron. Always interested in engineering, Boeing took his passion and applied it to airplanes. He was awarded the Guggenheim Medal for his contributions to the aviation industry. A dispute with government forced him to divide his company into three entities: United Aircraft Company, Boeing Airplane Company, and United Airlines. He lived to see his planes reach the jet age and retired focusing on his other interest of breeding thoroughbred horses.

Bono, Sonny (1935–1998)

Entertainer, politician. As a songwriter and backup singer, **Detroit**-native Bono worked with Phil Spector and the Righteous Brothers. With his then-wife, Cher, he achieved success in television and recording.

After their divorce, Bono turned to other pursuits and was elected mayor of Palm Springs, California, at the age of 50. In 1994, he won the GOP primary in California's 44th District and then election to the United States House of Representatives. Re-elected in 1996, Bono was named to the House Judiciary and National Security committees. He died in a skiing accident at the age of 62.

Borders Books

The first Borders was a downtown **Ann Arbor** used-book store owned by brothers Tom and Louis Borders. As they opened more stores, the brothers customized the book selection to fit each community. They sold the chain to Kmart in 1994.

Bottle Bill

Michigan was the first industrial state to enact a law requiring deposits on bottles and cans. The Beverage Container Act of 1976 set the highest deposit value, 10 cents, of any such law in the country, on beer, carbonated drink, and mineral water bottles. Refillable beverage bottles required a five-cent deposit. Supporters claimed the law would boost employment as it conserved energy and natural resources and lowered litter clean-up costs. The bill was opposed by retailers, labor unions, bottlers, and brewers, who predicted increased beverage prices and decreased manufacturing jobs. Although the state Legislature also opposed it, the bill won with 64 percent of the state vote and took effect December 3, 1978.

By 1986, as amendments to the bill were already in the works, Michigan was recycling over 95 percent of its refundable containers. The Michigan Department of Transportation reported an 80 percent drop in beverage container litter and a 38 percent drop in litter on state roadsides from the inception of the deposit.

The Bottle Bill was amended in 1988 to include wine coolers and canned cocktails. Another amendment the following year raised the five-cent deposit to a uniform 10 cents per container. At the same time, a provision was added to allow retailers a handling fee of 25 percent of unredeemed deposits, with the remaining 75 percent to go into the state's environmental fund. The original bill had provided no handling fee.

Brewing Industry

Beer was brewed in **Detroit** as early as 1836. By the eve of the **Civil War** there were at least 40 breweries in Michigan's largest city. In 1850, Bernhard Stroh, having learned the brewing trade in his homeland of Germany, founded the Lion Brewery in Detroit. Output at that time was about one barrel a day. By the time Bernhard Stroh died in 1882, the Lion Brewery, later renamed **Stroh Brewing Company**, was

the largest of more than 140 breweries in Michigan. Stroh sold its Detroit operation in 1999. Today Michigan brewing is a thriving cottage industry as microbreweries and brewpubs emerge throughout the state.

Bronson, Titus (1788–1853)

Founder of **Kalamazoo**. Bronson discovered the spot where he founded the city, originally named for him, while walking down an old westbound Indian trail. Although he was liked and respected, his eccentric and outspoken behavior eventually offended everyone. He was convicted of stealing a cherry tree, and villagers petitioned to change the city's name to Kalamazoo.

Brown, Cora Mae (1914–1972)

Legislator. Born in Alabama in 1914, she moved to **Detroit** as a child, graduated from Wayne State University Law School in 1948, and was admitted to the Michigan Bar that same year. She was the first African American woman in the Michigan State Senate, elected in 1952. She served two terms and earned a reputation as a supporter of **civil rights**.

Brown, Nancy (1870–1948)

Advice columnist. Born Annie Louise Brown, she used both Nancy and her married name, Mrs. J.E. Leslie, as pen names. She was one of the first advice columnists in the country and, unlike others, responded seriously to readers' queries about domestic and financial problems, coping with grief, and other social issues.

Not realizing the extent of her popularity, she invited readers to join her to view an exhibit at the new **Detroit Institute of Arts**. More than 30,000 showed up; the outing became an annual event.

During the Depression she asked readers to donate nickels and dimes to build a Peace Carillon at **Belle Isle**. Despite **Detroit**'s impoverishment, enough money was raised to build the monument, which was named for Brown.

Michigan's brewing industry today caters to gourmet tastes in beer.

B

Brûlé, Étienne (*c.* 1592–1633)

Explorer. Sent to look for the Northwest Passage, he lived among the Algonquins and learned their language, then became an interpreter between the Indians and French. He is thought to be the first European to travel down the **Detroit River**. He was nicknamed King of the Coureurs de Bois, French settlers who left their land for the **fur trade**.

Buick, David (1854–1929)

David Buick founded the Buick Motor Company.

Auto maker. Scottish native David Buick moved to **Detroit** with his family at age 2. Around the turn of the twentieth century, Buick saw his first motorcar and became obsessed with automobiles. He turned his passion for cars into the Buick Motor Company and set himself up as president in 1904. Today, over 17,000,000 cars bearing his name have rolled off assembly lines. The inventive Buick also developed a process for heat-binding porcelain to wrought iron to make white bathtubs, at the time a much-sought-after status symbol.

Bunche, Ralph (1904–1971)

Diplomat. A consummate mediator and United Nations diplomat, he was the first person of color awarded the Nobel Prize for Peace (1950).

Bunche was born in **Detroit**, the African-American son of a barber and an amateur musician. When he was 10 the family moved to New Mexico. Two years later, after both parents had died, Bunche and his sisters moved to Los Angeles and his maternal grandmother's home. He graduated first in his class in high school and at the University of California at Los Angeles, where he majored in international relations. Bunche went on to earn a Harvard Ph.D. in political science and conduct research on how to decolonize colonial empires. In the 1930s at Howard University he led the political science department and collaborated on a groundbreaking study of U.S. race relations.

During **World War II,** Bunche helped write the charter that founded the United Nations. He became a master negotiator in Middle East disputes and drafted the U.N. Partition Plan for Palestine, the document that led to the creation of Israel. He had been chief aide to Count Folke Bernadotte, whom the U.N. appointed as mediator in the 1948 fighting between Arabs and Jews. Just four months into the process Bernadotte was assassinated and Bunche was named acting U.N. mediator. After 11 months of negotiating Bunche obtained signatures on armistice agreements between Israel and the Arab states. His ceaseless efforts earned him the 1950 Nobel Peace Prize. Bunche continued to work for the U.N., becoming undersecretary general in 1967.

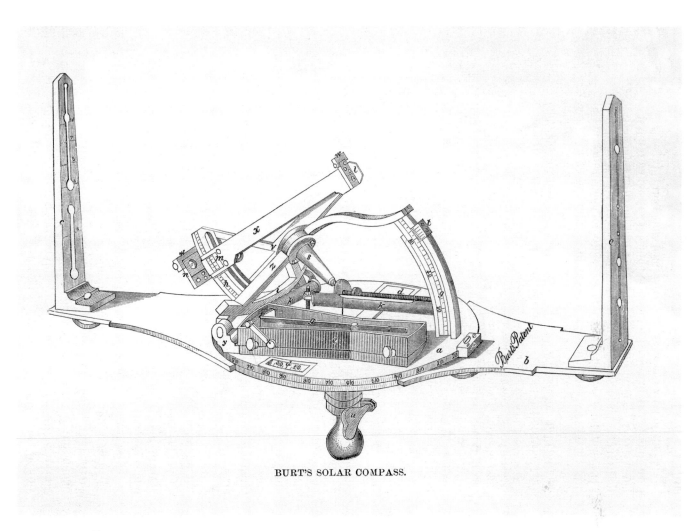

BURT'S SOLAR COMPASS.

Burstyn, Ellen (1932–)

Actor. Nominated five times for an Academy Award, Burstyn won the Oscar in 1974 for *Alice Doesn't Live Here Anymore.* The same year, she won Broadway's Tony award for *Same Time, Next Year.* She has served as president of Actor's Equity and co-president of the Actors Studio.

Burt, William Austin (1792–1858)

Inventor, surveyor, legislator. He settled in Macomb County in 1824 and was a member of both the Michigan territorial and state legislatures. He was Mount Vernon's first postmaster. He patented America's first typewriter and an equatorial sextant but is best known for his solar compass, patented in 1836, which was the prototype of today's solar compasses. As it was not affected by magnetic iron ore fields, Burt's compass was invaluable for surveying. Burt discovered the Marquette iron ore range in 1844. He was instrumental in establishing the Michigan-Wisconsin border and in dividing Michigan into townships.

Busfield, Timothy (1957–)

Actor, director. Although he broke into films in 1984, Busfield is best known for the role of Elliot Weston in the television drama *thirtysomething.* For this portrayal, he was five times nominated for an Emmy, winning the award in 1991. He also co-founded the B Street Theatre in Sacramento, California.

Today's solar compasses hearken back to William Burt's design of 1836.

C

Cadillac, Antoine de la Mothe
(*c.* 1658–1730)

Founder of **Detroit**. A minor French nobleman, he sought his fortune in America. After living in the east, he became a favorite of the Comte de Frontenac, governor of New France, in present-day Quebec. Frontenac sent him to the frontier post at Michilimackinac. Cadillac believed an area along the **Detroit River** would offer a better vantage point against the British so he went to France to plead his case and was granted land to create the post. He founded Detroit, which he called Fort Pontchartrain, in

The daughter of Antoine de la Mothe Cadillac was baptized here at the Ste. Anne de Detroit church.

Calumet Theatre. Just one of the buildings that bears testimony to Calumet's affluence, which was brought about by the copper mining boom of the late 19th century.

1701. He later established posts in Alabama and Louisiana before being recalled to France.

Cadillac, Marie Therese Guyon (1671–1746)

French settler. The first female European settler in Michigan, she arrived from France in 1702 to join her husband, **Antoine de la Mothe Cadillac**, in what is present-day **Detroit**. Her ten years at Fort Pontchartrain were spent teaching Christianity to **Native Americans** and raising a family on the frontier.

Calumet Historic District

In the mid-19th century, explorers discovered the remains of ancient mines and stumbled upon one of the richest copper deposits in the world. That discovery led to a **mining** boom that developed the settlement of the **Upper Peninsula**, with consequences felt around the world. Michigan soon robbed Cornwall, England, of its position as world leader in copper production, and many Cornish miners relocated to Calumet.

With financial backing from Boston investors, Alexander Agassiz, a Harvard-trained scientist and son of a world-renowned geologist, merged two companies in 1871 to form the Calumet and Hecla Mining Company. C&H became the dominant player among the 400 or so companies that worked the Copper Country mines from 1872 to 1920. Fifty percent of U.S. copper mined during the 1870s came from C&H, one of the longest lived and innovative of the mining companies. Stock that had gone for $1 a share early on was worth $1,000 a share by 1907. Nearly 20 years later, the company still paid a stock dividend of 700 percent.

Of all the boomtowns that sprang up around the copper fields, Calumet was the most sophisticated. Schools, a library, a hospital, and utility companies were well maintained with copper money.

The Calumet Historic District represents the operation of C&H and its influence on the 19th-century copper industry. The area, in

Louis Campau—"the Father of Grand Rapids."

Houghton County, is a National Historic Landmark and is listed on the National Register of Historic Places.

Campau, Louis (1791–1871)

Called the Father of **Grand Rapids**, Louis Campau founded a trading post there in 1826. Although some credit him with being the first permanent white settler, he was actually second, after a Baptist minister. Campau's biggest claim to fame is that in 1831, he purchased what is now the entire downtown business district from the federal government for $90.

Capitol Hill School

Restored to its former glory, the Capitol Hill School in **Marshall** is a children's museum that depicts a 19th-century primary classroom. Built in 1860, the two-room schoolhouse was one of three Gothic Revival schools erected in the city. Named for its proximity to the intended state capitol, it was used until 1961.

Carriage Industry

The industry required an abundance of wood, and heavily forested Michigan became a national leader. By the late 1890s Michigan employed 7,000 workers in more than 125 carriage factories, primarily in **Detroit**, **Flint**, **Grand Rapids**, Jackson, **Kalamazoo**, **Lansing**, and Pontiac. Flint was the home of the **Durant-Dort Carriage Company**, which later evolved

C

Horse-drawn carriages shared Michigan's streets with trams and automobiles.

The carriage industry evolved into the auto industry.

into General Motors. The prominence of Durant-Dort and other companies, along with parts suppliers such as Cornwall Whip Socket Company and Imperial Wheel Company, earned Flint the nickname Vehicle City.

Durant-Dort was the brainchild of marketing genius **William C. Durant**, who bought the patent for a two-wheeled cart with a comfortable leaf-spring suspension, partnered with J. Dallas Dort to handle production, and created a company that produced 4,000 vehicles in 1886, its first year of operation. The production line expanded to four-wheeled carriages and wagons and, briefly, bicycles. By 1900, Durant-Dort made more horse-drawn vehicles than any other company in the country. Other companies were created as spin offs from this, including Flint Axle Works and Flint Varnish Works. The company peaked in 1906, with the production of 56,000 vehicles by 1,000 employees, and ceased operations in 1917.

Other carriage-makers in Flint included the W.A. Patterson Company and Flint Wagon Works, which opened in 1882 and, two years later, became the city's first incorporated company. Its factory burned to the ground in 1900 but was rebuilt. For a time the Wagon Works owned the Buick Company, which it sold to General Motors.

Carter, Betty (1930–1998)

Jazz and blues singer. Born Lillie Mae Jones in **Flint**, as a child she studied piano at the Detroit Conservatory of Music. After winning a talent contest, she became a regular in **Detroit** clubs and sat in with visiting artists such as Dizzy Gillespie and Sarah Vaughan. Notably unpredictable, she never received the acclaim of Vaughan and other peers. Lionel Hampton nicknamed her Betty Bebop; the name stuck. She won a Grammy in 1988 for her album *Look What I Got!* She performed at the White House in 1994 and three years later received a National Medal of Arts.

Casino Gambling

In 1996, voters approved three licensed casinos to be built in **Detroit**, with tax revenue to go to public education, capital improvement, youth programs, and city tax relief. An additional 17 casinos throughout the state are run by **Native American** tribes that, as sovereign nations,

MotorCity Casino still bears the sign of its original owner, Wagner Baking Co., creator of Wonder Bread.

allow the Michigan Gaming Control Board certain oversight duties.

Cass, Lewis (1782–1866)

Statesman. A native of New Hampshire, Cass lived in Ohio for several years before the **War of 1812**. He rose to brigadier-general during the war. He was appointed military and civil governor of the Michigan Territory in 1813 and served 18 years, during which he led the territory toward statehood. He was appointed President Andrew Jackson's secretary of war in 1831 but resigned in 1836 to become ambassador to France. He remained in that position until 1836, then returned to **Detroit**. In 1845, he was elected to the U.S. Senate.

Cass was an ardent supporter of western expansionism. With the outbreak of the U.S.–Mexican War in 1846, the nation's confidence that the war would result in new territories in the Southwest helped push him into the Democratic presidential nomination in 1848. During the campaign, he proposed the idea that new territories should decide for themselves whether or not to allow slavery. The doctrine of "squatter sovereignty" satisfied neither the proslavery nor antislavery camp, and he lost the election to Zachary Taylor.

The following year, Cass was re-elected to fill the Senate seat he had left vacant. He remained in the Senate until 1857, serving as president *pro tempore* during the Thirty-third Congress.

His final appointment was as President James Buchanan's secretary of state. He resigned when Buchanan refused to make a decisive response after South Carolina seceded from the union. He returned to Detroit to write about his life.

Cass founded the Michigan Historical Society and designed the state's coat of arms.

Catton, Bruce (1899–1978)

Historian, author, editor. Growing up around

Lewis Cass, who designed Michigan's coat of arms.

Chandler, Elizabeth Margaret (1807–1834)

Chandler earned notoriety when she was 18 for her poem *The Slave Ship,* which described the "innate nobility of a slave." It drew critical acclaim in the abolitionist movement and she became editor of "The Ladies Repository" section of the antislavery magazine *The Genius of Universal Emancipation.* Chandler moved to Tecumseh in 1830 and in 1832 formed the Logan Female Anti-Slavery Society, which

The Pulitzer Prize-winning author, Bruce Catton.

Elizabeth Chandler, the anti-slavery campaigner.

Civil War veterans, he became fascinated by the war and wrote many books about it; he won a Pulitzer Prize for *A Stillness at Appomattox.* He also wrote about his home state, including *Michigan: A Bicentennial History.* He was editor of *American Heritage Magazine* from 1954 until his death.

Central Time Zone

While most of Michigan lies within the Eastern Time Zone, four counties on the western edge of the **Upper Peninsula** are in the Central Time Zone. Life in Menominee, Dickinson, Iron, and Gogebic counties is one hour later than in the rest of Michigan. People in these and neighboring U.P. counties often say when scheduling a meeting, "Is that my time or your time?"

Chaffee, Roger (1935–1967)

Astronaut. The **Grand Rapids** native always wanted to touch the stars. He became a pilot with the U.S. Navy and in 1963 was among the pilots chosen for Apollo I. During a countdown simulation in January 1967 at Kennedy Space Center in Florida, a flash fire destroyed the capsule. Chaffee was killed.

Opposite: Walter Chrysler established the Chrysler motor company in 1924.

would later establish a main link in the **Underground Railroad**. She contributed proceeds from her published writings to abolish slavery. Chandler was inducted into the **Michigan Women's Hall of Fame** in 1983.

Chandler, Zachariah (1813–1879)

Statesman. Born in New Hampshire, he moved to **Detroit** and became wealthy as the owner of a general store. He used his money to champion his ideals, including the **Underground Railroad**. Elected mayor of Detroit in 1851 as a Whig, he helped found the **Republican Party** three years later. He served in the U.S. Senate from 1857 to 1875, when he was appointed Secretary of the Interior under President Ulysses S. Grant. He headed Rutherford B.

Zachariah Chandler was elected mayor of Detroit in 1851.

Hayes' presidential campaign in 1876. He was re-elected to Congress in 1879 but died shortly after taking his seat.

Chaney, Alice (n.d.)

Mariner. Licensed as a Great Lakes ship captain in 1900, she was the first woman to pilot a ship on the Great Lakes.

Charles H. Wright Museum of African American History (*see* Wright Museum of African American History, Charles H.)

Checker Cab

Checker Cab vehicles were first produced in **Kalamazoo** in 1922 by Russian immigrant Morris Markin's Checker Cab Manufacturing Company, later the Checker Motors Corporation. The distinctive cars, yellow with black-and-white checkerboard stripes, had roomy interiors and small collapsible seats, for extra passengers, behind the front seats. Production ceased in 1982.

Chevrolet, Louis (1878–1941)

Automaker. Louis Chevrolet was the creator and founder of Chevrolet Motor Company. His first interest was bicycles and he loved racing. As he got older, racing cars was his main passion. Moving from La Chauxde-Fonds, Switzerland, to North America in his early 20s he caught the eye of **William C. Durant**, founder of General Motors, and raced a Buick in the fifth Indy Car race ever run. The relationship Chevrolet formed with Durant led to the formation of the Chevrolet Motor Company in 1911. Soon after the formation of the company Durant branched off on his own and built several racing cars, which his brother drove, that won at the Indianapolis 500.

Chrysler, Walter (1875–1940)

Automaker. Walter Chrysler was always interested in finding out how engines worked. His first job was as a janitor for Union Pacific

Railroad. He quickly worked his way up to locomotive engineer. His interest in engines and how they worked took him to work in the automobile industry with Buick Motors. He used his philosophies for reorganizing and improving production with Buick, increasing the company's output from 45 to 800 cars a day in just eight years. In 1924 he began his own company, Chrysler Corporation, that soon after absorbed the Maxwell Motor Company and became the third largest automobile maker in America.

City of Champions

In 1935, three teams brought championship fever to **Detroit**. After four World Series losses, the **Detroit Tigers** faced the Chicago Cubs for the pennant and won the series. The second winning team was the **Detroit Red Wings**, who defeated Toronto for the Stanley Cup. The **Detroit Lions** beat the New York Giants for their first NFL Championship.

City of Milwaukee

Sole survivor of the traditionally designed **Great Lakes** car ferries, the steamer, built in 1931 for the Grand Trunk Western Railroad fleet, has a four-track enclosed deck that can hold 22 freight cars.

Transporting railroad cargo across the often stormy Great Lakes was challenging but essential for the economic development of the northern Midwest. Until 1892, the contents of railroad cars were emptied onto package freighters, shipped to their destination ports, and loaded back onto railroad cars. In November of that year, a specially designed craft was launched that could carry 24 loaded cars. The Great Lakes car ferry, still running, became the largest open lake train ferry system in the world, linking 26 port cities. Of the 39 ferries eventually built for the service, one of them still holds the world's record for greatest annual mileage.

Shipping declined during the Depression. The *City of Milwaukee*, last of six sister ships

commissioned, was often leased to other railroads, including the Ann Arbor Railroad, and ferried war materials during **World War II**. The ferry was officially chartered to the **Ann Arbor** fleet after Grand Trunk's car ferry service ended in 1978 and was retired in 1982.

The *City of Milwaukee* was listed on the National Historic Landmark registry and also the National Register of Historic Places on December 14, 1990. Visitors may tour the ferry, berthed at Manistee Lake, during the summer. Days vary.

City Opera House

Built in 1891, it was the first public building in **Traverse City** to have electric lights. The 1,200-seat Victorian building, designed by E.R. Prall, has a 43-foot ceiling, hardwood maple floors, and excellent acoustics. The hall closed in 1930. A restoration project is under way.

Civilian Conservation Corps Museum

The Civilian Conservation Corps was formed during the Great Depression to "put Americans back to work." Between 1933 and 1942, more than 100,000 young Michigan men performed a variety of conservation and reforestation projects thereby revitalizing the Michigan state park system and improving campgrounds in Michigan's national forests. The CCC planted 484 million trees, spent 140,000 days fighting forest fires, and constructed 7,000 miles of truck trails, 504 bridges, and 222 buildings.

When the program was discontinued during **World War II**, many alumni donated their photographs and artifacts to the museum in North Higgins Lake State Park near Grayling.

Civil Rights

The United States was built upon the proposition that its inhabitants had an inalienable right to life, liberty, and the pursuit of happiness. Some of the men who designed the nation's system of laws were slave owners, so it did not occur to them to include African Americans in their vision of the country's inhabitants entitled to those rights.

African Americans were unwilling **immigrants**, as slave traders kidnapped them in their homelands and forced them into servitude in the United States. The battle for civil rights for African Americans and other immigrants has been long and bloody. The U.S. Constitution was amended in the mid-1860s in an effort to ban racial discrimination, but the practice continued.

Slavery was concentrated in the rural south, where plantation owners got rich off the work of unpaid laborers. Many African Americans, after winning their freedom, moved to the more industrial north in hope of finding work in factories.

Michigan was an attractive destination in the late 1800s and early 1900s because jobs were plentiful. The young and growing automobile industry in **Detroit** offered well-paying jobs, and automakers even recruited workers from the south. African Americans who migrated north soon learned that they were still treated as second-class citizens. Blacks realized they needed an organized effort to attain and protect their civil rights. They created the **National Association for the Advancement of Colored People** in New York in 1909. The Detroit branch, founded three years later, remains the largest chapter in the nation.

In theory, African Americans were free to live anywhere. In practice, they were not welcomed into all-white neighborhoods. And most of Detroit consisted of all-white neighborhoods. African Americans carved out a neighborhood of their own. It became known as Black Bottom.

Whites had little recourse when their employers integrated the workplace, but things were different in their own neighborhoods. In 1925, Ossian Sweet, an African American physician, bought a house in a mostly white neighborhood on the east side of Detroit. Anticipating trouble, Sweet had asked family and friends to stay with him for a few days.

Police guarded the place but were ineffectual against a gathering crowd. On the second evening of the Sweets' integration, a white mob assembled outside the home and began to pelt it with rocks. Shots were fired from inside the house, and a white man across the street was killed. All 11 people in the Sweet house were arrested and charged with murder.

Famed lawyer Clarence Darrow was hired by the NAACP to defend the Sweets. Darrow stressed to the jury that if it had been a black mob closing in on a white family, the whites would have reacted just as the Sweets did. The jury couldn't agree on a verdict, so the 11 went

East Lansing, March 1960. Black students protesting against segregation practices.

free. When the prosecution retried Henry Sweet, the doctor's brother, the verdict was "not guilty."

Detroit slowly became more integrated, but race relations remained strained. In 1943, a fight between blacks and whites on the city's **Belle Isle** escalated into a riot that resulted in death and destruction. Rumors of white-on-black and black-on-white crime traveled over the Belle Isle bridge and into the surrounding neighborhoods. The riot lasted almost two days and cost 34 lives and millions of dollars in property damage.

While a mob mentality was battering the streets of Detroit, cooler heads were conspiring within the NAACP. The organization took to the courts to ensure equal treatment for people of color. In the 1940s it successfully challenged agreements between home buyers and sellers to exclude African Americans from certain neighborhoods. A decade later, as the courts were being asked to end separate-but-equal education, the Detroit NAACP led a charge against segregation in public housing.

The summer of 1967 brought what is considered Detroit's darkest hour. Tension between police and the black community was common in many large cities. When Detroit police raided an after-hours club frequented by African Americans, it lit a spark that caused a five-day blaze of rioting. Before the unrest ended, riots would break out in New York City, Cleveland, Chicago, Atlanta, Newark, and Washington, D.C.

Detroit police could not control the looters and arsonists who started on the west side and headed east, leaving a path of destruction. City police got assistance from state troopers, the National Guard, and even the U.S. Army. The death toll reached 43. About 1,200 others were injured, and police arrested more than 7,000. Economic damages were estimated at between $40 million and $80 million.

The 1967 riot contributed to "white flight," in which whites left the city for what they perceived to be safer suburbs. As the population shifted to a black majority, its leadership began

to reflect that change. City residents elected their first African American mayor, **Coleman Young**, in 1973. He held the post for 20 years.

Unfortunately, the riots overshadow some of the civil rights triumphs in Detroit. In 1963, Detroiters wanted to mark the 20th anniversary of the Belle Isle riot in a positive manner. The Reverend Martin Luther King Jr. agreed to lead a Walk to Freedom down Woodward Avenue, one of Detroit's main arteries. King was joined by politicians, labor leaders, and about 125,000 other believers in civil rights. In a speech that followed at **Cobo Hall**, King said, "I have a dream this afternoon that one day right here in Detroit, Negroes will be able to buy a house or rent a house anywhere that their money will carry them…" Later that year, King delivered a variation of those remarks at the Lincoln Memorial in Washington, D.C., and his "I Have a Dream" speech made history.

Civil rights struggles in Michigan were not solely based on white vs. black animosity, and they were not limited to Detroit.

Vincent Chin, a 27-year-old Asian American, was beaten to death in 1982 in a Detroit suburb. The altercation began in a bar where Chin's friends had thrown a bachelor party for him. Two white auto workers started taunting Chin, blaming him for the economic downtown their industry was experiencing. Their ignorance was immediately apparent: Chin was of Chinese ancestry, and the American autoworkers were feeling the pinch because of Japanese competition.

Nevertheless, the pair followed Chin out of the bar, caught up with him a short distance away in a parking lot, and bludgeoned him with a baseball bat. The men who killed Chin were fined $3,000 and sentenced to probation. The punishment was considered offensively inadequate by Asian Americans and other civil rights activists.

On the west side of the state, two nights of violence erupted in 2003 when a 28-year-old African American motorcyclist died after a police chase. The incident in Benton Harbor was blamed on the chase as well as on segregation and resentment toward police in the impoverished town.

Governor **Jennifer Granholm** appointed a task force to "help restore opportunity and hope" to the city. The group's duties included reviewing educational and employment opportunities for minorities and finding ways to improve police-community relations.

Equality in employment, education, and housing continues to be a challenge for African Americans. In the mid-1960s, President Lyndon Johnson suggested the creation of affirmative action programs. The idea was to earmark a percentage of jobs and slots in higher education to minorities as a means of righting past discriminatory wrongs. Requiring employers and colleges to welcome a certain number of blacks was designed to level the playing field in the employment arena.

The 1970s brought a court challenge by a white man who was denied admission to the University of California. Allan Bakke complained that giving seats to minorities who were less qualified than he amounted to reverse discrimination. The Supreme Court upheld affirmative action but struck down the quota system of admitting African Americans.

Thirty years later, affirmative action admissions programs were attacked at the **University of Michigan**. In a 2004 opinion poll, the court ordered the school to redesign its system of evaluating applicants, but it reiterated the legality of the program. Attempting to correct past injustice is defensible, the court said, because society is better off when schools and other institutions have a diverse population.

Civil War

The Civil War pitted brother against brother and friend against friend. The controversy over slavery is generally seen as the main cause for the war. But other issues, such as the debate over state rights and the economic aspects of the agricultural South versus the industrial North, were also a cause of conflict.

From the beginning, Michigan was against slavery. It was during an election year that tensions increased between the Northern and Southern states. South Carolina was particularly vocal about the Republican nominee for president, Abraham Lincoln. A moderate candidate, Lincoln was determined to stop the spread of slavery. South Carolina claimed it would secede from the United States if Lincoln was elected president. On December 20, 1860, South Carolina left the Union. Mississippi and Florida left in January 1861. Alabama, Georgia, Louisiana, and Texas followed.

There was no turning back. On April 12, 1861, the newly established Confederacy of the United States fired on the Union forces at Fort Sumter in Charleston Harbor. The war would last until 1866.

When the president sought volunteers to subdue the Southern forces, more than 90,000

Michigan Civil War flag, one of many designs

1ST INFANTRY MICHIGAN VOLUNTEERS

Michigan & Pennsylvania Association Camp, circa 1864

Michiganders heeded the call to arms. Among that number, 1,661 were African American soldiers. At the urging of Governor **Austin Blair**, the state legislature voted to give Lincoln all its available resources. In addition, Blair was given the authority to raise two regiments of militia to help fight in the war.

Recruiting warriors was not a problem for this **Great Lakes** state. Willing volunteers were disappointed when they had to be turned away because Michigan had filled its quota of men. Many of these men joined units from other states.

The First Michigan Infantry Regiment, organized at Fort Wayne in **Detroit**, was made up mostly of men from the southern part of the state. Formed in April 1861, the regiment was the first to reach Washington. When Lincoln saw the soldiers marching through the streets of the capital, he said, "Thank God for Michigan."

The state's soldiers and their families were supported by private and public sources. The

Ulysses S. Grant was stationed in Detroit for part of 1849 and again from 1850 to 1851.

state legislature passed the Michigan Soldier's Relief Act, which contributed money to soldiers' families. In addition, private **Michigan Soldier's Relief Association** groups provided medical care and supplies to soldiers. Throughout the state, citizens held patriotic rallies for departing soldiers and celebrations for returning veterans. In other cities, soldiers' homes were built to help seriously wounded veterans recover from their injuries.

Michigan soldiers were involved in every major battle of the Civil War. General Israel B. Richardson, with the Second Michigan Infantry, fought at the Battle of Antietam. He was killed rallying the federal forces near Bloody Lane. Lt. Col. **Benjamin F. Pritchard** and the men of the Fourth Michigan Calvary captured Confederate President Jefferson Davis in May 1865 as he tried to escape through Georgia.

Many historians consider the Battle of Gettysburg the turning point of the Civil War. Michigan's Cavalry Brigade, led by General **George Armstrong Custer**, was among the regiments that contributed to the victorious outcome of the Union on those Pennsylvania fields. On the final day of the battle, the Michigan Seventh Regiment helped hold back Pickett's charge, the last significant effort by the Confederate Army to defeat the Union forces.

Clovese, Joseph (1844–1951)

Civil War veteran. Born into a slave family of 15, he ran away to join the Union Army and served with the 63rd Negro Infantry during the siege of Vicksburg. He was the last surviving black **Civil War** veteran and attended the last meeting of the **Grand Army of the Republic,** in 1949, when he was 105.

Cobb, Ty (1886–1961)

Sports legend. Ty Cobb may have been baseball's greatest player, if not the game's fiercest

Of the 90,000 Michigan soldiers who fought in the Civil War, more than 1,600 were African American.

C

*Ty Cobb was the first inductee
into the Basketball Hall of Fame.*

competitor. His batting accomplishments are
legendary: a lifetime average of .367, 297
triples, 4,191 hits, 12 batting titles (including
nine in a row), 23 straight seasons in which he
hit over .300, three .400 seasons, and 2,245 runs.
The Georgia Peach stole 892 bases during a 24-
year career, primarily with the **Detroit Tigers**.

In 1936, Cobb became the first inductee
into the Baseball Hall of Fame, with 222 out of
a possible 226 votes.

Cobb played 24 seasons of baseball and
invested his earnings wisely, mostly in General
Motors and Coca-Cola stock, which made
him very wealthy and he was probably baseball's first millionaire.

Cobo Hall

Madonna, KISS, and **Bob Seger** all leaped to
superstardom from the stage of this 12,191-seat
auditorium, famous for its superb acoustics. In
its 40-plus years as one of the state's premier
entertainment venues, Cobo has hosted sporting and civic events, family shows, and even
U.S. presidents.

Martin Luther King Jr. previewed his "I
Have a Dream" speech at Cobo two months
before he delivered the history-making speech
at the Lincoln Memorial in Washington, D.C.,
in 1963.

Coleman, Mary (1914–2001)

Judge. She was elected to the Michigan

Cobo Hall, where Martin Luther King Jr. previewed his "I Have a Dream" speech.

Supreme Court in 1972, the first woman to hold that honor. She became the court's chief justice in 1979 and retired in 1982. Her contributions to Michigan's judicial system included revising the state's probate and juvenile justice codes and drafting most of the state's first child protection legislation.

Colon

After Percy Abbott visited magician **Harry Blackstone Sr.** there, the town of 1,200 did a transformation act and ever since has been known as the Magic Capital of the World. In 1933, the Australian magician opened **Abbott's Magic**, the world's largest magic company. Many of the most famous magicians from David Copperfield to Doug Henning have shopped there, and Blackstone was for a short time Abbott's business partner. Since 1934 Abbott has sponsored the annual Magic Get-Together, which attracts thousands of professional and amateur conjurers.

Blackstone spent summers in Colon creating new illusions and rehearsing his show, which he then took on the road during the winter.

There's more magic memorabilia at the Colon Community Museum, located on a street named for the town's most famous resident. Housed in an 1893 church, the museum chronicles the town's first pioneer families but also has an area devoted to Blackstone and Abbott. The museum, at 219 North Blackstone Road, is open Tuesday, Thursday, and Sunday, from 2 to 4:30 p.m.

Mary Coleman was the first woman to be elected to the Michigan Supreme Court.

Colon Opera House, home to the many magic shows that have been performed in Colon over the years

Even the local cemetery attracts conjurers. Both **Harry Blackstone Sr.** and **Harry Blackstone Jr.** are buried there. Other permanent residents include Bill Baird, "The Magnificent Fraud"; illusionist Jack Gwynne, comic magician Donald Monk Watson; Robert Lund, who opened the American Museum of Magic; Don Alan McWethy, star of the 1960s television show *Don Alan's Magic Ranch*; and Ricki Dunn, a pickpocket, comedian, and inventor of magic tricks.

Columbia

Typical of the propeller-driven excursion ships of the early 20th century, the *Columbia* is the nation's oldest remaining passenger steamship. Excursion steamers, used throughout the country, were built to take passengers on day trips; *Columbia*'s route ran between **Detroit** and **Bob-Lo Island** in the **Detroit River**. Its builder was the Detroit Dry Dock Company, who gave it a rare propulsion engine which was never altered.

Columbia, designed by famed ship architect **Frank E. Kirby**, was listed on the National Register of Historic Places in 1979 and became a National Historic Landmark in 1992. It is docked at Nicholson Terminal in Ecorse, pending restoration.

Comerica

After more than a century of baseball at **Tiger Stadium** at "The Corner" of Michigan and Trumbull avenues, the **Detroit Tigers** moved into Comerica Park in 2000. Located in **Detroit**'s Foxtown area, the stadium seats 40,000. With no upper-deck outfield seating, Comerica Park claims to offer the best view of a downtown skyline.

The $360 million ballpark has a sunken playing field, a Ferris wheel, a baseball museum, and one of the largest scoreboards in sport. When the Tigers hit a homerun, the two tigers on top of the scoreboard roar and the center-field fountain shoots water into the air.

Constitutional Convention

Michigan's first constitutional convention was held in the territory's capital of **Detroit** from May 11 to June 24, 1835. Territorial Gov. **Stevens T. Mason** believed Michigan had a right to be a state, despite the refusal of Congress to endorse a state constitutional convention. In fact, Congress refused to recognize Michigan as a state until the dispute over the Toledo strip was settled. **Michiganders** and Ohioans were fighting over a 468-square-mile stretch of land in a border dispute. The mean-spirited struggle, known as the **Toledo War**, ended by Congressional decree.

While Congress debated that disagreement, 91 delegates from Michigan drafted and adopted Michigan's first constitution, declaring the territory a state and preserving the rights of its voters. On October 5 and 6, 1835, the new constitution was adopted by a vote of 6,299 to 1,359.

Michigan joined the union on January 26, 1837, when President Andrew Jackson signed a bill making Michigan the nation's 26th state. That also ended the battle over the Toledo Strip, as Michigan accepted a congressional proposal that gave Toledo to Ohio. Instead, Michigan was given the western **Upper Peninsula**, a 9,000-square-mile chunk of land

The Columbia *is the oldest passenger steamship in America.*

Comerica Park is the new home of the Detroit Tigers.

C

later found to contain vast resources of timber, iron, and copper.

Michigan's 1835 constitution proved far-sighted in that it called for a public education system under the direction of a state superin-tendent, the first state constitution to do so, and safeguarded federal land-grant funds from diversion to uses other than education. The constitution also authorized the state govern-ment to build a transportation infrastructure.

Modern political scientists have praised the constitution's provisions regarding state offi-cials. Only the governor, lieutenant governor, and legislators—the offices voters could most easily follow—were to be elected. Other offi-cials, whose qualifications might be more obscure, were to be appointed. Elections were to be held in odd-numbered years so as not to divert voters' attention from national elections.

Despite its progressive clauses, the consti-tution left much room for improvement in the area of suffrage for the state's African American and female populations: only white men were allowed to vote. Over the years, Michigan vot-ers repeatedly rejected proposals to give African Americans the vote. Until passage of the Fifteenth Amendment to the U.S. Constitution, which barred such discrimination, whites-only remained status quo. Women, faring slightly better, were given the vote in Michigan a year before ratification of the **Nineteenth Amendment** to the U.S. Constitution granted all American women full suffrage.

The 1935 state constitution allowed the people of Michigan to decide every 16 years if another constitutional convention was neces-sary to propose revisions. Michigan has had five more conventions, the most recent in 1961 to 1962. The state has had three additional con-stitutions, including the current one, adopted in 1963. Two other constitutions were drafted but rejected by the citizens.

The first constitution is now housed at the State Archives of Michigan in Lansing. A fragile document, it is now publicly displayed only in January during Statehood Day celebrations.

Copper Harbor Lighthouse

Copper Harbor ship traffic expanded rapidly in the 1840s, and in 1849 a stone light tower was put into service. The station received a Fresnel light in 1856. The lighthouse ceased function-ing in 1927. Topped with a copper roof, the building today houses a nautical museum that is part of **Fort Wilkins State Park**.

Coppola, Francis Ford (1939–)

Filmmaker. As a child, the **Detroit** native made 8mm short features from home movies. The son of composer and musician Carmine Coppola, he was groomed for a career as a musician.

While doing graduate work in film at the University of California, Los Angeles, he assisted director Roger Corman on a series of moderately budgeted films. Corman assigned him to various roles as dialogue director, sound man, and associate producer.

While filming *The Young Racers* in Ireland in 1962, Coppola proposed a low-budget film to Corman. *Dementia 13* was shot in only nine days and was Coppola's first feature from his own screenplay. The film more than made back its meager budget and became a cult favorite among horror enthusiasts.

With George Lucas, Coppola created inde-pendent film production company American Zoetrope in 1969. His film *The Godfather*, direct-ed in 1971, became one of the highest-grossing movies in film history, and Coppola won an Oscar for the screenplay.

In 1974, Coppola directed *The Conversation*, which won the Golden Palm Award at the Cannes Film Festival, as well as Academy Award nominations for best picture and best original screenplay. The same year, Coppola wrote the screenplay for *The Great Gatsby* and *The Godfather, Part II* was released. The *Godfather* sequel rivaled the original with record-setting success at the box office and six Academy Awards, an unprecedented high for a sequel that has not been repeated since.

He continues to make films and also owns a successful winery in California's Napa Valley.

Cornish Pasty

Favorite portable meal for **Upper Peninsula** miners, a Cornish pasty is a hearty meat pie filled with onions, beef, and potatoes. **Immigrant** miners from Cornwall, England, carried the specialty into the U.P.'s copper mines in the 1880s. The still-popular meal is made and sold in Upper Peninsula cafés and bakeries.

Coughlin, Father Charles (1891–1979)

Priest. After studying in Toronto, in 1926 the Ontario native was ordained and became pastor of the Shrine of the Little Flower in Royal Oak. There he became known as the Radio Priest and the Fighting Priest because of his

controversial broadcasts on WJR. An estimated 30 million listeners tuned in during the 1930s. Coughlin was considered a social watchdog by some, an anti-Semite by others.

Coughlin also published a magazine, *Social Justice,* in which he expressed pro-Nazi opinions. The magazine was barred from the mail by the U.S. government for violation of the Espionage Act and ceased publication in 1942.

Coughlin was silenced by his superiors but continued his parish duties until his retirement in 1966.

Cranbrook Educational Community

Detroit News owners George Gough Booth and Ellen Scripps Booth funded Finnish architect

Cranbrook brought together some of the most gifted art students in the world, with a faculty to match.

Eliel Saarinen to transform their Bloomfield Hills estate into an artists community, which opened in 1932 to great success. The Booths, like Saarinen, believed that art could not be taught directly but must be a shared process. With art students from around the world, the Cranbrook Academy of Art became a living record of the emerging character of American architecture. World-renowned Swedish sculptor **Carl Milles,** who joined Saarinen on the faculty, created more than 70 sculptures to complement Saarinen's design. Students lived their art, creating everything from the overhead light fixtures to the rugs on the floors.

The Booths' house, designed by **Albert Kahn,** is the oldest manor home in metropolitan **Detroit**. The grounds around the house were designed by Booth himself.

Today Cranbrook includes the Academy of Art, a graduate-level program in the fine arts; the Institute of Science, a natural history and science museum and research facility; a contemporary art museum; and an independent school system from pre-kindergarten through to high school. There is also a resident program for high-school students.

Cranbrook, named for the English village where Booth's ancestors lived, was listed on the State Register in 1972 and the National Register of Historic Places the next year. It was listed as a National Historic Landmark in 1989.

Crane, Caroline Bartlett (1858–1935)

Pastor, reporter, social reformer. The daughter of a steamboat captain, she could navigate the Mississippi River, which won her an interview with Mark Twain.

After her ordination, she became pastor of the First Unitarian Church of **Kalamazoo**, later the nonsectarian People's Church, and led the congregation to open a public kindergarten, women's gymnasium, training programs, and club for Kalamazoo's "young colored people."

Appalled at the unsanitary conditions in slaughterhouses, she lobbied a bill through the

Caroline Bartlett Crane's Everyman's House took first place in the Better Homes of America contest of 1924.

Michigan legislature to regulate meat packing. She organized the Women's Civic Improvement League to promote public health projects, and the Charity Organizations Board. She also designed the award-winning **Everyman's House**.

Crane, C. Howard (1885–1952)

Architect. Departing from classical European traditions and combining Old World sophistication with Hollywood glamour, **Detroit**'s C. Howard Crane turned picture theaters into palaces with his dazzling architectural designs. A leading theater architect of the 1920s, he was in demand nationwide for his "Picture Palace Gothic" style. He built 52 theaters just in Detroit.

Cultural Center Historic District

The intellectual center of **Detroit** encompasses the Detroit Public Library on the east side of Woodward Avenue and the **Detroit Institute of Arts** and Rackham Building on the west side. The layout came from a 1913 plan based on the City Beautiful movement, the philosophy that urban beauty would inspire civic virtue.

Curtis, Christopher Paul (1954–)

Children's author. He received both the Newbery Medal and the Coretta Scott King Award for his novels *The Watsons Go to Birmingham* (1996) and *Bud, Not Buddy* (2000). He began *The Watsons* while working assembly at the **Flint** Fisher Body Plant. His most recent book is *Bucking the Sarge.*

The Cultural Center Historic District is within walking distance of Wayne State University's main campus.

C

Custer, George Armstrong (1839–1876)

Civil War General. Ineffectual while he lived, Custer rose to mythological fame in death. He grew up in Monroe, though he was born in Ohio, and enrolled at West Point, where he graduated at the bottom of his class. He was court-martialed shortly after graduation but escaped punishment because of the desperate need for officers brought on by the outbreak of the **Civil War**.

Fearlessly aggressive, he distinguished himself in the First Battle of Bull Run and in the Virginia and Gettysburg campaigns, and his cavalry units were instrumental in forcing Confederate Gen. Robert E. Lee to retreat. However, his units suffered frightful losses, even by the standards of the Civil War.

After the war, as lieutenant-colonel of the Seventh Cavalry, he led a failed campaign against the Southern Cheyenne. In 1867, he was court-martialed again, this time for absence during the campaign, and suspended. Gen. Philip Sheridan, a friend from the war, reinstated him a year later.

Custer led one of three forces charged with defeating the Lakota tribes in 1876. In contradiction to orders, he advanced ahead of the other units. On June 25, he approached what appeared to be a large Indian village and, contemptuous of Indian warfare, split his forces into three for an immediate attack. Thousands of Lakota Sioux, Cheyenne, and Arapaho warriors surrounded his 210-man unit and killed them all. Tales of the battle at Little Big Horn, fueled by his widow, made Custer a hero. Over the next century, under closer examination, Custer's Last Stand became a symbol of failure.

General George Armstrong Custer was famously killed at the Battle of Little Big Horn.

D

de Angeli , Marguerite (1889–1987)

Author. Over 50 years, the Lapeer native wrote and illustrated 28 children's books and illustrated more than a dozen others. She won the 1950 Newbery Medal for *The Door in the Wall.* She was among the first inductees to the **Michigan Women's Hall of Fame**.

DeLorean, John (1925–)

Auto industry executive. While with General Motors, DeLorean designed the Pontiac GTO and Gran Prix, but he left the company in 1973 to form the DeLorean Motor Company. His visionary, radical first car, the DeLorean, featured a stainless steel body and gull-wing doors. Approximately 8,500 of the cars were built between 1981 and 1983. Financial problems plagued the company, and DeLorean was arrested in 1982, charged with smuggling cocaine and money laundering to support his operations. He was later acquitted of the charges on the basis of government entrapment.

The DeTour Lighthouse marks the meeting point of Lake Huron and Lake Superior.

DeTour Reef Light

Since 1931, the Art Deco lighthouse has stood at DeTour Reef to mark the meeting point of Lake Huron and Lake Superior at the mouth of the St. Mary's River. In 1998, representing dozens of Michigan's lighthouses, it was used as the "poster lighthouse" on the list of America's 11 Most Endangered Historic Places of the National Trust for Historic Preservation.

Detroit

Founded by the French in 1701, Detroit was first called Fort Pontchartrain. It was renamed Fort Detroit in 1751. A remnant of the early settlement, **Ste. Anne de Detroit Catholic Church**, still stands beneath the entryway to the **Ambassador Bridge**. Fort Detroit was one of the few British posts that successfully withstood the siege of **Pontiac**'s Rebellion. Construction of a new fort north of the original settlement, and on higher ground, was ordered in 1778. Fort Lernoult was built at the site of present-day Fort and Shelby streets in downtown Detroit.

At the turn of the century, Detroit was still a small town busily engaged in making stoves, beer, and carriages, but Detroit's first automobile, built by **Charles Brady King**, changed that. It was driven for the first time on March 6, 1896, and was the beginning of Detroit's transformation into the Motor Capital of the World. The pioneering spirit of men like **Ransom E. Olds**, **Henry M. Leland**, and **Henry Ford** led

PLANT OF THE DETROIT STOVE WORKS, JEFFERSON AVENUE.

Detroit to far outclass all competitors. Assembly line techniques were known by the mid-19th century, but it was Henry Ford who brought them to their peak with the introduction of the moving automobile assembly line at the **Highland Park Ford Plant** in 1913. Ford Model T production immediately increased from seven and a half per hour to 146 per hour, firmly anchoring Detroit's position as the Motor City. On February 9, 1942, all auto assembly lines in Detroit ceased production of civilian vehicles; they manufactured only military vehicles until the end of **World War II**. By 1943, Detroit produced about 10 percent of all U.S. military output.

America's pioneer radio station, **WWJ**, began regularly scheduled broadcasts on August 31, 1920. *The Detroit News* announced the first radio newscast, which included state, country, and congressional primary election returns.

On November 11, 1929, while the world celebrated Armistice Day, Detroit and Windsor celebrated the opening of the **Ambassador Bridge**, so named because it represented long-standing good relations between old allies, the United States and Canada. When it opened, it was the longest suspension bridge in the world.

Detroit is home to three national sports teams, and in 1935, all brought home championships. The **Tigers** won baseball's World Series, the **Lions** won the NFL Football Championship, and the **Red Wings** won hockey's Stanley Cup.

Motown, Detroit's other nickname, comes from **Berry Gordy**'s **Motown** Records, which opened in 1959. Under Gordy's leadership, the company became one of the largest music producers in the nation. The Motown Sound was new to the music world and catapulted unknown black youths to singing stardom during the early 1960s.

On June 23, 1963, Rev. Martin Luther King Jr. previewed his "I Have a Dream" speech before 125,000 Detroiters after the Walk to

Detroit's nicknames included Stove Capital of the World.

D Freedom down Woodward Avenue. Michigan State senator and former Tuskegee Airman **Coleman A. Young** was inaugurated as Detroit's first black mayor in 1974. Young remained in office through 1993. The subsequent election of mayors Dennis A. Archer and Kwame M. Kilpatrick ensured that blacks would continue to lead Detroit for over 30 years.

Still known as the Motor City, Detroit is also a great steel center and a leading manufacturer of pharmaceuticals, office equipment, paint, rubber products, salt, and more than half the garden seed used in the U.S.

Detroit Arsenal Tank Plant

Detroit Arsenal was the first plant built for the mass production of American tanks. It was designed in 1941 by architect **Albert Kahn** and run by Chrysler. When the United States entered **World War II**, Detroit Arsenal Tank Plant was called upon to build M3 and M4

Sherman tanks. The plant built 22,392 tanks during the course of the war and went on to supply tanks to the military until 1996. The plant relocated to the city of Warren and is now used for research and development.

Detroit Historical Museum

The museum, which celebrates **Detroit**'s 300-year history, was dedicated with great hoopla on July 24, 1951, the 250th anniversary of the city's founding by **Antoine de la Mothe Cadillac**. Exhibits include a working assembly line and recreations of Detroit streets over the decades. The museum's educational programs, including the interactive Detroit Storyliving, serve thousands of school children each year. The museum, at 5401 Woodward Avenue, Detroit, is open Tuesday through Friday, 9:30 a.m. to 5 p.m., Saturday 10 a.m. to 5 p.m., and Sunday 11 a.m. to 5 p.m.

Detroit (the "Motor City") has a thriving relationship with its cross-river neighbor, Windsor, Canada. Bottom left is the Horace E. Dodge and Son Memorial Fountain in Hart Plaza.

D

Detroit Industry

Henry Ford commissioned Mexican painter Diego Rivera to paint the 27 fresco panels, which pay tribute to the American worker. Rivera's radical politics and many of the images he created drew much controversy, but **Edsel Ford**, Henry's son, defended Rivera. *Detroit Industry,* on the walls of the **Detroit Institute of the Arts**, remains Rivera's most important piece in America.

Rodin's famous sculpture The Thinker, *which has been on display outside the Detroit Institute of the Arts since it first opened in 1888.*

Detroit Institute of the Arts

The DIA has come to symbolize the strength and diversity of the people of **Detroit** and its surrounding cities. With its collection of more than 65,000 works, ranging from African Cultures and Ancient Islamic art to European paintings and contemporary art, the DIA offers one of the largest and most expansive art collections in the country.

A painting of four women in Greek mythology called *Reading the Story of Oenone,* by the American painter Francis D. Millet, was the museum's first piece for Detroit's public collection. It was purchased for $2,500 with the proceeds from a temporary art exhibit in 1883 organized by William H. Brearley, advertising

The exterior of the Detroit Institute of the Arts

manager of the Detroit *Evening News,* and held in a temporary hall. Close to 135,000 people attended the show during its 10-week run. Inspired by the success of his venture, Brearley persuaded 40 of Detroit's most prominent families to donate $1,000 each to build a museum. Many others contributed and in 1884, *Evening News* founder James E. Scripps gave an additional $50,000. The Romanesque-style Detroit Museum of Art opened on East Jefferson and Hastings on September 1, 1888, with Rodin's famous sculpture *The Thinker* proudly on

display out front, where it continues to be admired. Among the museum's most famous works are paintings done by Diego Rivera in 1932 on the garden walls inside the DIA. In the fresco panels, entitled **Detroit Industry**, the artist depicts scenes of workers on the assembly line at the **Ford River Rouge Plant**, along with paintings of himself and his wife, Frida Kahlo, at the DIA.

Detroit Lions

The Detroit Lions were welcomed into the National Football League in 1934, when **Detroit** radio executive George A. Richards purchased the Portsmouth (Ohio) Spartans for nearly $8,000 and moved them to the Motor City. The Lions name was chosen by Richards to symbolize the hope that the team would be the monarch of the league, just as the lion is the monarch of the jungle.

The Lions started play in the University of Detroit Stadium and won their first NFL Championship in 1935. After moving to Briggs Field in 1938, the Lions dominated the NFL, with four division titles and three league championships, in 1952, 1953, and 1957. The team boasted Hall of Fame players Jack Christiansen, Lou Creekmur, Bill Dudley, Bobby Layne, Doak Walker, and Alex Wojciechowicz.

After last winning the league championship in 1957, the Lions continued to reach for another championship but suffered a long drought until winning the division championship in 1983 with superstar running back Barry Sanders. During the 1990s they reached the playoffs six times, a franchise record.

The Lions moved to the Pontiac Silverdome in 1975 and played there for 37 years. They moved to a new 65,000-seat domed stadium, Ford Field in Detroit, in 2002. William Clay Ford purchased the team in 1964 for $4.5 million.

Detroit News **and** *Detroit Free Press*

The *Free Press* grew out of a weekly newspaper, first published May 5, 1831, called the *Democratic Free Press and Michigan Intelligencer.* In 1835, the paper started publishing daily, and the name was changed to the *Detroit Free Press.* It was the state's first daily newspaper and is Michigan's oldest paper in continuous publication. The *Detroit News* started as the *Detroit Daily News* on July 7, 1845, and was renamed the *Evening News* in 1873. In 1905, the *News* merged with the *Detroit Tribune* and became the *Detroit News.*

The papers were fierce competitors, the *Free Press* known as more liberal, the *Detroit News* considered conservative. With the rise of 24-hour cable TV networks, the appetite for newspapers declined and circulation dropped off. Although neither newspaper was failing, in the 1980s, a controversial joint operating agreement was approved that combined the papers' business and production operations. The editorial operations remain separate. The new

The Detroit Institute of the Arts was designed by Paul Phillipe Cret to complement its neighbor, the Detroit Public Library.

The Detroit News Building also houses the Detroit Free Press.

company, called Detroit Newspapers, is co-owned by the parent companies of the *Free Press*, Knight-Ridder, and the *Detroit News*, Gannett. The newspapers publish separately during the week and combine weekend and holiday publication as the *Detroit News and Free Press*.

The marriage proved to be rocky. Profits were still low, and the change was difficult for readers and staff. When Detroit Newspapers wanted to cut staffing in 1995, six of the newspaper unions, with 2,500 members, went on strike. It turned out to be a nasty affair, erupting into violence as police clashed with strikers and some journalists crossed the picket lines to get back to work. The strike ended in 1997.

Detroit Opera House

Opened in 1922 as the Capitol Theater, it was designed by **C. Howard Crane**, in Italian Renaissance style. The movie palace had superb acoustics. It opened and closed under different names until it was restored to its original appearance in 1989. The **Detroit** landmark stands at 1526 Broadway.

Detroit Pistons

The Detroit Pistons are one of the National Basketball Association's oldest franchises. Automobile-piston magnate Fred Zollner founded the team in 1940 as the Fort Wayne Zollner Pistons, and a year later they joined the National Basketball League. They shifted to the Basketball Association of America in 1948 and then the NBA when the BAA and the NBL merged in 1949. One of eight teams in the Central Division of the Eastern Conference, they qualified for the playoffs in each of their first five seasons but lost every time. After moving to **Detroit** in 1957, the Pistons continued one of the longest droughts in the history of professional sports, enduring 41 years before winning their first NBA championship in 1989.

The late 1980s and early 1990s showed the Pistons to be one of the top teams in the NBA. They won back-to-back titles in 1989 and 1990,

with such featured players as **Isiah Thomas**, Bill Laimbeer, Joe Dumars, Rick Mahorn, and Dennis Rodman. In the 1990s the Pistons faded as the Chicago Bulls emerged to dominate the Eastern Conference.

Over the years, many players have received awards of distinction, including three Eddie Gottlieb Trophy winners for Rookie of the Year, and six numbers have been retired. Three Pistons have been inducted into the Basketball Hall of Fame (Dave Bing, 1989; Bob Lanier, 1992; and George Yardley, 1996). The Pistons, wearing jerseys of red, white, and blue, play at the Palace of Auburn Hills.

Detroit Plaindealer

Detroit's first successful African American newspaper was started in 1883 to advocate for black interests throughout the Midwest. The paper attracted well-known writers such as activist Ida B. Wells but, lacking proper community support, it ceased publication in 1894. The *Michigan Chronicle*, founded in 1943, continues to publish.

Detroit Red Wings

In 1926, Charles Hughes and a group of investors persuaded the **Detroit Athletic Club** to add a new team, the Detroit Cougars, to the National Hockey League. Four years later the team became known as the Detroit Falcons. In 1932, after millionaire James Norris bought the team, they became the Detroit Red Wings. Today **Detroit** is Hockeytown, as the Red Wings, nine-time Stanley Cup winners, have become one of the dominating hockey teams in history. They have inducted 33 players into the Hockey Hall of Fame.

The Red Wings got their name from Norris, who belonged to the Montreal Amateur Athletic Association, which had cycling roots. He decided the name would be perfect for a team playing in the Motor City.

Hockey is rich in tradition, especially in Detroit, with its history of an octopus thrown on the ice. The octopus mascot made its first

appearance in 1952 during a Stanley Cup play-off run. The eight tentacles were symbolic of the eight wins it took to collect the Stanley Cup. The Red Wings swept the series that year to win their fifth Stanley Cup, and the octopus has been a good luck charm ever since.

The Red Wings have had their share of ups and downs, but the motivation that helped build the team in 1926 has served to keep them alive for nearly 80 years. Home ice is the 19,983-seat Joe Louis Arena.

Detroit River

A 1908 *Detroit News* article compared the amount of goods that had passed to the port of **Detroit** via the Detroit River in the previous year to what had gone through London and New York during the same period. Detroit won hands down, with 67,292,504 tons, nearly double the tonnage of the two other cities combined. To move that amount of freight by boxcar would require a train that stretched three-quarters the way around the earth.

The Detroit River is unique in the world in connecting, rather than dividing, two sovereign nations. With annual crossings by 14,000,000 vehicles and 8,000 commercial ships, the river is the busiest international border in North America and comprises the world's largest metropolitan area along an international border.

Since the beginnings of the Common Era,

The Detroit Opera House was restored to its original appearance in 1989.

D

The Detroit River has both American Heritage River and Canadian Heritage River designations, intended to conserve and protect the river.

the river has been a major cultural and commercial artery. Remains of Indian cultures along the riverfront date back 2,000 years. By the time the river carried the first Europeans, it had been used by **Native Americans** for centuries as a passageway to hunting and trapping areas. In the past 300 years it has carried everything from furs to "hooch" to human commerce—runaway slaves.

French **fur traders** were the first Europeans to navigate the river. Roads came much later; the river was their only means of transporting their goods. Living among the Indians, the fur traders traveled as their neighbors did, by canoe. **Antoine de la Mothe Cadillac**, founder of Detroit, arrived by way of the river.

By the mid-1700s, French settlers were invited to the area with the promise of farm implements and animals. They settled on both sides, always near the river, which provided water for drinking and washing.

In 1760, after defeating the French, the English found their way down the river. When the French and Indians formed a coalition to drive them out, they were saved by proximity to the river and the troops and supplies that sailed down it.

After the **War of 1812**, as soldiers returning to their homes in the East told of the plentiful land in Michigan, settlers began to head west. They were joined by **immigrants** from Germany, France, and Britain. The opening of the **Erie Canal** in 1825 helped travel to the **Great Lakes** and cities along the river thrived.

Michigan, by virtue of the **Northwest Ordinance**, prohibited slavery, but in 1850 Congress passed the Fugitive Slave Act, which enabled slave owners to follow runaway slaves even into free states and take them back. The Detroit River became the number one station for conducting slaves along the **Underground Railroad** to Canada.

The Detroit River joins two friends, the United States and Canada.

The river was used for smuggling of a different kind during the 1920s and '30s. The narrow river—less than a mile across at some points—provided a quick dash into Canada for illegal liquor during **Prohibition**, and the myriad coves and islands along its 32-mile length offered protection from the U.S. Coast Guard. Rumrunners dragged booze under boats during the summer and skated or drove it across the frozen river during the winter. Enterprising bootleggers even constructed a pipeline between a Detroit bottler and a Windsor distiller.

Detroit Shock

The Detroit Shock is Michigan's women's pro basketball team. Founded in 1998, the team has played against the toughest WNBA teams in the nation. In 2003 the Shock, led by Coach Bill Laimbeer, won the WNBA Championship. The team plays home games at the Palace of Auburn Hills, which it shares with the men's pro team, the **Detroit Pistons**. The Shock also hosts a WNBA Girls' Basketball Camp in summers for aspiring young female athletes.

Detroit Symphony Orchestra

The orchestra played its first concert at the Detroit Opera House on February 26, 1914. Its founders were 10 society mavens who contributed $100 apiece and added 100 subscribers, at $10 each, to the membership rolls.

The orchestra's first music director, Boston church organist Weston Gales, left after three years. He was succeeded by renowned Russian pianist **Ossip Gabrilowitsch**, who insisted upon a new auditorium before he would take the position and oversaw the building of **Orchestra Hall**. Under Gabrilowitsch's direction, DSO became one of the country's premier orchestras, drawing such guest artists as Enrico Caruso, Marian Anderson, Isadora Duncan, and Igor

D

Stravinsky. Gabrilowitsch directed the DSO in the world's first radio broadcast of a symphonic concert, on February 10, 1922. He also led the orchestra's first performance at Carnegie Hall and its first recording, both in 1928.

DSO fell on troubled times after Gabrilowitsch's death. Financial woes forced the orchestra out of Orchestra Hall. It disbanded twice. By the 1950s, under music director Paul Paray, DSO was back on top and was one of the nation's most recorded orchestras.

In 1989, 50 years after leaving, DSO returned to make a renovated Orchestra Hall its home once again. The orchestra's weekly radio performances reach more than 1,000,000 listeners, making it the most widely heard symphony orchestra in the country. Musical director Neeme Järvi observes his 15th anniversary with the orchestra in 2005.

Detroit Tigers

On April 25, 1901, the Detroit Tigers took the field at Bennett Park for their first official American League baseball game. Named for the striped stockings they wore, the Tigers were led early by the legendary **Ty Cobb**, the

Ty Cobb led the Tigers to three AL pennants.

most famous Tiger of all. **Detroit** won three AL pennants in the early 1900s with Cobb, who achieved some of the most remarkable statistics in baseball history.

The club moved to its new home, Navin Field, in 1912. The field, named after team president Frank Navin, evolved into **Tiger Stadium**. For nearly a century the stadium was home to such greats as Mickey Cochrane, **Hank Greenberg**, Charlie Gehringer, Hal Newhouser, Denny McLain, Willie Hernandez, and **Al Kaline**. **Sparky Anderson**, Hughie Jennings, and Bucky Harris, all Baseball Hall of Famers, are among the memorable managers who have led the team.

Comerica Park, which opened its doors in 2000, signaled the beginning of a new era of Tiger baseball. Its Walking Hall of Fame, with a large collection of memorabilia, lets fans remember the great moments of the past. Opening Day brought a sold-out crowd of 40,000 people and a win, all in mid-30 degree weather.

The Tigers have played in six Hall of Fame Games and held the titles of American League East Champions three times and American League Champions nine times. They have won four World Series—1935, 1945, 1968, and 1984.

Detroit-Windsor Tunnel

The tunnel is the second busiest border crossing between the United States and Canada and the only underwater border crossing in the world open to private vehicular traffic. Finished a year after its competitor, the **Ambassador Bridge**, the two-lane tunnel is the primary connection between the downtown areas of the two cities, channeling 20,000 vehicles a day from one side to the other. The tunnel is 5,160 feet long and has a clearance of just over 13 feet. The roadway goes 75 feet below the surface of the **Detroit River**. The tunnel opened on November 3, 1930.

More than any other team, the Detroit Tigers are the hometown favorites.

The tunnel takes travelers directly from downtown Detroit to downtown Windsor, Canada.

D

Detroit Zoo

An animal lovers' destination for more than 75 years, the Detroit Zoo covers more than 125 acres of landscaped grounds. With its large open spaces and outdoor animal environments, it is considered one of the most modern zoos in the country.

The zoo opened at its current site on Sunday, August 5, 1928. More than 1,000 people entered during the first 15 minutes. An early popular exhibit was a pair of lion cubs. But it was the Indian elephant Paulina who became the undisputed queen of the zoo. When she arrived in 1928 the six-ton Paulina, who had performed in circuses prior to coming to the zoo, was immediately put to work moving heavy construction materials in preparation for the zoo's opening later that year. It is estimated she gave rides to half a million zoo visitors, mostly children. Last of the original zoo animals, Paulina died in 1950 at the age of 69.

The Detroit Zoo has been open since 1928.

Among the Detroit Zoo's newest attractions is the world's largest polar bear exhibit. In the Arctic Ring of Life, a 70-foot underwater tunnel takes visitors into the watery world of the zoo's seven polar bears. A four-acre great ape complex, snow monkey and Mandrill baboon compounds, reptile house, and free-flight aviary also are featured. A historic building on the grounds has been converted into the Wildlife Interpretive Gallery and contains an aquarium, butterfly garden, art gallery, and interactive exhibits. The Detroit Zoo is located in Royal Oak at 8450 West Ten Mile Road. Please call Detroit Zoo or check their website for opening times.

Dewey, Thomas (1902–1971)

Statesman. The Owosso native studied law at Columbia University and became the district attorney for the southern district of New York. His popularity as a gang-buster made him a shoe-in for governor in 1941. He lost the 1944

Diggs' victory at the federal level in 1954 marked the beginning of a 25-year career on Capitol Hill. In the early 1970s, he was a founder and the first chairman of the Congressional Black Caucus.

Diggs' political career ended after he was convicted of mail fraud and filing false payroll forms. Diggs was censured by the House in 1979. He was subsequently re-elected but resigned after being sentenced to prison.

Thomas Dewey lost the 1944 presidential election to Franklin D. Roosevelt.

Charles C. Diggs Jr. was the first African American from Detroit to be elected to the U.S. House of Representatives.

WELCOME HOME

presidential election to Franklin D. Roosevelt. He was so highly favored to win the 1948 election, a morning-after *Chicago Daily Tribune* headline famously proclaimed "Dewey Defeats Truman"—though Dewey had lost to Harry S. Truman. In 1952, Dewey decided not to run but to help Dwight D. Eisenhower win office. He went back to his law practice in 1955 after his third term as New York governor.

Dew, Gwen (1903–1993)
Reporter, photographer. Gwen Dew's fascinating narratives made the Albion native an international legendary reporter and photographer. Her experiences as a prisoner of war during **World War II** left an indelible impression on readers and helped cement her reputation for accuracy and integrity.

Diggs, Charles C., Jr. (1922–1998)
Legislator. Charles C. Diggs Jr. was the first African American Detroiter to be elected to the U.S. House of Representatives. His political career began in the 1950s when he took over his father's seat in the Michigan State Senate.

Charles C. Diggs Sr. was the first African American elected to the Michigan State Senate.

Diggs, Charles C., Sr. (1894–1967)

Legislator. Charles C. Diggs Sr. was a well-known mortician and prominent Detroiter. He ran the House of Diggs, a large funeral home.

In 1937, Diggs became the first African-American elected to the Michigan State Senate. In the 1940s he served time in prison for accepting bribes. He was re-elected despite that conviction, but fellow senators refused to allow him to occupy the office. His son, **Charles C. Diggs Jr.**, was elected to replace him.

Dodge, Horace (1868–1920) and John (1864–1920)

Automakers. Brothers Horace and John Dodge invented the first all-steel automobiles. The Niles natives began their road to success by producing bicycles, and in 1901 they opened a shop making stove parts. Later they moved on to building auto parts. They established the Dodge Brothers Company in 1910. Their first automobile made its appearance in 1914.

Dodge cars earned a reputation for ruggedness and were used as staff vehicles and ambulances in World War I. By 1920, Dodge

The beautifully designed gardens around the Alden B. Dow House (see entry on page 82).

was one of the industry's largest companies. Dodge is known to this day for its high-performance vehicles and durability.

Domino's Pizza

Thomas Monaghan founded **Ann Arbor**-based Domino's in 1960. A multi-billion-dollar business, Domino's pioneered the conveyor oven, dough trays, corrugated pizza boxes, and insulated transport bags. Today, Domino's operates 6,300 stores in more than 60 international markets. The world's number two pizza chain employs approximately 120,000 people.

Dossin Great Lakes Museum

The Dossin family, which made a fortune selling soft drinks, donated the money to start this museum of shipping and maritime history, as well as its first exhibit: their Miss Pepsi hydroplane, retired from racing because nothing else could compete. Other permanent exhibits in the 16,000-square-foot facility include the anchor of the **Edmund Fitzgerald** and the pilothouse of a freighter, where visitors can simulate steering the ship. There are also many changing exhibits. The museum, at 100 Strand Drive on Belle Isle, is open Saturday and Sunday, 11 a.m. to 5 p.m.

Dow Chemical

In 1897, Herbert Henry Dow created the **Dow Chemical Company** in Midland to extract bromides and chlorides from brine. The first product Dow sold commercially was bleach, but the company quickly broadened the range of products it developed.

Dow formed an agricultural division in 1908 to develop a spray for fruit trees. In the following years it started to focus on chlorine and exited the bleach business. Dow greatly expanded its business in the 1920s as it expanded into the production of elemental chlorine, phenol, magnesium, styrene, and Saran resins. In 1922, it introduced the chemical ethylene dibromide, which is used in ethyl gasoline.

Dow built its first plant, to produce magnesium, in 1930. The company began to produce plastic resins later in the decade. During **World War II**, Dow produced silicones, rubber, and magnesium for the military.

After the war, as the company continued to grow, it created subsidiaries such as Dow Corning. Saran Wrap, designed for commercial use in 1949, was introduced for household use in 1953. By 1960, Dow's annual sales had passed $1 billion.

In 1965, Dow introduced a one-shot measles vaccine. Three years later Dow's epoxy resins were used as a heat shield for Apollo 8 as it returned to earth. Dow followed this with products for automotive applications and Styrofoam plastic foam for the Alaskan pipeline.

In the following years, Dow produced napalm, the herbicide Agent Orange, compact discs, silicone breast implants, Handi-Wrap plastic film, and Scrubbing Bubbles bathroom cleaner. In recent years, Dow has been urged to take financial responsibility for one of the world's worst industrial disasters. An estimated 12,000 persons were killed by a gas leak at the Union Carbide plant in Bhopal, India, on December 3, 1984. Dow acquired Union Carbide in 2001.

Dow Historical Museum and Bradley Home and Carriage House

The museum offers history, artifacts, and photographs of Herbert H. Dow and **Dow Chemical Company**, chronicling Dow's contributions to chemistry and philanthropy in Midland. Also on the grounds are the Bradley Home, a Victorian Gothic house built in 1874, and a historical carriage house with a working blacksmith's forge. The museum and historical home, at 3200 Cook Road in Midland, are open Wednesday through Saturday 10 a.m. to 4 p.m. and Sunday 1 to 5 p.m., except major holidays.

Dow House and Studio, Alden B.

As the son of Dow Chemical Company founder Herbert H. Dow, Alden Dow had the financial means to study at leisure and develop his own style of architecture. He had an eye for European Modernism but he was also among the early participants in Frank Lloyd Wright's Taliesin Fellowship; he apprenticed at Taliesin in 1933. The association with Wright won him attention early in his career, but his style was all his own.

His master work was the one that began his architectural career: his own home. The house sat beside a stream on the grounds of his father's estate. A pioneer in organic architecture, Dow created a space of geometric shapes set into the gardens, balancing manmade rigidity against the randomness of nature—a nature he manipulated by rerouting the stream and planting trees and shrubs for their textures and colors. Spaces within the house flowed from one to another without the barriers of unnecessary doors. The colors and textures of carefully placed furniture, artwork, woodwork, and potted plants all contributed to what Dow termed "composed order."

Dow's papers, which document his philosophies on creativity as well as his architectural work and civic activities, are archived in the former playroom of the house. Collections of mid-20th century art and model trains also are on display.

The house, at 315 Post Street, Midland, is a National Historic Landmark and is listed on the National Register of Historic Places.

Dr. Nathan Thomas House (*see* Thomas House, Dr. Nathan)

Dunbar Hospital

Barred from practicing in white hospitals, 30 black **Detroit** physicians formed the Allied Medical Society, bought the home of a former real estate developer, and started a hospital to serve the African American community. The hospital, named for poet Paul Lawrence Dunbar, also sponsored Detroit's first training program for black nurses. Within 10 years, demand forced the hospital into a larger building; its name was changed to Parkside General Hospital. The original building, at 580 Frederick, was saved from demolition in 1979 and now is a historic site and museum.

Durant-Dort Carriage Company

Historical marker. From 1985 to 1913, Durant-Dort was headquarters of **William C. Durant**'s carriage and automobile businesses. The office building, at 315 West Water Street, Flint, is a National Historic Landmark and is on the National Register of Historic Places.

Durant, William C. (1861–1947)

Industrialist. He dropped out of high school in **Flint** to work in his grandfather's lumberyard. In 1885, with J. Dallas Dort, he founded the Flint Road Cart Company, later called the **Durant-Dort Carriage Company**. In 1904, he invested in the failing Buick Motor Car Company, which he expanded into General Motors by incorporating Cadillac, Oldsmobile, and parts manufacturers.

After the foundering GM was taken over by a bank, Durant joined **Louis Chevrolet** in 1911 to form the Chevrolet Motor Company. He regained control of GM in 1916 but was again forced out, in 1920, and started Durant Motors, which closed in 1933. By 1935, Durant was bankrupt.

In 1885 William C. Durant founded the Flint Road Cart Company, later called the Durant-Dort Carriage Company.

E

Eastern Market Historic District

Founded in 1841 to serve the German community, this market moved to its present site in the 1850s. The first sales shed was built in the open-air market in 1891; the area now includes 80 structures and plans are in the works to upgrade the area. With the development of supermarkets, customers' shopping habits changed and more food processors and wholesalers moved to the area to accommodate them. Parts of the **Underground Railroad** ran under the market and the area is now on the National Register of Historic Places. The market, at 2934 Russell Street, Detroit, is open Monday through Friday 5 a.m. to noon and Saturday 5 a.m. to 5 p.m.

Detroit's Eastern Market is now on the National Register of Historic Places.

Edison Depot Museum

Science presentations, hands-on interactive exhibits, and live theater performances document the life of Thomas Alva Edison, from boyhood through his successful years as an inventor. The museum, at 1115 Sixth Street, Port Huron, is open 1 to 4:30 p.m. daily, Memorial Day through Labor Day, and Wednesday through Sunday for the rest of the year.

Edison, Thomas (1847–1931)

Inventor. Born in Ohio, he grew up in Port Huron. He created a number of his 1,093 inventions at a laboratory in Menlo Park, New Jersey. In the 1920s, he and his good friend **Henry Ford** moved the lab to **Greenfield Village**, Ford's museum in Dearborn.

Edmonds, Sarah (1854–1898)

Soldier, spy. Edmonds joined the Union army at the start of the **Civil War** in 1861 by concealing her identity and calling herself Frank Thomas. After serving in many legendary battles, including the

Battle of Bull Run, she volunteered to go behind enemy lines as a spy. To gather information, she disguised herself as a young black man. After contracting malaria, and fearful of revealing her sex, she left the army. She eventually wrote to Congress and was granted a soldier's pension. She was the only woman inducted into the **Grand Army of the Republic**.

Edmund Fitzgerald

At 729 feet long and 13,632 tons, until 1971 it was the largest carrier on the **Great Lakes**. It was the first carrier to ship over a million tons of ore through the **Soo Locks**.

On November 9, 1975, the *Fitzgerald*, captained by Ernest M. McSorley, left Superior, Wisconsin, carrying 26,000 tons of iron ore to **Detroit** and was joined by the *Arthur M. Anderson*, bound for Gary, Indiana. That night, warned of an impending storm, the two ships steered a northerly course across Lake Superior seeking protection along the Canadian coast before they eventually turned southeast to

Whitefish Point, Michigan, and their respective destinations. The *Fitzgerald* never made it.

Late the following afternoon, the *Fitzgerald* radioed another ship, the *Avafors*, that it had lost its radars and was listing. Then it radioed the *Anderson*, "We are holding our own." Shortly thereafter, the *Fitzgerald* disappeared from the *Anderson*'s radar. Evidence suggested that the ship, with its 29-member crew, sank quickly. There were no distress signals, and wreckage of two lifeboats recovered by the U.S. Coast Guard indicated that no attempts had been made to abandon ship.

Although the cause of the disaster was never determined, a report released by the Coast Guard on April 15, 1977, speculated that the ship's cargo hatch covers had not been sealed properly, allowing the cargo hold to flood as waves rolled over the deck. The

Thomas Edison invented, among other things, the kinetoscopic camera, an early form of cinematography.

The steamer Edmund Fitzgerald *with a cargo of iron ore*

Sarah Edmonds disguised herself as a man so she could fight in the Civil War.

E

hatchways had been scheduled for repair after the shipping season ended.

The disaster was immortalized in Gordon Lightfoot's 1976 ballad *The Wreck of the Edmund Fitzgerald*. The ship's bell, recovered on July 4, 1995, is on display at the **Great Lakes Shipwreck Museum**.

Eldredge, Todd (1971–)

Ice skater. Todd Eldredge is the most successful American skater never to win an Olympic medal. He won U.S. titles as a novice, junior, and senior skater. He is a six-time U.S. National Men's Champion, taking the title in 1990, 1991, 1995, 1997, 1998, and 2000. He has also medaled six times at the World Championships, winning the gold in 1996, the silver in 1995, 1997, and 1998, and the bronze in 1991 and 2001. An elegant skater, he is known for his spinning ability. He retired from Olympic-eligible skating in 2002.

Many famous Detroiters are buried in Elmwood Cemetery.

Elmwood Cemetery

The **Detroit** cemetery, with its garden-like landscaping, was founded in 1846. The 54,000 markers read like a history book—Territorial Governor **Lewis Cass**, geologist **Douglass Houghton**, and distiller Hiram Walker are here, as are mayors, governors, senators, and **Civil War** veterans, including 28 generals.

Enberg, Dick (1935–)

Born in Armada, Dick Enberg was a premier sportscaster for almost four decades. The graduate of Central Michigan University and Indiana University is a veteran of eight Super Bowls, four Olympics, and almost 20 Wimbledon tournaments. His awards include 13 Emmys, nine Sportscaster of the Year awards, the Ronald Reagan Media Award, and the Victor Award as the top sportscaster of the past 25 years. He is only the fourth sportscaster to be honored with a star on the Hollywood Walk of Fame.

The Erie Canal made it practical for immigrants to the United States to move west.

Erie Canal

In the early 19th century, pioneers moving westward from the Eastern seaboard had to overcome the absence of roads and navigable rivers, as well as the obstacle of rugged terrain. Many decided that the trail was too formidable and opted to stay in the East. The Erie Canal, the most famous and successful of America's early towpath canals, breached the barrier of the Appalachian Mountains and linked Lake Erie with the Hudson River.

The ancestor of the Erie Canal was the Western Inland Lock Navigation Company, which was chartered by the New York State Legislature in 1792. It was not a financial success, barely raising enough in tolls to pay for itself. Nevertheless, many prominent commercial and political leaders called for the creation of a state-built canal that would cross New York to link the Hudson River with points west. On July 4, 1817, ground was broken for the Erie Canal at a site near Rome, New York. Before the canal was completed in 1825, its builders would have to overcome rivers, swamps, and hills.

The completion of the Erie Canal was a significant moment in Michigan history. The canal greatly facilitated the transportation of passengers and freight between the Eastern seaboard and Michigan ports. Any large-scale movement into Michigan was hampered by the difficulty settlers had in reaching the territory. Transportation to Michigan by water was dangerous—some said it was more dangerous to travel on Lake Erie than on the Atlantic Ocean. Heading north by land to reach **Detroit** was almost as treacherous. First it was necessary to cross the Black Swamp, in northwestern Ohio, which was virtually impassable in rainy weather. Black fly infestations and the lack of roads prevented many from attempting the crossing. The threat of fever brought on by the noxious

The canal was officially opened by New York Governor DeWitt Clinton as he poured a keg of Lake Erie water into New York Harbor.

E

gases from the Black Swamp deterred others. With plenty of good land still available in Ohio, few wanted to brave the hazards to continue to Michigan. Improved transportation helped pave the way for one of the great land booms in all of American history as settlers poured into the state during the early 1800s, especially the 1830s. The majority of the newcomers came by way of the **Great Lakes**, making the journey from Buffalo to Michigan by steamship or sailing ship, aided in great part by the Erie Canal.

The Erie Canal was 360 miles long and connected New York with the Great Lakes via the Hudson River. Locks were built to overcome the 571 foot difference between the level of the river and that of Lake Erie. In the early days, the canal was not very large, but it could move Michigan's grain and wool to markets in the east, thereby providing Michigan with a market for its commodities, an enticement to settlers. The boats used on the canal were generally flat bottomed and usually hauled grains, wood, whiskey, and meat. The canal was enlarged between 1836 and 1862.

Everyman's House

Designed by social reformer **Caroline Bartlett Crane**, the five-room model home took first place in the Better Homes of America contest of 1924. The $7,249.71 price tag included a basement, brick fireplace, water softener, oak floors, and other optional features that could be omitted to lower the cost to about $5,000, within reach of the average American family. Rather than a dining room, wasted space for most of the day, Crane put in a mother's room, adaptable for any use. More than 20,000 tourists viewed the house the year it opened. It still stands, nearly unchanged, on Westnedge Hill in **Kalamazoo**.

Explorers

The Michigan Territory was discovered by the white man almost by accident. Explorers seeking a Northwest Passage were among the first to pass by *Michi-gama,* Algonquin for great

waters. Access to the **Great Lakes** and Michigan was easy from the north, and the French, having founded New France (Quebec) were eager to extend their boundaries.

In 1618, Samuel de Champlain sent young **Étienne Brûlé** on a journey that Champlain hoped would find the Northwest Passage, which many believed connected North America to the riches of Asia. Champlain probably chose Brûlé because he was an eager young man who loved living and took full advantage of any opportunity. This included working for the fur merchants as well as the administration of New France, a conflict of interest. Brûlé searched for years. While the details of the journey are sketchy, he probably passed through Sault Ste. Marie in 1621. He was killed by members of the Huron Tribe in 1632.

A few years later, Champlain sent out **Jean Nicolet** on a similar mission. Nicolet was so sure he'd reach Asia that he packed a suit of silk robes to wear at the court of the khan, the emperor of China. In the summer of 1634, Nicolet, an employee of the fur company known as the Hundred Associates, threaded his way in a birch canoe from Georgian Bay through the straits of Mackinaw, and thus discovered Lake Michigan. He later traveled along Wisconsin rivers and made it as far south as the modern Green Bay, Wisconsin. There he met the Winnebago Tribe. Nicolet arrayed himself in the silk robes and walked about firing pistols from both hands, declaring he had come among them to make peace. He continued his journey through Illinois, possibly reaching the Mississippi River later in 1634. He drowned in 1642 in a boating accident near Quebec City.

While Nicolet never found the passage to Asia, he did find furs. Pelts of beaver and other animals brought high prices in the European market, and by 1650, scores of adventurous **fur traders**, mostly young Frenchmen or Canadians, were paddling down the St. Lawrence River and onto the lakes to trade.

The traders fell into two groups. The *coureurs des bois*, or runners of the woods, journeyed on foot through regions of thick forests. The *voyageurs*, or voyagers, paddled canoes along the Michigan rivers and streams. The voyagers were actually responsible for more trading than were the runners. The French wanted only to trade, not to settle, and their attitude hurt the **Native American** population. The Indians abandoned their crops and did little but hunt fur-bearing animals to trade with the French. Some Indians became addicted to brandy that the French brought in return for pelts. Others were killed by diseases, like smallpox, which had been unknown before the French arrived.

Rationalization for French exploration of the land included the adventure of it, visions of wealth and empire, and the determination of missionaries to bring Christianity to the Indians. In 1641, two Jesuit priests, Charles Raymbautt and Isaac Joques, reached the rapids of Sault Ste. Marie. Twenty-seven years later, Father **Jacques Marquette** established a mission on **Mackinac Island** and named it **St. Ignace**. Historians consider this mission the first European settlement in Michigan. Explorer

Robert Cavelier La Salle came to America to explore the new land, settle it, and claim some of it for France. In 1671, he visited Mackinac Island with Father Marquette. Shortly thereafter, an old friend and trader, **Louis Jolliet**, arrived with orders for Marquette to accompany him on a journey to explore the Mississippi. Marquette went, but in October 1674 his failing health forced their return to Sault Ste. Marie. Marquette died en route in 1675. His remains were returned to St. Ignace by Indian converts and placed in a chapel there.

Antoine de la Mothe Cadillac, commandant at **Fort Michilimackinac**, decided in 1669

Explorations of Michigan began by accident and ended because of a series of wars.

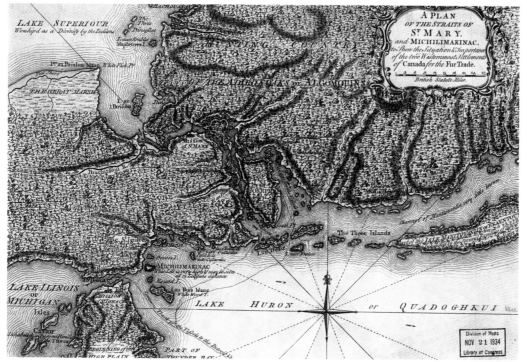

A 1781 "Plan of the Straits of St. Mary and Michilimakinac, to Shew the Situation and Importance of the two Westermost Settlements of Canada for the Fur Trade."

E that another post was needed to the south. Fearing a Native American affiliation with the British, Cadillac led one hundred soldiers to the *place du detroit*, the "place of the strait," in his view an obvious location for a major post. The river was narrow enough that a cannon could be fired from one side to the other but substantial enough to provide a defense. The surrounding **Great Lakes** and waterways meant easy travel from most major points. Cadillac founded a trading post there, Fort Pontchartrain, which later became known as LaVille d'Etroit, modern-day **Detroit**. In 1701, a log fort rose along the shore. It was partially destroyed by the Indians in 1703 but was later rebuilt. Cadillac was named governor of the Louisiana Territory in 1710, but he was so unpopular that he was recalled to France and imprisoned in the Bastille.

LaSalle and Father Louis Henepin sailed to the Straits of Mackinac in 1679, aboard the **Griffon**, a ship LaSalle had built. It was the first commercial sailing ship on the Great Lakes. LaSalle sailed from Lake Erie to Lake Michigan and along the Michigan coast, where he erected Fort Miami on the site of the present-day city of St. Joseph. LaSalle believed forts providing protection would entice settlers to the west. In 1681, LaSalle led a party of 40 men to the Mississippi River, which they traversed in canoes. They reached the Gulf of Mexico in

April 1682. Five mutineers from a later expedition shot and killed Lasalle. He was so unpopular with his men, they did not even bury him.

The demise of exploration in Michigan came primarily because of wars fought between the British and the French. In 1689, war broke out between the two countries, interrupting trade as far west as Minnesota. The French and Indian War, which started in 1754, again interrupted trade, as most licensed traders and their voyagers were called east to fight. The Quebec Act in 1774 made the western Great Lakes and all land north of the Ohio River part of Quebec, subject to its laws and regulations. The American Revolution in 1776 caused some traders to avoid areas south and west of the Great Lakes and to go north and west instead. As part of the **Northwest Ordinance**, Michigan became part of the Northwest Territory in 1787. This put Michigan under British control, as it remained throughout most of the **War of 1812**. The British were more interested in settling than in exploring. The dangerous waters of the Great Lakes and poor traveling conditions to the south, combined with the political unrest, slowed the influx of settlers until the opening of the **Erie Canal** in 1825. The United States government was in control, and Easterners were ready to see what lay to the west.

Fair Lane

As other wealthy families moved to Detroit's eastern suburbs, Henry Ford took his family in the opposite direction, to his hometown of Dearborn. The 2,000-acre estate was close enough for him to tend to business, yet remote enough for him to feel the seclusion of a natural setting. He named the estate for the area in Ireland where his ancestors had lived.

It took a year, more than 500 men, and nearly $2 million to complete the estate before the Fords took residence in 1916. The 31,000-square-foot house was built of Marblehead limestone and included an auditorium and a library. Thomas Edison, a close friend, had his own suite of rooms.

Included on the grounds were Ford's private laboratory, staff cottages, a pony barn, gardens, a manmade lake, a greenhouse, and a small working farm. The estate had its own hydroelectric powerhouse, connected to the house by a 300-foot tunnel.

After the deaths of Henry and Clara Ford, the Ford Motor Company bought the estate to house its corporate archives. In 1957, the company donated part of the estate to the University of Michigan to create a Dearborn campus.

A Michigan Historical Marker was erected at the estate in 1978. The house is listed on both the State Register and the National Register of Historic Places and is a National Historic Landmark. Fair Lane, at 4901 Evergreen Road in Dearborn, is open to the public daily, except Saturday, from January through March.

Henry Ford's birthplace in Dearborn. He later built his large estate, Fair Lane, in his hometown.

Fayette Historic Townsite

With its proximity to limestone and hardwood forests, its large dock, and two blast furnaces, Fayette was one of the **Upper Peninsula**'s most productive iron-smelting operations. The

About 500 people lived and worked in Fayette during the 24 years its blast furnaces operated.

Preservation efforts have given Ferry Street a rebirth.

reconstructed town, at Fayette Historic State Park in Garden, includes a museum and a 26-point walking tour. Museum hours are 9 a.m. to 7 p.m. daily, mid-May through mid-October.

Ferber, Edna (1885–1968)

Author. Ferber became a working journalist immediately upon her graduation from high school. In her mid-20s, while recuperating from an illness, she wrote her first short story and novel. Both were published within a year. A series of 30 Emma McChesney stories were published in national magazines, and her first play dealt with the same heroine. In 1924, Ferber won the Pulitzer Prize for her novel *So Big*. She also wrote *Showboat*, *Cimarron*, *Giant*, and *Ice Palace*. *Showboat* was made into a musical and three movies. *Giant* was also adapted for the screen. Ferber wrote two autobiographies, *A Peculiar Treasure* and *A Kind of Magic*.

Ferry Street

East Ferry Street in **Detroit** was a tony address in the 1890s. The block that runs between Woodward Avenue and John R. Street was lined with mansions owned by prominent Detroiters.

By the 1990s, those original owners were long gone and many of the mansions had fallen into disrepair. But Ferry Street, like so much of Detroit, experienced a rebirth.

The house built by **Charles Lang Freer** is a mainstay of the block. Freer was a businessman and art collector. Thanks to his donation, the Freer name graces a gallery at the Smithsonian Institution. The Merrill-Palmer Institute has owned and occupied the Freer House since about 1920, and the integrity of the shingle-style architecture has been retained.

Freer's neighbor to the west was his business partner, Frank J. Hecker. Hecker's mansion, which sits on the corner of Woodward Avenue, was inspired by a French chateau. For years, Detroiters knew the mansion as the home of the Smiley Brothers Music Company. The building now houses a law firm.

A cluster of mansions on the south side of Ferry Street was refurbished beginning in the 1990s, thanks to the efforts of preservationists. The Queen Anne and Romanesque Revival buildings were turned into a sprawling bed and breakfast, with 42 rooms spread over four mansions and two carriage houses.

Ferry Street is in the heart of Detroit's **Cultural Center Historic District**, close to the **Detroit Institute of Art**, the Detroit Public Library, and Wayne State University.

Finney House Barn

Strategically located near the **Detroit River**, Finney House Barn was the last stop before freedom along one line of the **Underground Railroad**. Seymour Finney, a tailor turned hotelkeeper, was an ardent abolitionist. He built the barn, part of his hotel business, in 1846, and sheltered fugitive slaves until they could cross the river to Canada.

Fire of 1805

When Michigan's first territorial governor, General **William Hull**, arrived in **Detroit** on July 1, 1805, he found nothing but ashes—the settlement had been leveled by fire three weeks before.

Legend has it that the town's baker was smoking as he hitched his pony to a wagon and that a gust of wind blew burning tobacco from his pipe into a pile of hay in his barn. Although townspeople came running, their fire-fighting equipment was so crude it did nothing to prevent the fire from spreading, and soon all that remained of the settlement was the fort and a few military buildings along the **Detroit River**.

The townspeople found shelter in the fort and in improvised tents and shacks. Father **Gabriel Richard**, the city's clergyman, sailed down the river, calling on farmers to help their neighbors.

Hull traveled to Washington, D.C., where Congress authorized appropriation of 10,000 acres to rebuild. He was accompanied by Judge **Augustus B. Woodward**, who created a visionary plan for the city based on Pierre L'Enfant's radial-street design of Washington. Woodward, however, worked on an even grander scale, with 120-foot-wide avenues feeding into open circles. To the 900 citizens of Detroit, the plan seemed absurd, and it was widely derided. Although building was begun according to Woodward's vision, much of it was later undone.

Surveying the ruined city, Father Richard had observed, *"Speramus meliora; resurget cineribus"* ("We hope for better days; it shall rise from its ashes."). His words still serve as Detroit's motto and appear on the city seal.

Father Gabriel Richard, who assisted in the Fire of 1805 rescue operations

F

First Bessemer Steel Mill in the United States

Eureka Iron Works in Wyandotte, opened in 1854, was the first plant in American to use the revolutionary process, which allowed inexpensive mass production of steel from pig iron by removing impurities from the molten iron.

The first Bessemer steel mill in the United States. Eureka Iron Works lasted only a few decades, but the company discovered a salt bed under the town of Wyandotte. That opened the way for the chemicals industry.

First Border-to-Border Interstate Highway

Interstate 94 was completed in 1967, after nearly two decades of construction. Initially it ran 205 miles, between **Detroit** and New Buffalo. Later the highway was extended northeast to Port Huron, creating a new international border crossing with a direct connection to the nation's interstate system.

First Concrete Road

In response to the demand for smoother roads by bicyclists and early auto owners, a concrete road was built in **Detroit** in 1909. America's first paved road, a mile-long stretch of Woodward Avenue, took less than three months to build and cost $13,534.59.

First Four-Lane Divided Highway

It was built in Ypsilanti during the 1940s. As U.S. involvement in **World War II** escalated, improved roads were needed to move bombs and workers. The highway carried 42,000 workers to and from the Ypsilanti bomber factory.

First Four-Way Traffic Stop

Detroit Police Lieutenant Williams Potts invented the signal so fewer officers would need to direct traffic on the city's busy streets. Everyone agrees it was on Woodward Avenue, though the intersection is up for grabs: some say Fort Street, others say Michigan Avenue. But within a year, the city had installed 15 more.

A piece of Interstate 94 extended toward the border with Canada.

First Michigan Colored Regiment

The all-volunteer regiment, recommissioned as the 102nd U.S. Colored Troops, was organized at Camp Ward in **Detroit** from August through October 1863. The original 900-man regiment comprising both cavalry and artillery units, picked up more men during its 19 months of fighting in South Carolina, Maryland, Georgia, and Florida. All told, about 1,400 served in the regiment; about 140 were killed. Seventeen of

Woodward Avenue, the first concrete road, is still in the heart of Detroit.

About 1,400 African Americans fought in the Civil War as members of the 102nd U.S. Colored Troops.

the veterans are buried in **Elmwood 18 Cemetery** in a military area designated as a national historic site. A **Michigan Historical Marker** was placed at Duffield School, on the former site of Camp Ward.

First Snowplow

The nation's first snowplow was designed by Edward C. Levy, Munising's public works superintendent, in 1922. It consisted of two 10-foot-by-20-foot retractable wooden wings mounted on runners. The wings made it possible to plow all city streets, country roads, and small alleys. The introduction of rotary angle and front-mounted V-plows soon made the wing design obsolete.

First State Prison

The Jackson prison, opened in 1839, was unusual in that it had individual cells with inmates working in groups during the day. In the 1880s, under Warden H.F. Hatch, emphasis

The Fisher Building was designated a National Historic Landmark in 1989.

shifted from simply warehousing inmates to rehabilitating them. The original building was replaced in the 1930s with a new structure, the world's largest walled prison.

First Telephone Company

The Michigan Telephone and Telegraph Construction Company, the nation's first phone company, turned on service to Michigan businesses in October 1877. Less than a year later, the **Detroit** Telephonic Exchange offered lines for private homes. In January 1880, the world's first international telephone line opened between **Detroit** and Windsor.

First to Ban Capital Punishment

In 1828, a **Detroit** man, Patrick Fitzpatrick, was convicted in Canada of rape and murder and hanged. Seven years later, his former roommate confessed to the crime. Citizens of Michigan were so repulsed by the case that in 1847 they abolished capital punishment, becoming the first English-speaking territory in the world to do so.

First to Fluoridate

Grand Rapids was the first U.S. city to implement a community water fluoridation program. In 1945, the city adjusted the fluoride level in municipal water to 1.0 parts per million, the level at which fluoride begins to combat the demineralization process that causes tooth decay.

Fisher Building

Often described as **Detroit**'s largest art object, the building was commissioned by the seven Fisher brothers as a home for their auto body company. The Fishers, pioneers in closed body design, made year-round automobile travel possible.

The brothers told architect **Albert Kahn** to spare no expense. Abandoning the ground-hugging buildings of the past, Kahn followed the lead of **Eliel Saarinen**, designer of Chicago's Tribune Tower, and created a 28-story high-rise at a prime location. A quarter of the

$9 million price tag went toward art work and the most luxurious materials available. The Art Deco building, Kahn's masterwork, featured plasterwork, stone carving, and ornamental bronze by the most important craftspersons of the day. Dozens of exotic marbles decorated its vaulted arcade. The building was filled with works by artists such as Geza Maroti, an important figure in the European Arts and Crafts movement.

In addition to Fisher's headquarters, the building housed dentists, bankers, a tearoom, a theater—everything to entice automobile owners, who happily handed their cars over to white-suited valets. On the fourth floor, nurses watched children in a skylight nursery complete with a carousel. Babysitting was free.

Kahn's building was honored by the Architectural League of New York in 1930.

The surviving Fisher brothers sold the building to a real estate company in 1974. The building, still fully occupied, is meticulously maintained. It was listed on the National Register of Historic Places in 1980 and was designated a National Historic Landmark in 1989.

Fisher, M.F.K. (1908–1992)

Food writer. The Albion native created a new genre by filling her off-beat books with philosophy, anecdotes, and reminiscences. Her books include *How to Cook a Wolf*, *Here Let Us Feast: A Book of Banquets*, *An Alphabet for Gourmets*, and *Two Towns in Provence*.

Flint

Flint's history begins in 1819, when a **fur trader** named Jacob Smith opened a trading post, calling it the Grand Traverse. Settlers trickled in, led by Jacob Stevens in 1825. The town changed names several times and eventually became known as Flint River, translated from an Indian name, *Pawanunking*, meaning "river bed." In 1836, the name was shortened to Flint. The city was incorporated in 1855.

Flint came into its own with the growth of the auto industry. **Louis Chevrolet** produced

his first car there. **David Buick** took his auto company there. And Flint was the headquarters of **William C. Durant**, who put it all together and created General Motors Corporation.

But the same industry that provided Flint's lifeblood also brought it unwanted notoriety. First came the sit-down strike of 1937, one of the most significant events in Flint's history. Workers at Fisher Body Plant No. 1 spontaneously stopped working on the night of December 30, 1936. Plant No. 2 followed suit, and the strike spread to other GM plants. The workers maintained control of the plant until an agreement was reached with GM on February 11, 1937. When the dust cleared, the UAW had grown from a fledgling union into the bargaining agent for GM employees.

In 1989, filmmaker **Michael Moore** used

Michigan boasted both the first phone lines to private homes and the first international exchange.

F

his hometown as the focus of the documentary *Roger and Me*, about the collapse of the auto industry and its effects on the cities that lived and breathed automobiles.

The city experienced another setback on June 8, 1953, when it was hit by the deadliest tornado ever recorded in the U.S. The twister killed 116 persons and injured 844 more.

Flint lies in the southern half of Genesee County and is its county seat. In recent years the city has felt the benefits of a residential population shift from metropolitan **Detroit** to northern suburbs and into southern Genesee County. The area's more affordable housing and easy commutes are turning this once blue-collar county into a white-collar community. The area has one of the nation's highest median family income rates. It's at the center of a north-south interstate highway corridor that makes it convenient to both the lower part of the state and to the Canadian border.

Flint hosts a campus of the **University of Michigan**. Other educational institutions include Kettering University, formerly General Motors Institute, one of Michigan's premier engineering schools. The city's Longway Planetarium, Michigan's largest, is among the top 20 in the United States. More than 600,000 visitors a year are attracted to **Flint Cultural Center**, a 30-acre campus that is home to nine major cultural institutions, including the **Sloan Museum**. The Flint Institute of Music, also on the cultural center campus, enrolls nearly 3,000 students in its School of Performing Arts, Michigan's largest performing arts school and among the largest in the country.

Flint, the hometown of controversial filmmaker, Michael Moore

Flint Cultural Center

Established in 1957, it is a coming-together on a single campus of nine arts and humanities organizations that work together to strengthen Flint's understanding of its diverse cultures. The center includes a theater, planetarium, and institutes of art and music. The **Sloan Museum** also is on the campus.

Flint School of Performing Arts

A program of the Flint Institute of Music on the **Flint Cultural Center** campus, it's the largest performing arts school in Michigan and, with nearly 3,000 students, one of the largest in the country. It offers classes for all ages, including preschool, and has its own junior ballet company and orchestras.

Flint Sit-Down Strike

One of the most important events in U.S. labor history, the strike transformed the fledgling **United Auto Workers** from a collection of locals into the major union of the American automobile industry. The UAW had been organized August 26, 1935, by auto workers aiming to negotiate for higher wages and better working conditions. Early in auto industry history, the factory environment was hazardous. There were few safety devices, and accidents were common. Auto workers were under constant pressure to increase production but had no job security.

On December 30, 1936, UAW workers at three General Motors factories stopped production, striking for higher wages and better working conditions. They occupied the plant for more than six weeks, battling security guards, police, and even the National Guard. Supporters slipped in food from the outside; the strikers slept on car seats.

Police armed with tear gas tried to overrun the plant on January 11, 1937. They were met with a barrage of auto parts and torrents from the factory's fire hoses. From outside, the union's women's auxiliary smashed windows to undermine the effects of the tear gas. The

Automobile Workers!

Attend Your Own

STATE-WIDE PICNIC

Enjoy a Holiday of Fun and Sport for the Entire Family

FOR THE GROWN-UPS—Fishing—Baseball—Boating
FOR THE KIDS—Merry-Go-Round—Teeter-Totters—
Swings—Rides. . . . FOR EVERYBODY—Swimming—
Races—Contests—Prizes.

SPEAKERS:

FRANK MURPHY
Labor's Candidate for Governor

HOMER MARTIN
President, International Union, United Automobile Workers of America

A Real Workers' Holiday at

DODGE PARK NO. 1, ISLAND LAKE
Two Miles Southeast of Brighton on Route 16

SUNDAY SEPTEMBER 6, 1936
(Sunday Before Labor Day)

ADMISSION FREE
All Automobile Workers Invited

Sponsored by

**International Union, United Automobile Workers
of America**

The United Auto Workers mixed picnics with politics as president Homer Martin spoke at a 1936 family event.

"bulls," as the strikers mocked them, retreated after several failed attempts to break in. The strikers referred to the skirmish as the Battle of Bulls Run.

The strike ended February 11, after GM, via intermediary Gov. **Frank Murphy**, agreed to bargain with the UAW. A final agreement was signed March 12. Almost immediately,

Edsel Ford, far right; on the left is Alfred P. Sloan

UAW membership jumped from a handful to 100,000.

Ford, Edsel (1893–1943)

Automotive design visionary. A quiet, unassuming man, Edsel Ford was fated to live in the shadow of his celebrated father, **Henry Ford**. He was president of the Ford Motor Company from 1919 until his death, when his father resumed control. His legacy is seen in his work as an auto stylist, from the Ford Model A to Lincoln Continental. In 1938 he created the Mercury line as a bridge between Ford and Lincoln. One of **Detroit**'s major philanthropists, Ford financed the Diego Rivera mural *Detroit Industry* at the **Detroit Art Institute** and was an early investor in the **Detroit Red Wings**.

Edsel Ford was president of the Ford Motor Company from 1919.

Ford, Elizabeth Ann (Betty) (1918–)

First lady, humanist. After her first marriage ended in divorce, she married **Gerald R. Ford** during his successful 1948 campaign for Congress. As her husband rose through the political ranks, Ford raised the couple's four children and stayed active in women's political organizations.

As first lady, Ford spoke openly about her battle with breast cancer in 1974 and helped raise public awareness of the disease. Equally frank about her battle with alcohol and drug addiction, she helped remove the stigma associated with addiction. She co-founded the Betty Ford Center, considered one of the best addiction treatment centers in the country.

Ford Foundation

Initiated by Henry and Edsel Ford as a local philanthropy, the foundation has become an international organization that funds knowledge building initiatives throughout the world. Since 1936, it has provided more than $12 billion in grants, projects, and loans. It has been headquartered in New York since 1950.

Ford, Gerald R. (1913–)

Thirty-eighth president of the United States. In August 1974, at the height of the Watergate conspiracy scandal, President Richard M. Nixon resigned, elevating Ford to the

presidency. Ford is the only president of the United States not to have been elected to either the presidency or the vice presidency.

Prior to serving as vice president, Ford had had a distinguished career in the U.S. House of Representatives, serving as a Republican congressman for Michigan from 1949 to 1973. In 1965 he became minority leader of the House. After Vice President Spiro Agnew resigned from office in late 1973, Ford was confirmed and sworn in on December 6, 1973.

Ford was born in Omaha, Nebraska, as Leslie L. King Jr. His parents separated two weeks after his birth and his mother took him to **Grand Rapids** to live with her parents. The Ford name came from his mother's second husband. Ford was a gifted student and athlete at the **University of Michigan**. He received a law degree from Yale, graduating in the top 25 percent of his class. During **World War II** he served in the Navy in the South Pacific.

One of the most difficult and controversial decisions of Ford's presidency was his granting of a pardon to Richard Nixon. During his term

Ford coped with rising inflation, energy shortage fears, and a divisive war in Southeast Asia. He survived two assassination attempts.

Ford won the Republican nomination for president in 1976 but lost the election to Democratic challenger Jimmy Carter.

Ford, Gerald R., Library and Museum

The only separated presidential library and museum, the library is in **Ann Arbor**, where President Ford went to college, and the museum is in his hometown of **Grand Rapids**. Both focus on post-**World War II** American history. Permanent museum collections include a replica of the Oval Office and a multimedia 1970s pop culture gallery. The library, at 1000 Beal Avenue, Ann Arbor, is open Monday through Friday, 8:45 a.m. to 4:45 p.m. The museum, at 303 Pearl Street NW, Grand Rapids, is open every day 9 a.m. to 5 p.m.

Ford, Henry (1863–1947)

Auto industry titan. When historians identify persons who most influenced 20th-century America, the name Henry Ford is inevitably found near the top of the list. His early achievements in the **auto industry** sparked an economic boom in Michigan that also spurred

Gerald Ford inherited the presidency after Richard M. Nixon resigned. He served only one term.

Henry Ford's Model T was the first automobile to be constructed by purely mass-produced methods.

Henry Ford sits on a piece of farm machinery, one of his inventions.

the growth of America's middle class by putting average people into reliable, low-cost automobiles.

Ford, son of Irish immigrants, was born on a farm in the Dearborn area. A natural mechanic, he became an engineer with the Edison Illuminating Company in **Detroit** in 1891 and met **Thomas Edison**, with whom he formed a lifelong friendship. His interest in the internal combustion engine led him to construct his first self-propelled vehicle, the Quadricycle, in 1893. In the early 1900s he focused on building racing machines, including the famous 999, driven by the legendary **Barney Oldfield**. He was backed financially by local lumber dealer William H. Murphy.

Ford formed the Ford Motor Company in 1903 and set himself up as vice president and chief engineer. His early cars were produced in plants on Mack Avenue and at Piquette and Beaubein streets. But the 1910 startup of the huge **Highland Park Ford Plant** put Ford's stamp on history. There he perfected the continuously moving assembly line. He also instituted the $5 work day. Mass production of the Model T, soon dubbed the Tin Lizzie, resulted in a cheap, reliable car for an eager public. More than 15 million Model Ts, available for as little as $290, were built at Highland Park before production was shifted in the late 1920s to the **River Rouge** complex and the new Model A.

Ford's assembly line techniques were also used in building the popular Ford Tri-Motor 12-passenger airplane, which Admiral Richard Byrd used to explore the South Pole. During **World War II**, thousands of B-24 Liberator bombers were assembled at a Ford plant at **Willow Run**.

In spite of his many achievements, Ford was known as an autocratic leader who sometimes stubbornly resisted change. In the late 1920s, the company lost its supremacy to General Motors when Ford was slow to replace the Model T with the new Model A. Ford was the last of the Big Three automakers to allow unionization in his plants; in the infamous 1937 **Battle of the Overpass**, Ford security guards beat union organizers attempting to pass out literature at the Rouge plant. In 1941, when Ford finally allowed the **United Auto Workers** to hold elections, the resulting union contract was more generous than those with General Motors and Chrysler.

Ford's personal beliefs also tarnished his image. Anti-Semitic articles in the *Dearborn Independent*, his newspaper, resulted in libel suits against Ford. He issued a public apology.

Ford created a dynasty within the company. His son, **Edsel Ford**, was a visionary designer. A grandson, **Henry Ford II**, is often credited with turning the company's fortunes around after World War II. A great-grandson, William Clay Ford Jr., currently is board chair and chief executive officer of the Ford Motor Company.

The Ford family has left an indelible imprint on **Detroit**. Among major institutions that owe their existence to the Fords' generosity are the Henry Ford Hospital and the **Henry Ford Museum and Greenfield Village** historical complex, now known simply as the Henry Ford.

Ford, Henry, II (1917–1987)

Industrialist. The son of **Edsel Ford** and grandson of **Henry Ford**, Henry II rejuvenated the Ford Motor Company after **World War II**. He became president in 1945 and brought in a cadre of executives, nicknamed the Whiz Kids, who overhauled operations. Following the 1967 riots in **Detroit**, he announced plans for the **Renaissance Center**, a riverfront complex.

Ford, Henry, Museum and Greenfield Village

Established in 1933 in Dearborn, Greenfield Village was created by **Henry Ford** to "give people a true picture of the development of the country both culturally and technologically." The village of nearly 100 buildings and the museum cover more than 255 acres and span more than 300 years of change. While Ford had some of the structures built, many were brought from their original locations. These include Noah Webster's birthplace, the Wright brothers' cycle shop and home, and **Thomas Edison**'s Menlo Park and Fort Myers laboratories. A replica of Independence Hall is located at the entrance of the village, and a town hall,

William H. Murphy sponsored Henry Ford's early efforts to build an automobile.

F

general store, courthouse, school, and white-spired church paint a portrait of simpler times for tourists. It all reflects Ford's view of what was important in the history of America. Craft and trade demonstrations, including glass blowing, pottery making, and blacksmithing are presented.

Inside the museum, some of the most popular exhibits include "The Automobile in American Life," which shows the impact the car had on 20th-century America, and "Made in America," an exhibit that models the history of the United States' industrial evolution. Also on exhibit are a folding camp cot used by George Washington, the rocking chair in which Abraham Lincoln was sitting when he was shot at Ford's theater, and five presidential limousines, including the one in which John F. Kennedy was riding when he was assassinated.

Seasonal events, historic recreations, and "live demonstrations of American ingenuity," draw more than a million visitors every year.

The Henry Ford Museum demonstrates the impact the car had on 20th-century America.

Ford River Rouge Complex

One of the industrial wonders of the world, the complex was a marvel of self-sufficiency. **Henry Ford** hired industrial architect **Albert Kahn** to design the 2,000-acre complex; by the late 1930s, Kahn had created more than two dozen single-story buildings of glass and steel.

Although Ford's plan, when he bought the land in 1915, was to use the site to smelt iron and build tractors, by 1927 the site included everything needed to produce a car: blast furnaces, a steel-rolling mill, foundries,

The mission of the Henry Ford Museum is to use authentic American artifacts and stories to provide rare educational experiences.

open-hearth steel mills, glass and tire plants, metal-stamping facilities, and an engine plant. The complex had its own dock and power plant. The various facilities were connected by 90 miles of railroad track and endless conveyor belts. At its peak, it employed 120,000 workers. Nowhere else in the world was there a plant of such industrial efficiency.

Many of the most important buildings are still there: The Dearborn Assembly Plant, built in 1917, still houses the main assembly line, and energy still is supplied from the power house built in 1921. None of the buildings in the complex, however, remains in its original configuration. All have been adapted as production techniques have changed. Today it takes only a few seconds to produce a car at River Rouge.

The plant, at 3001 Miller Road, Dearborn, was listed on the National Register of Historic Places and as a National Historic Landmark in June 1978, two years after its listing on the State Register. A **Michigan Historical Marker** was placed there in September 1977.

Fort Mackinac

Established by the French in 1714 on the island of Michilimackinac, the fort was intended to

Every few seconds, a car is turned out at the Ford River Rouge plant.

guard traders as they traveled between fur trading outlets. Control of the fort bounced from the French to the British to the Americans back to the British and finally back to the Americans. The American Army remained until 1894, when the fort and surrounding park were put under the care of the **Mackinac Island** State Park Commission. In 1904, Michilimackinac State Park in Mackinac City was added to the commission's responsibilities.

Fort Michilimackinac

Built by the French in the early 1700s, the fort was less a military facility than a fortified trading post. French fur traders used the fort as a stopping-off place for supplies as they traveled

Fur traders sought protection at Fort Mackinac as they traveled their trading routes.

F

from Montreal around the Great Lakes. Its strategic location also made it ideal for seeking alliances with the region's Indian tribes.

The British, following their victory in the French and Indian War, took control of the fort in 1761 and continued to use it as a major outpost in the fur trade. Their harsh policies were not welcomed by the nearby Ottawa and Chippewa, who had lived comfortably under French occupation and were primed by Chief **Pontiac** for his 1763 rebellion.

On June 2, 1763, the tribes staged a lacrosse game outside the fort walls; the women who watched from the sidelines had weapons hidden under their robes. The British, in a festive mood and easily diverted as they celebrated the birthday of King George III, were taken by surprise. Most were killed as the tribes attacked the fort.

Michilimackinac has been more intensively excavated than any other French site in the United States. The longest continually running archeological dig in the country, it is open to the public each summer. The fort has been restored as a living-history museum. A **Michigan Historical Marker** was erected there in 1958. The site is on both the State Register and National Register of Historic Places and is a National Historic Landmark.

Fort Wilkins

In 1844, the army's Fifth Infantry was dispatched from **Detroit** to construct and garrison a fort at Copper Harbor. This was in response to settlers' pleas for protection from resentful Indians, primarily the Chippewas. The fort was named for then-Secretary of War William Wilkins. Shortly after the fort's construction, miners discovered copper mines, and the rush was on.

Fort Wilkins was abandoned in 1846, reopened in 1867, and officially discontinued as a military post in 1870. Today it has been restored and is a state park in conjunction with the **Copper Harbor Lighthouse**.

Fort Wilkins, abandoned in 1870, remained nearly intact and was restored as a state park.

Fox Theatre

Built by William Fox, owner of 20th Century Fox, and designed by renowned local architect **C. Howard Crane**, the Fox Theatre opened just in time for the stock market crash of 1928. Despite the financial hard times, the Fox thrived as an affordable way to escape the depression of the time. The Fox showed its first film, *Street Angel*, on September 21, 1928.

In the 1940s, when the focus was on **World War II**, the Fox premiered movie reels for the public. Crowds came to see vaudeville shows, big band performances, and war movies. The 1950s brought wide-screen films and epic movies such as *Ben Hur*, as well as comedians

who performed several times a day to crowds totaling over 37,000.

In the 1960s people flocked in to see the popular **Motown** show, the Motown Revue, but in the 1970s the theater fell on hard times. As the downtown area declined, the theater strove to maintain its popularity and catered to the African American market with blaxploitation films, kung-fu, and horror movies.

In the 1980s, public interest turned back to older times, and the Fox brought in gospel singers, silent movies, and classic films. In 1987, the Ilitch family chose to invest in the Fox, which was, by this time, beginning to be badly in need of repair. The family spent $12 million over 18 months to renovate the Fox. The theater reopened in November 1988.

The Detroit Fox Theatre is one of the top-grossing theaters of its size in the world and still manages to draw in a wide variety of audiences and performers.

Frankenmuth

The city of Frankenmuth, also known as Michigan's Little Bavaria, is one of the state's top tourist attractions, welcoming 3 million people every year. Shops styled to copy Alpine architecture line Main Street while banners sporting the blue and white of the Bavarian flag hang from every light pole. Restaurants serve food cooked in the Bavarian tradition, and locally brewed beer provides libation. A 35-bell carillon in the Bavarian Inn's Glockenspiel tower plays selected melodies followed by a presentation of carved wooden figures that tells a Brothers Grimm tale on the hour.

The town was originally settled in 1845 by 15 Franconians, primarily from Mittelfranken, Bavaria. Led by their Lutheran pastor, the group was intent on bringing faith to the native people of the region. The Chippewas, however, preferred their own ways and retreated west. The Franconians stayed put in their

The Fox Theatre, the largest remaining 1920s movie palace, has hosted everything from silent films to retrospectives, vaudeville to Motown.

The Bavarian Inn, a classic example of Frankenmuth's Alpine architecture. One of the highlights of the year in Frankenmuth is the Bavarian Festival. Each year 100,000 people go for the music, food, and parades.

F

new settlement along the Cass River, clearing forests, planting crops, and brewing beer. They named their settlement Frankenmuth, meaning "courage of the Franconians."

One family of descendants, the Zehnders, traveled to Bavaria in the mid-1950s and found what they needed to perk up their town. In food and style, the town began to imitate the style of its Bavarian counterparts. A Bavarian Festival was established, and in 1962, a sister-city agreement with the Mittelfranken community of Gunzenhausen was signed.

Along with Zehnder's restaurants, another popular tourist site is Bronner's Christmas shop. The shop displays over 50,000 ornaments and has expanded to include a Tannenbaum section and a Bavarian Corner.

Frankensteen, Richard T. (1907–1970)

Union organizer. He came to prominence with the **Battle of the Overpass**, when he was beaten by security officers while leafleting outside the **Ford River Rouge** plant. He rose to vice president of the **United Auto Workers** in 1937

Richard Frankensteen became vice president of the United Auto Workers in 1937.

but was ousted in a power struggle. He ran unsuccessfully for mayor of **Detroit**.

Franklin, Aretha (1942–)

Musician. Dubbed the Queen of Soul, Franklin boasts a string of soul hits rooted in the sound of gospel music. She began singing with her sisters in the **Detroit** church where her father, the Rev. L.C. Franklin, was pastor. At 14, she made her first recordings of gospel music.

The first female inductee into the Rock and Roll Hall of Fame, Franklin rose to prominence in the 1960s with releases such as *Respect*, *Chain of Fools*, and *Baby I Love You*. Widely respected, she sang at Dr. Martin Luther King's funeral and at President Bill Clinton's first inauguration.

Frederik Meijer Gardens and Sculpture Park (*see* Meijer Gardens and Sculpture Park, Frederik)

Freer, Charles Lang (1856–1919)

Industrialist. One of the founders of Peninsular Car Company, he was an avid collector of Asian and American art. He willed his collection to the Smithsonian Institution and also provided the institution with funds to build a gallery to display the artwork. The Freer Gallery of Art includes the famous Peacock Room, an example of American painter James McNeill Whistler's interior design work.

Fresh Air Society

The Fresh Air Society was founded in 1902 to provide outdoor recreational activities for immigrant women and children. Its day trips to **Belle Isle** evolved into camping experiences, and today the society runs the largest camp in North America. FAS was among the incorporating members of the Jewish Welfare Federation.

Frost, Robert (1874–1963)

Poet. He was writer-in-residence at the **University of Michigan** in **Ann Arbor** from

Robert Frost, the Pulitzer Prize-winning poet.

1921 to 1923. While there, he completed a book of poetry, *New Hampshire*, that won him the Pulitzer Prize. Other collections by Frost, considered America's finest poet, include *Mountain Interval*.

Fudge

The sweet, usually chocolate, confection is a favorite souvenir for Michigan tourists. Since the late 1880s fudge has been made and sold on **Mackinac Island**. Visitors lured into a shop by the aroma watch the candy as it is mixed and cooled on marble slabs. "Fudgie" is the locals' affectionate term for Michigan tourists.

Furniture Industry

In the early 1800s industrialists took advantage of Michigan's large hardwood forests and cheap immigrant labor in establishing a furniture industry in western Michigan. The city of **Grand Rapids** holds a unique position in the history of American furniture. For more than 150 years it has been a center for furniture design and manufacturing, starting with the first cabinetmakers who arrived in the mid-1830s. Increased railroad access by the 1860s and '70s also helped the fledgling industry expand as it began to ship its products throughout the United States.

The Grand Rapids companies furnished the homes of a growing Victorian middle class with high-quality mass-produced furniture—chairs, tables, and coat racks, as well as bedroom and dining room suites. After Grand Rapids furniture makers displayed exceptional pieces at the Centennial Exposition in Philadelphia in 1876 the city became known as the Furniture Capital of America.

While Grand Rapids was Michigan's best-known city for the manufacture of furniture, it was not the only one. **Detroit**, Grand Ledge, Monroe, and Holland also built large quantities of furniture. By 1890 Michigan employed some 7,000 people in 178 furniture factories across the state.

Grand Rapids' reputation as the center of American furniture manufacturing continued well into the 20th century, and while High

A furniture maker plies his craft at Baker Furniture in Grand Rapids.

F

Point, North Carolina, may have overtaken Grand Rapids' position in the residential furniture industry, Michigan is still a dominant force in the office furnishings industry.

Fur Trade

The buying and selling of furs was a major industry in America throughout its early history. The key animal in the fur trade was the beaver; beaver hats were in style all over Europe in the 1700s. The fur trade linked fashionable women in Paris to New York exporters, frontier traders, and Indian trappers. The pelts of beavers, muskrats, otters, and minks went one way; kettles, blankets, axes, and muskets went the other.

President George Washington reasoned that only a government-run fur company would be strong enough to challenge the British in the newly formed Michigan Territory. In 1795, Congress voted to establish a company that would secure furs from the Indians in exchange for an assortment of goods. The government created the Office of Indian Affairs to conduct the fur trade. It set up trading posts in **Detroit** and on **Mackinac Island** and stocked them with goods. Paid agents were to buy, store, and transfer furs from the trading posts to Washington, D.C., where they would be sold at auction. The agents would then buy goods and take them back to the posts to sell or trade.

One of the licensed traders was a French descendent named **Louis Campau** who, in 1826, opened a trading post on the left bank of the Grand River. Once it was up and running, he opened another at the native village of Brock-a-tinck about 25 miles downriver along the O-wash-to-nong. That site is now in the heart of downtown **Grand Rapids**. Most fur traders used Detroit as their home base to sell furs and acquire supplies that they would haul to the valley in back packs, weighing about 125 pounds each, to trade with the Indians.

Competition arrived in 1808 when John Jacob Astor founded the American Fur Company. He had studied the fur trade and

Native American trapper and fur trade agent. Mackinac Island, circa 1910.

mastered the trading concept. Astor turned his sights west to Michigan and made his move to challenge the government facilities. He targeted Michigan for his fur trade using Detroit as his base and Mackinac Island as the western headquarters where most furs were bought, packed on boats, and sent to the East Coast. Unlike most government agents, Astor's agents lived with the **Native Americans** and supplied them with goods and credit as needed. Astor's company was so efficiently operated that the government shut down its own companies in 1822.

By the late 1820s and into the 1830s, the fur trade began to decline. The trade had only worked when the Indians had control of the lands. The loss of the Indians to assist with trapping and maintaining the trading system was perhaps as important at the depletion of the beavers and other fur-bearing animal populations. The real death knell was changing tastes in fashion. As Astor noted from Paris in 1832, "They make hats of silk in place of Beaver."

Gabrilowitsch, Ossip (1878–1936)

Pianist and conductor. He studied under Anton Rubinstein at St. Petersburg Conservatory and conducted the Munich Konzertverein Orchestra before becoming music director of the **Detroit Symphony Orchestra**. He oversaw the building of **Orchestra Hall**. He was married to concert singer Clara Clemens, daughter of Mark Twain.

Garland Stove

In 1880, **Detroit** was considered Stove Capital of the World. One of the largest companies, the Michigan Stove Company, built a massive replica of its Garland Stove kitchen range. The World's Largest Stove debuted at the 1893 World's Columbian Exposition in Chicago. Carved of oak, painted to look like metal, it stood 25 feet high, 30 feet long, and 20 feet wide and weighed 15 tons. Following the exposition, it became a tourist attraction in downtown Detroit until 1965, when it was moved to the Michigan State Fairgrounds. In 1974 it was disassembled and stored at the Fort Wayne Military Museum. In 1998, the stove was restored and displayed at the Michigan State Fair.

General Motors Building

It was world headquarters for the automotive manufacturing giant for more than 75 years. A massive symbol of the power and prestige of the automotive industry, the General Motors Building was completed in 1923 during downtown **Detroit**'s building boom. Prior to occupying the building, General Motors had rented office space in New York and Detroit. For many years the building was considered the largest office complex in the world.

The General Motors Building became company headquarters in the era of Alfred P. Sloan, who pushed GM ahead of its competitors.

Internationally-known architect **Albert Kahn** designed the Urban Beaux-Arts style limestone edifice. Approximately 1,800 offices were housed in the General Motors Building, which consists of a long central block with four projecting wings on the front and back. The innovative design allowed natural light and greater air circulation for employees who worked in a time before air conditioning.

Developed to house a wide scope of activities under one roof, the 15-story structure contained an auditorium and exposition halls, auto display rooms, shops, a gymnasium, café, and lounges. One of Detroit's most famous signs became the red glowing "General Motors" letters atop the building. The building was designated a National Historic Landmark in 1978.

General Motors vacated the structure in 1999 and moved its headquarters to a location in the **Renaissance Center**. Since then the building has been renovated, retaining the historic appearance of the exterior and first floor interior. Currently the building, now called **Cadillac** Place after Detroit's founder, houses a variety of state government agencies.

The building is located at 3044 West Grand Boulevard.

G

Over the years, Gerber has branched out into baby skin care products, in addition to its baby foods.

Gerald R. Ford Library and Museum (*see* Ford, Gerald R., Library and Museum)

Gerber

Hand straining food for their infant gave Dorothy and Daniel Gerber the idea to produce baby food at the family's Fremont Canning Company. Baby Sally was the first food analyst. Ads featuring the Gerber Baby, Ann Turner Cook, made Gerber foods an instant success. Gerber, Fremont's largest employer, buys much of its produce from local farmers.

Gerrish, Winfield Scott (n.d.)

Logger. After seeing a locomotive at the 1876 Centennial Exposition in Philadelphia, Gerrish realized lumbermen could extend their operations farther from the riverbank if they used a narrow-gauge locomotive to transport logs. He organized a six-mile rail line into areas that had been too remote to harvest. His inventiveness shortened the life of Michigan's forests.

Giant Tire

On Interstate 94 near **Detroit** Metro Airport is a landmark like no other. The big tire that sits

The Giant Tire has been a Detroit landmark since 1964.

next to the highway is not an optical illusion, nor did it come off an even bigger truck. The tire was designed and built as a Ferris wheel in 1964 for the World's Fair in New York. The 80-foot high spectacle was a big draw at the Transportation pavilion. When the fair ended, the tire's owner, U.S. Rubber, removed the

Ferris wheel seats. It was moved to Michigan and reassembled outside the company's headquarters in Allen Park.

Gibson Mandolin-Guitar Manufacturing Company

The company started in Orville Gibson's **Kalamazoo** mandolin workshop and branched out into guitars, banjos, and ukuleles as they became popular in the 1920s. Gibson was one of the first companies to produce electric guitars. The company, long considered a symbol of quality, moved its headquarters to Nashville in 1981.

Gipp, George "The Gipper" (1895–1920)

Football player. Immortalized in Knute Rockne's "Win One for the Gipper" locker room speech, Laurium native George Gipp is arguably the best college football player of all time.

At Notre Dame, he aspired to be a baseball player, but Rockne was so taken with Gipp's natural, graceful athleticism, he recruited him for the football team. Gipp was a runner, passer, punter, kicker, kick returner, and defensive back. He rushed for 2,341 yards and 21

touchdowns and threw for an additional 1,789 yards. He scored 156 points during his career.

Gipp died of an infection at the age of 25, two weeks before being named Notre Dame's first All-American.

Gordy, Berry, Jr. (1929–)

Record producer and film executive. Through his Motown Records, he brought black music into mainstream American culture. In the mid-1950s, following army service and stints as a boxer and a Ford production worker, he began to write R&B songs, scoring with Jackie Wilson's recording of his *Reet Petite*. He started Motown Records with a borrowed $800 and developed a stable of stars that included **Stevie Wonder**, the Four Tops, the Temptations, and

the **Supremes**. After relocating Motown to Los Angeles in 1970, he tried his hand at directing (*Mahogany*, 1975) and producing (*Lady Sings the Blues*, 1972). He sold Motown Records in 1988, the same year he was inducted into the Rock and Roll Hall of Fame.

Grand Army of the Republic

The GAR was the nation's first national veterans organization. Membership was open only to **Civil War** veterans. The organization held annual reunions, cared for indigent widows and orphans, and became a powerful political force in lobbying for veterans pensions. The GAR instituted Memorial Day on May 30, 1868.

The Michigan chapter, with members throughout the state, peaked at more than

Although membership in the Grand Army of the Republic was restricted to Civil War veterans, the organization lasted into the 1940s.

21,000 men in 1893. The **Detroit** Post, one of the five in the city, was nicknamed the Millionaire Post, as it limited itself to the state's elite.

The last Michigan encampment, in 1940, comprised six veterans, including **Orlando LaValley**, the last surviving veteran born in Michigan.

Grand Hotel

Mackinac Island has always been known as a historic oasis, giving those who venture there the chance to travel back in time to the 1830s. In 1886, the Michigan Central Railroad, **Grand Rapids** & Indiana Railroad, and the **Detroit** & Cleveland Steamship Navigation Company formed the Mackinac Island Hotel Company to provide better accommodations for those

Grand Hotel, Mackinac Island, became a National Historic Landmark in 1989.

traveling to Mackinac. Land was purchased, and construction on what is now the Grand Hotel began. The following year, the Grand Hotel opened at rates of $3 to $5 per night. In 1890, the Grand Hotel's front porch, the longest in the world, was constructed.

The Grand Hotel has hosted famous visitors, including Mark Twain and the casts of movies filmed there. In more than 100 years, W. Stewart Woodfill and the Musser family have been the only owners. The Grand Hotel is on the State Register and National Register of Historic Places. It became a National Historic Landmark in 1989

In addition to its beauty and prestige, the hotel is home to a full 18-hole golf course, a private cottage, and many themed rooms, including five named for former first ladies. In each room, the namesake assisted in the decor. Although guests could once rent rooms for a few dollars a night, rates have risen as the hotel has become more exclusive. After 6 p.m., men and women are expected to wear formal dress while in the hotel. Weddings, corporate gatherings, and private parties are booked on a regular basis.

Grand Rapids

Like most cities in central Michigan, Grand Rapids has been involved in the auto industry. But it's better known as Furniture Capital of America, a nickname it's held for more than a century.

The city's furniture industry started in 1837 with **William Haldane**, who opened a shop in his home. The area's plentiful hardwood lured more craftsmen over the following decades. A display of Grand Rapids furniture at the 1876 Centennial Exposition in Philadelphia clinched local furniture makers' reputation and flooded them with orders.

A bird's eye view of Grand Rapids ("the Furniture Capital of America"), from 1868.

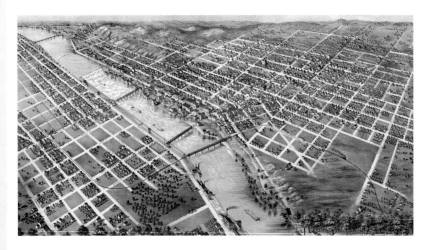

Furniture markets, first held in 1878, attracted buyers from all over the world. The business evolved into two industries, residential furniture and business and institutional furniture. Not surprisingly, **Steelcase**, which began in 1912 as the Metal Office Furniture Company, is one of Grand Rapids' major employers.

Located in the southwestern part of the state, Grand Rapids is Michigan's second-largest city, with about 200,000 residents. It's the county seat of Kent County and sprawls out into a metropolitan area that has a population of over a million. The central city is bisected by the Grand River, from which it took its name.

More than 2,000 years ago, the Grand River Valley was populated by the Hopewell Indians, also known as the Mound Builders. By the time the Ottawa arrived, some 300 years ago, the Hopewell had disappeared. The first Europeans, missionaries and fur traders, arrived in the 1820s and lived in relative peace alongside the Ottawa, trading metal and textiles for fur pelts. In 1826, Louis Campau, a French trader, set up a trading post and settled in. Five years later, he paid the government $90 for what is now Grand Rapids' downtown business district, and seven years after that, in 1838, his settlement incorporated as a village. Grand Rapids grew quickly. The first formal census, in 1845, recorded 1,510 residents. On May 1, 1850, when the village was upgraded to a town, the population was 2,686. By the turn of the century, it was close to 83,000.

In 1916 Grand Rapids became one of the first cities in the country to adopt a commission-manager form of government, with an at-large mayor, commissioners elected by ward, and a city manager hired by the commission. Although it's been amended, the 1916 city charter is still in effect.

Grand Rapids is proud of its reputation as a leader. In 1880, Grand Rapids Electric Light and Power Company flipped the switch on the nation's first hydroelectric turbine, firing up 16 brush-arc lamps at the Wolverine Chair

La Grande Vitesse *("the grand rapids"), a stabile by Alexander Calder, was dedicated in front of Grand Rapids City Hall in 1969. The area became known as Calder Plaza.*

Factory. In 1945 Grand Rapids was the **first American city to fluoridate** its water. The vacuum cleaner was invented there. And Grand Rapids was the boyhood home of Michigan's only U.S. president, **Gerald R. Ford**. Grand Rapids hosts the **Gerald R. Ford Museum**.

Grand Rapids School Furniture Company

In 1886 it began to produce student desks comprising a desktop and book box connected to a seat and back. Following the desk's success, the company expanded into other types of durable furniture and by 1889 was the world's largest chair manufacturer. The name was changed to American Seating Company in 1926.

Grand Traverse Lighthouse & Museum

One of the oldest lighthouses on the **Great Lakes**, it stands at the northern entrance to the Manitou Passage. Exhibits in the restored lighthouse chronicle the history of Great Lakes mariners. The museum, at 15550 N. Lighthouse Road, Northport, is open May through December. Hours vary.

G

Granholm, Jennifer (1959–)

Governor. Granholm made history in 1998 as Michigan's first female attorney general. She topped that feat in 2002 by becoming the state's first female governor.

Born in Vancouver, she came to the United States at age 3 and became a citizen at 21. She attended the University of California at Berkeley, the first in her family to graduate from college. After earning a law degree at Harvard University, she moved to Michigan to practice.

As a U.S. prosecutor in **Detroit** in 1990, she achieved a 98 percent conviction rate. Nearly unknown when she ran for attorney general, she won nonetheless and became the lone Democrat in a Republican administration.

Great Lakes

Lakes Superior, Michigan, Huron, Erie, and Ontario comprise the Great Lakes, the largest system of fresh, surface water in the world. The Great Lakes contain roughly 18 percent of the world supply of fresh water; only the polar ice caps contain more. The Great Lakes cover more than 94,000 square miles and drain more than twice that much land. They hold an estimated 6 quadrillion gallons of water, about nine-tenths of the United States' fresh water supply. Spread evenly across the contiguous 48 states, the lakes' water would be about 9.5 feet deep. The Great Lakes basin is home to 25 million people in the United States and 8.5 million in Canada. The lakes span more than 750 miles east to west.

The Great Lakes affect our way of life in many ways including weather, climate, wildlife, and habitat. They are an important part of the physical and cultural heritage of North America and have played a major role in the history and development of the United States and Canada.

Outflows from the Great Lakes are relatively small, less than one percent per year, in comparison with the total volume of water and large surface area. Both the large volume and surface area make the lakes susceptible to a wide range of pollutants, which enter the lakes from a variety of sources and are retained and concentrated in the system. The Great Lakes are also susceptible to pollutants that fall with rain or snow and as dust on the lake surface.

Michigan is the only state that touches four of the five Great Lakes.

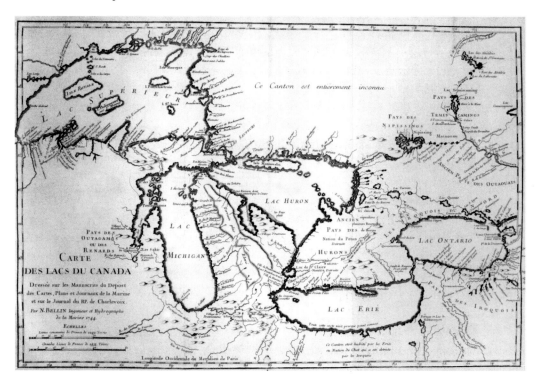

The Great Lakes have evolved during the 10,000 years since the retreat of the last glacier. The first Europeans found a fairly stable system, but soon **logging**, farming, and fishing brought about profound ecological changes. Industrialization and urbanization followed, stressing the Great Lakes system even more. By the late 1960s growing concern about the condition of the Great Lakes resulted in new investment, control, and regulation of pollutant discharges and other improvements. The first Great Lakes Water Quality Agreement between the United States and Canada, in 1972, formalized the efforts. Continued recognition of the needs for an ecosystem approach resulted in new agreements that have greatly improved the condition of the Great Lakes, but the wise management needed to maintain the use of lake resources requires continued strong public, political, and governmental awareness and action.

The Great Lakes all have different characteristics. Lake Superior is the largest in terms of volume, and the deepest and coldest of the five. Lake Michigan, the second largest, is the only one entirely in the United States. Lake Huron contains the Georgian Bay and is the third largest of the lakes by volume. Lake Erie is the smallest by volume and is exposed to the greatest effect from urbanization and agriculture. Lake Ontario is the smallest in area of the Great Lakes.

Great Lakes Chamber Music Festival

In a remarkable partnership among religious and cultural institutions, the festival has been sponsored since 1994 by **Detroit** Chamber Winds & Strings together with organizations representing the Catholic, Jewish, and Protestant faiths. Each June, 20 concerts are played, many hosted in the sponsors' venues.

Great Lakes Lore Maritime Museum

The museum charts the history of **Great Lakes** navigation, from **Native American** traders to modern-day captains. Annual inductees are

More than a tenth of the population of the U.S. and more than a quarter of Canada's population live in the Great Lakes basin.

G

A tribute to Hank Greenberg, left, makes him a permanent fixture at Comerica Park. At right is a tribute to Ty Cobb.

added to the hall of fame. The museum, at 367 N. 3rd Street, Rogers City, is open Tuesday through Saturday 11 a.m. to 5 p.m. and Sunday noon to 5 p.m.

Great Lakes Shipwreck Museum

The only museum of its kind, it features artifacts from 13 local shipwrecks and a tribute to the *Edmund Fitzgerald*. It shares Whitefish Point with the oldest active lighthouse on Lake Superior. The museum, at 18335 North Whitefish Point Road, Paradise, is open every day May 1 through October 31, 10 a.m. to 6 p.m.

Greektown

Greeks first came to **Detroit** in the late 1880s and formed a community centered on Monroe Street, between Beaubein and St. Antoine streets. Three historic churches anchor the area. One, the **Second Baptist Church**, was an important stop on the **Underground Railroad**. Historic Trapper's Alley, site of Detroit's early **fur trade**, is also nearby.

Greektown narrowly escaped the wrecking ball in the late 1940s, when the area was slated

for a new judicial center. Today Monroe Street is a bustling entertainment district filled with ethnic restaurants, coffeehouses, Old World bakeries, unique shops, and nightclubs.

Green, Al (1946–)

Singer. He grew up in **Grand Rapids** and began to perform gospel when he was nine. In the early 1970s he had six consecutive Top Ten hits, including "Let's Stay Together." With his unmistakable mix of baritone and soaring falsetto, he was the top male soul singer in the world before becoming a preacher and, in 1979, dropping secular music to sing only Christian music.

Although he continues to preach at Full Gospel Tabernacle in Memphis, he returned to secular music in the mid-1980s. He was inducted into the Rock and Roll Hall of Fame in 1995.

Greenberg, Henry Benjamin "Hank" (1911–1986)

Baseball legend. Among the first major leaguers to enlist, he missed four seasons during **World War II** and still hit 331 career home runs. He was named Most Valuable Player at first base (1935) and left field (1940), among three players to win the award at different positions. His ninth-inning grand slam on the last day of the 1945 season nailed the pennant for the **Detroit Tigers**.

Greenberg slugged the Tigers to a pennant race in 1934. The schedule against the Boston Red Sox called for games on the Jewish High Holidays. Greenberg, a Jew, hit two homers on Rosh Hashanah that won the game. He refused to play on Yom Kippur. The Tigers lost.

Griffiths, Martha (1912–2003)

She was a feminist before the term gained popular usage. From 1954 to 1974, she represented southeastern Michigan in the U.S. House of Representatives. She was the first woman to sit on the **Detroit** criminal courts bench, the first female lieutenant governor of Michigan, and the first woman to serve on the powerful House Ways and Means Committee. When Congress was debating **civil rights** legislation in the early 1960s, Griffiths was pivotal in adding women to the list of protected classes.

Martha Griffiths was the first woman to sit on the Detroit criminal courts bench.

G

*Wirt Rowland's Guardian
Building stands out from
Detroit's other skyscrapers.*

She later helped shepherd the ill-fated Equal Rights Amendment out of committee for a full House vote.

Griffiths' intelligence and sharp tongue were well known. In the mid-1960s, when airline stewardesses were to remain single, she learned that an airline had fired a stewardess for getting engaged. Griffiths rebuked an airline executive: "What are you running, an airline or a whorehouse?"

Griffon

The first sailing ship on the Great Lakes, it was built by **Robert Cavelier La Salle** and launched in 1678. It vanished on its maiden voyage, taking with it five crew members and a load of furs. It has never been found.

Guardian Building

Detroit's post-World War I economic boom favorably impacted the city's largest banking institutions. In 1928 the Union Trust Company began work on a 40-floor skyscraper on Griswold Street, considered Detroit's Wall Street. The finished structure, which opened in 1929, is called the Guardian Building after the Guardian Detroit Union Group, the 1930 company that developed from Union Trust.

Detroit architect Wirt Rowland designed the narrow rectangular edifice, which is clad in a striking tangerine-hued brick, specially created for the structure and soon dubbed Guardian brick. Along lower floors run bands of pink granite, buff Mankato stone, and green, tan, and red-brown glazed tile and terracotta. Building entrances feature stepped arches accented with **Pewabic** tile.

The architectural design of the building, which covers a city block, resists categorization, with a dizzy but harmonic combination of Aztec, American Indian, exotic modern, and jazz age influences fused with French, Dutch, and American arts and crafts details.

The three-story barrel-vaulted lobby contains intricate designs in Rookwood and Pewabic tiles. Other sumptuous details

incorporated into the lobby or banking hall were stained-glass windows, hand-painted ceilings, rare Numidian marble, and a Tiffany clock. The building soon became known as the Cathedral of Finance.

Over the years several companies have owned the Guardian Building. In late 2003, DTE Energy Company sold the building to a real estate group that is developing new retail plans for it. The Guardian Building is at 500 Griswold Street.

Guest, Edgar (1881–1959)

Poet, syndicated columnist. In 1895, Guest became a copy boy for the *Detroit Free Press*, where he worked for almost 65 years. At its peak, his column, "Breakfast Table Chat," was syndicated to more than 300 U.S. newspapers. Guest wrote more than 11,000 poems, many presenting an often-sentimental view of daily life. His 1961 *A Heap o' Livin'* begins with the now-classic line: "It takes a heap o' living to make a house a home. ..."

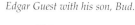

Edgar Guest with his son, Bud.

H

Haldane, William (1807–1896)

Furniture maker. The first of the great **Grand Rapids** craftsmen, he opened a shop in his home at Pearl Street and Ottawa Avenue, where he made furniture using only a foot-powered lathe. Later he added water-powered machinery, then converted to steam. Some of his pieces are on display in the Grand Rapids Public Museum.

Haley, Bill (1925–1981)

Rock-and-roll icon. Bill Haley and His Comets recorded "(We're Gonna) Rock Around the Clock" in 1955 and added a new dimension to American music. Beginning as a country singer, Haley later formed a new band, the Saddlemen, who would become the Comets, the first rock-and-roll band in history.

The group's first million-seller was "Shake, Rattle, and Roll," but its success was eclipsed by "Rock Around the Clock," which sold 45 million copies. Haley recorded 10 more chart-toppers, and his music was featured in many movies, most notably *Blackboard Jungle*.

Haley, a Highland Park native, died of a heart attack in Harlingen, Texas.

Hamilton, Eva McCall (1871–1948)

Legislator. The **Grand Rapids** Republican was the first woman in Michigan's Legislature. Elected as a senator from the Sixth District in 1920, she served one term.

William Haldane, whose furniture designs are on display in the Grand Rapids Public Museum.

Hansbury School, Bertha

Opened in 1925, it was the first music school in **Detroit** in which African American children were taught music by an all-black faculty. The school, which included a nursery and kindergarten, also taught etiquette, history, and interpretive dance. Founder Hansbury chose teaching over a career as a concert pianist.

Harmon, Tom (1919–1990)

Football player, broadcaster. The **University of Michigan**'s first Heisman Trophy winner, in 1940, and an All-American halfback in both 1939 and 1940, Harmon scored 237 career points for the Wolverines. He rushed for 2,134 yards and scored 33 touchdowns. He scored 16 additional touchdowns through the air.

After college, Harmon served as a pilot in **World War II**, earning a Purple Heart and a Silver Star. He played with AFL New York Americans in 1941 and NFL Los Angeles Rams in 1946–47.

Paving the way for other athletes, he became a radio and television commentator and hosted a nightly sports broadcast.

Harris, Julie (1925–)

Actor. Harris has been nominated for Broadway's Tony award ten times and has won the award more than any other actor—five times, including for *I Am a Camera* in 1952 and *The Belle of Amherst* in 1977. She has starred in more than 30 New York productions. Harris was nominated for the Academy Award for her work in *The Member of the Wedding*. In television, she has been nominated for nine Emmys, winning the award for *Little Moon of Alban* and *Victoria Regina*. Harris was born in Grosse Pointe Park.

Harrison, Jim (1937–)

Poet, novelist, essayist, screenwriter. His novels, published in 22 languages, include *A Good Day to Die* and *Sundog*. He has written nine volumes of poetry, including *After Ikkyu*, and in 2000 published his first children's book, *The Boy Who Ran to the Woods*. His only work of non-fiction is *Just Before Dark*.

Hartwick Pines Logging Museum

Visitors return to Michigan's 19th-century **logging** era at the Hartwick Pines Logging Museum. The museum is located within the Hartwick Pines State Park, site of one of Michigan's largest remaining stands of virgin white pine. A visitor center, logging camp

buildings, and other exhibits tell the stories of the lumberjacks, rivermen, and lumber barons. A paved trail leads to a 300-year-old pine, a remnant of the ancient forests. The park, northeast of Grayling on State Route 93, is open daily. The visitors' center and buildings open from 9 a.m. to dusk Labor Day to mid-October and weekends for the rest of the year.

Laura Haviland displays the kinds of shackles used to restrain runaway slaves.

Haviland, Laura (1808–1898)

Social activist. With her husband, Charles, she founded the Raisin Institute, one of the first de-segregated schools in the country. She was stationmaster of the first **Underground Railroad** station in Michigan. She also worked in the temperance movement and established a number of schools for dependent children.

Heathkit

Its earliest incarnation, the Heath Aeroplane Company, was known for aircraft and replacement parts. In 1926, founder Edward Bayard Heath introduced the Parasol, a mail-order

Hartwick Pines Logging Museum sits within one of Michigan's largest stands of virgin white pine, the state tree.

airplane in kit form, that foretold the future of his company, though Heath himself was not there to see it. The Parasol proved so successful that Heath decided to market additional kits. He crashed and died while testing a midwing airplane design.

After **World War II**, Howard Anthony, who had bought the Heath Company, as it was then known, designed an oscilloscope from war-surplus electronics parts and marketed it as a mail-order kit for $39.50. Anthony believed that anyone who had simple instructions, a few hand tools, and the time could assemble his kit. Following the success of the oscilloscope, Heath added amateur radio and hi-fi component kits. Heathkits were wildly popular, and enthusiasts waited breathlessly for the amateur electronics and radio magazines that announced new products. The company eventually branched out into kits for ham radios, radio controls, home electronics, satellite TV stations, furniture, and even a Thomas organ. In the 1960s, under several owners, Heath added retail store sales and authorized service centers. The company stopped making do-it-yourself kits in the mid-1980s.

Today, as Heathkit Educational Systems, the Benton Harbor company specializes in technical education curricula, courseware, and hardware for schools and training centers.

Heidelberg Street

Artist Tyree Guyton's canvas is a city block. In 1986, the native Detroiter got fed up with drug dealers taking over abandoned houses on Heidelberg Street, where he grew up. His Heidelberg Project, begun as a campaign to clean up a decaying street, has attracted visitors from all over the world and been the subject of a documentary film.

Guyton closed off access to the abandoned buildings by covering them with discarded items, such as toys, highway signs, kitchen appliances, chairs, and luggage. He fastened dozens of stuffed animals to one tree. He secured bicycles to another tree, so it looked as

*The community is invited to work
on the Heidelberg Street houses
Tyree Guyton decorates.*

H

if the bikes were riding up the trunk. He painted faces on automobile hoods. He covered his grandfather's house with bright polka dots.

A dingy block of questionable safety was transformed into a tourist attraction. Yet, not everyone appreciated the change. Neighbors complained the project was hindering development. Public officials called the whole thing an eyesore.

On a Saturday morning in 1991, when the media and much of the city were still asleep, bulldozers pulled up to tear down the houses. Guyton responded by creating free-standing sculptures in the now-vacant lots. Over the years, the project has continued to grow despite the controversy and continued fights with authorities.

Guyton has received numerous awards and honors. He has been named Michigan Artist of the Year and Michiganian of the Year and was given the **Spirit of Detroit** Award by the same city council that later demanded he remove the artwork.

Hemingway, Ernest (1899–1961)

Novelist, journalist. Hemingway spent his early summers exploring the woods and waterways of the northern Lower Peninsula. He was the first American wounded in World War I; at the conclusion of the war, he returned to Europe to cover world events. During the 1920s, he lived and worked in Paris. His terse, realistic style was unmistakable.

Hemingway's novels include *For Whom the Bell Tolls*, *The Sun Also Rises*, *Death in the Afternoon*, and *The Old Man and the Sea*. His short works, such as "My Old Man," "Up in Michigan," "Big Two-Hearted River," and "The Killers," were also notable. Hemingway won the Nobel Prize for Literature in 1954.

Henderson-Ames Company

The **Kalamazoo** company was among the nation's major producers of uniforms, swords, and regalia for military associations, secret societies, and other organizations. Governor **Hazen Pingree**'s administration was marred by

Ernest Hemingway Cottage (Windemere). Hemingway spent his early summers in the northern Lower Peninsula.

scandal after state officials allowed the company to buy used military uniforms at salvage prices, jack up the prices, and sell them back to the state.

Henry Ford Museum (*see* Ford, Henry, Museum and Greenfield Village)

Herbert H. Dow Historical Museum and Bradley Home and Carriage House (*see* Dow Historical Museum)

Heston, Charlton (1924–)

Actor. After service in **World War II**, he managed a playhouse in North Carolina. In 1947, he went to New York, where he played his first Broadway role in *Anthony and Cleopatra*. After some success in television, he moved to Los Angeles. He achieved widespread success playing epic characters including Moses, El Cid, and Ben Hur, for which he won the Academy Award in 1959. Known as much for his activism as his acting, Heston was president of the Screen Actors Guild from 1966 to 1971. A staunch conservative, he was a long-time spokesperson for the National Rifle Association. In July 2003, he received the Presidential Medal of Freedom. Heston grew up in St. Helen.

Hiawatha

Hiawatha, a chieftain of the Iroquois, brought about the union of the Five Nations of the Iroquois to survive the aggression of the strong Algonquin. The poem *Song of Hiawatha*, by American poet Henry Wadsworth Longfellow, recounts his legendary accomplishments in the area now know as Michigan.

Highland Park Ford Plant

Many of the principles still used in mass production, most notably the continuously moving assembly line, were perfected at Highland Park. Development of the building began in 1908, when **Detroit** industrial architect **Albert Kahn** designed a series of brick, glass, reinforced concrete, and steel buildings. In a formula still seen today, large, open floors were created to allow efficient arrangement of machines, and expansive windows brought in additional light for a more pleasant productive working environment. Ground was broken in 1909 and by January 1910 the Highland Park factory was in partial operation.

Man dressed as the 16th-century American-Indian chieftan, Hiawatha

Henry Ford introduced progressive economic ideas at the Highland Park Ford Plant.

Henry Ford had already standardized parts at the plant. Now cars flowed in a continuous stream on a moving assembly line. In October 1913 the Ford Motor Company reduced the time it took to assemble a Model T from nearly 13 hours to 93 minutes. By 1920 the plant was turning out a car every minute.

An economic innovation—the $5 work day—was introduced at Highland Park in January 1914. When most industry wages were just 30 cents an hour, it was a stunning business move aimed at curing high employee turnover. At the same time, Ford moved from two nine-hour shifts to three eight-hour shifts, meaning the assembly line never stopped. At its peak, the plant employed 70,000.

Mass production halved the price of a Model T. Its accessibility helped create America's working middle class.

Ford stopped assembling cars at Highland Park when the 1928 Model A went into production at its massive **River Rouge Complex**.

The Highland Park plant was designated a National Historic Landmark in 1978. The building, which is in disrepair and closed to the public, is at 91 Manchester Avenue.

Jimmy Hoffa, leader of the Teamsters Union, who went missing in 1975.

Hill Auditorium

Architect **Albert Kahn** worked with renowned acoustical engineer Hugh Tallant to design the auditorium, on the **University of Michigan** campus, as a "monument to perfect acoustics." Since its opening in 1913, it has attracted a Who's Who of appreciative performers, including Enrico Caruso, Pablo Casals, Marian Anderson, and Isaac Stern.

Historic Fort Wayne

The first of **Detroit**'s forts to be built by Americans, it was strategically placed at a river bend as part of a border defense against the British. Included in the plans were state-of-the-art cannons, but they became irrelevant after the United States and Britain signed a diplomatic treaty.

From the **Civil War** through the Vietnam War, the fort was used as an induction center for Michigan troops. It was the primary procurement site for weapons and vehicles made in Detroit during the two world wars.

The fort, at 6325 West Jefferson Avenue, is open Saturday and Sunday, 11 a.m. to 4 p.m., from Memorial Day weekend through Labor Day weekend.

Hoffa, Jimmy (1913–?)

Union organizer. The leader of the Teamsters Union from 1957 to 1971, Hoffa was suspected of having ties to organized crime. Because of his skills as an organizer and his mob-related friends, Hoffa stirred dislike among both government officials and the AFL-CIO, which expelled the Teamsters.

Hoffa was convicted of jury tampering in 1967 and served four years in prison before President Richard Nixon commuted his sentence, on the condition that he refrain from further union activities. However, by 1975, he was trying to regain control of the Teamsters.

Hoffa disappeared in 1975. His body was never found, and he was officially declared dead in 1983.

Holland-Dozier-Holland

The song-writing team of Brian and Eddie Holland and Lamont Dozier composed many of the songs that propelled **Motown** Records artists to stardom, including "Nowhere to Run," the **Supremes'** "Stop! In the Name of Love" and "You Can't Hurry Love," and the Four Tops' "Standing in the Shadows of Love." They had dozens of Top Ten hits before leaving Motown in 1967 to form their own labels, Invictus and Hot Wax. After prolonged legal wrangling with Motown over royalties, they were forced to stop writing songs, but they continued as producers. They were inducted into the Rock and Roll Hall of Fame in 1990.

Holland Tulip Festival

In 1927, Holland High School biology teacher Lida Rogers suggested annually planting tulips to celebrate the city's Dutch heritage. In the fall

Windmill Island, Holland, Michigan. The world takes note of the Holland Tulip Festival, which ranks internationally among the 20 best festivals.

H

of 1928, three quarters of a million bulbs were planted in Holland to pay homage to the fields of tulips that carpeted the Netherlands.

Tulip Time officially began in May 1929. In the early 1930s Tulip Time was an eight-day festival that centered around the annual flower show. Other events included high school students performing Dutch folk dances and wooden shoe carvers practicing their trade. A Tulip Time festival office opened in 1933, and the Holland Chamber of Commerce began to promote the event as an attraction to tourists. The festival thrived as more events were added and the Dutch costumes worn by participants became more authentic. During **World War II**, however, all Tulip Time activities except the flower show were canceled.

In 1946, the event returned in an abridged four-day version, and the following year more than six miles' worth of tulip bulbs were planted for the enjoyment of Tulip Time tourists. Due to the popularity of the festival, it was expanded to ten days in 1991.

What started as a lavish floral decoration blossomed into a festival that now draws more than a million tourists each year. Tulip Time features the traditional street scrubbing, three parades, more than a dozen music and variety shows, and 1,600 Klompen dancers. It ranks among the top 20 festivals in the world.

Hopkin, Robert (1832–1909)

Artist. He was the leading painter in mid- to late-19th century **Detroit**. Opening his own studio in 1853, he painted seascapes, landscapes, and decorative works. Some of his most well-known decorative projects were the interiors of the **Detroit Opera House** and the Cotton Exchange in New Orleans.

Houghton County Historical Museum

The museum promotes Houghton County through its exhibits of artifacts and antiques. Features include the Copper Country Railroad Heritage Center on the former site of North America's largest copper mill. The museum, at 5500 Highway M-26, Lake Linden, is open every day June through September, 10 a.m. to 4:30 p.m.

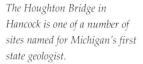

The Houghton Bridge in Hancock is one of a number of sites named for Michigan's first state geologist.

Houghton, Douglass (1809–1845)

Geologist. One of the nation's pioneering geological and mining scientists, he was named Michigan's first state geologist at age 28. He discovered salt, copper, and iron deposits that greatly impacted the fledgling state's economy. A city, county, and lake bear his name.

Howe, Gordie (1928–)

Hockey player. Howe played for 25 years with the **Detroit Red Wings**, beginning in 1946. During the course of his career, he was the league's leading scorer six times. Howe was among the Top Ten NHL scorers for 21 consecutive years, from 1949 to 1970. He was a member of the All-NHL first team 12 times; he was NHL Most Valuable Player six times. He retired briefly in the early 1970s, returning to play in the WHA and IHL. He was inducted into the Hockey Hall of Fame in 1972.

Hudson, Joseph Lowthian "J.L." (1846–1912)

Merchant. Hudson was 35 when he opened his first men's and boys haberdashery, in 1881, in the **Detroit Opera House**. Following the success of that store, he opened a 49-acre, 25-floor store on Woodward Avenue. Hudson inaugurated merchandising principles and policies that continue to be the retail industry standard, and by the 1930s Hudson's was the third largest chain of department stores in the country.

Hudson also dabbled in **Detroit**'s fledgling auto industry. With other businessmen, he formed the Hudson Motor Car Company, and the first Hudson rolled off the line July 3, 1909.

Hull, William (1753–1825)

Soldier. He was appointed first governor of the Michigan Territory in 1805. During the **War of 1812**, he surrendered **Detroit** to the British without a fight. He was court-martialed and sentenced to death for cowardice, neglect of duty, and unbecoming conduct. President James Madison commuted his sentence.

Hurlbut Memorial Gate

Architects Herman A. Brede and Gustave Mueller created the elaborate Beaux Arts arch that separates the East Jefferson waterworks from the rest of the world. The **Detroit** landmark, named for Chauncey Hurlbut, the 19th century water commissioner who willed his fortune to beautify the waterworks, is on the State Register and the National Register of Historic Places.

William Hull was appointed first governor of the Michigan Territory in 1805.

H

Hurlbut Memorial Gate (see page 131) is a familiar Detroit landmark.

Huron, Lightship No. 103

Ancient cultures moored lightships where lighthouses could not be built. The United States began to use lightships in 1819, eventually establishing 116 lightship stations along the coasts and on the **Great Lakes**.

No. 103, also called the Huron, was launched May 1, 1920, and saw general service on Lake Michigan before being assigned permanently to the head of Lake Huron Cut in 1935. Originally a steamship, it was converted to diesel in 1959.

When the ship weighed anchor and departed its station 11 years later, on August 20, 1970, it was the last lightship on the lakes. It was replaced by a lighted buoy.

The city of Port Huron took control of the ship in June 1971 and moved it to Pine Grove Park, where it was dedicated as a historical monument. A year later it was ravaged by

vandals; it was restored and rededicated. From 1973 to 1977, it was used as a training ship by the local naval reserve.

In all, the United States built 179 lightships. Although some have been preserved, No. 103 is the only surviving Great Lakes lightship. It is a National Historic Landmark and is listed on both the State Register and the National Register of Historic Places.

Hussey, Erastus (1800–1889)

Merchant, publisher, politician, and abolitionist. As **Battle Creek**'s "stationmaster" along the **Underground Railroad**, he conducted more than 1,000 runaway slaves into Canada. He helped establish the **Republican Party** and served as both a state senator and state representative.

Hutton, Betty (1921–)

Singer, comedian. The original Blonde Bombshell during **World War II**, the Battle Creek native rose to prominence in the 1940s. Her movie career included playing Annie Oakley in the 1950s film *Annie Get Your Gun* and a nonsinging role in *Miracle at Morgan Creek*, one of her few serious dramatic roles.

Huron, *Lightship No. 103, is the only surviving Great Lakes lightship.*

I

Iacocca, Lee (1924–)

Industrialist. Lee Iacocca graduated from Lehigh University in 1945 and received a master's degree in engineering from Princeton University in 1946. He was hired as an engineer by the Ford Motor Company, but soon moved to sales and management. Iacocca was responsible for the design of the phenomenally successful Ford Mustang. He was made president of Ford, but left in a dispute with **Henry Ford II** in 1978. Moving to the financially distressed Chrysler Company, he dramatically cut costs, sought government loans, introduced the K-Car and the minivan, brought the company back from the brink of bankruptcy, and repaid the loans ahead of schedule. He retired in 1992.

Ice Cream Soda

Fred Sanders opened the doors of his first store on Woodward and Gratiot in **Detroit** on June 17, 1875. He began by selling candy, later adding ice cream and baked goods. By the end of the year, Sanders had 57 stores in the metropolitan area.

In the summer of 1876, the sweet cream soda was a popular drink among customers. One night Sanders found that his entire stock of sweet cream had soured. Promising customers something just as good, the next day Sanders substituted ice cream for the sweet cream. He delighted customers and created a new confectionery sensation.

Immigrants

America is a land of immigrants, and nowhere is that seen more clearly than in Michigan. People from various nations, and from other parts of the United States, went to the **Great Lakes** State seeking economic opportunities, religious freedom, and racial equality. The arrival of new

Immigrants stoke the growth of all Michigan industries, including agriculture.

I immigrants provided the fuel that propelled Michigan's growing industries.

In the early years of the Michigan lands it was the French Canadian **explorers**, fur trappers, and Jesuit missionaries who first ventured into the wilderness, settling in the 1660s by the rapids at Sault Ste. Marie and then moving south after explorer **Antoine de la Mothe Cadillac** established a village called **Detroit** in 1701. British settlers were not far behind, competing in the **fur trade** and making early ventures into farming. When the state was young, Scandinavians—hearty Swedes, Norwegians, Danes, and Finns—saw reminders of their own virgin forests when they went to work in the mid-19th century **logging** camps, felling the tall pine timber and driving it to the sawmills of the Saginaw Valley and western Michigan.

Starting in the 1840s, immigrants surged into the **Upper Peninsula** seeking their fortunes in Copper Country and the iron ranges. Among those were the Finns and English miners from Cornwall, who stayed after the mines closed to leave their own cultural imprints on the Upper Peninsula. Hancock has become the Finnish cultural center of the United States with **Suomi College**, the only college in the country founded by Americans of Finnish descent.

In the mid-19th century, hard-working people from Holland developed a broad swath of farmland from **Grand Rapids** to Lake Michigan. Tulip fields and wooden shoe festivals are two reminders of that heritage. The Dutch also played a role in the area's **furniture industry**. Immigrants from Poland settled in several areas of Michigan, most notably in Detroit and nearby Hamtramck, a town that by 1920 had become the most predominantly Polish community in the nation.

Newcomers into Michigan also included a great migration from southern states during the early decades of the 20th century. While African Americans had lived in Michigan since before the **Civil War**, many moved northward to the Detroit area to work in the huge assembly plants springing up in support of an infant but growing **auto industry** that offered wages of $5 a day. Blacks settled in communities such as Black Bottom and established businesses in **Paradise Valley**. Other Americans were encouraged to move into Michigan during **World War II**, when more than 600,000 were employed in the assembly plants. So many Kentuckians were living in Ypsilanti that wags began to call the town "Ypsitucky." European immigrants—some of them refugees from the war—also worked in the factories and, in a strange quirk of fate, Germans and Poles found themselves assembling the very bombers and tanks that would destroy their homelands.

The auto industry also played a role in establishing Detroit's large Arab community. The **Highland Park** and **River Rouge** Ford assembly plants attracted Muslims from Lebanon and other areas of the Arab world who began to settle in Highland Park and Dearborn, near the Rouge Plant.

Interlochen Center for the Arts

What Joseph E. Maddy began in 1928 as a summer orchestra camp for high school students has grown and evolved to become a national cultural treasure. Interlochen is the premier site in the country for the training of young musicians, performers, visual artists, and writers.

The center still offers a summer arts camp, which draws talented students from all 50 states and throughout the world for four to eight weeks of intensive training, and its arts academy has graduated more Presidential Scholars in the Arts than any other high school in the country. Interlochen alumni include New York Philharmonic Orchestra director Lorin Maazel, jazz musicians Chris and Daniel Brubeck, soprano Jessye Norman, actors Tom Hulce and Linda Hunt, and CBS correspondent Mike Wallace.

In 2000, **Interlochen** merged with an independent school near Traverse City. The resulting Interlochen Pathfinder school serves children in preschool through eighth grade and includes a summer camp. The center also has a public radio station.

The Interlochen Arts Festival presents more than 750 concerts annually. Students and faculty are joined by the nation's most eminent artists. Featured performers have included the Mormon Tabernacle Choir, the Boston Pops Esplanade Orchestra, Bernadette Peters, Bonnie Raitt, Lyle Lovett, and Koko Taylor.

Interlochen attracts more than 265,000 visitors each year. The 1,200-acre campus, 13 miles south of Traverse City, is surrounded by forests and glacial lakes.

International 500 Snowmobile Race

In early February each year, Sault Ste. Marie hosts the world's premier snowmobile race. During the eight-hour marathon, daredevil riders zip around a one-mile oval 500 times. Speeds on the straightaways reach 100mph.

Isle Royale National Park

Wolves, beavers, loons, and moose, dense stands of spruce and fir, carpets of wildflowers, and crystal waters and rugged shoreline characterize Isle Royale National Park. Isle Royale is a remote archipelago of Lake Superior islands northwest of the **Upper Peninsula**. Park activities include trout fishing, sightseeing cruises, shipwreck dives, and hiking to historic **lighthouses** and copper **mining** sites. There are no roads in the park; travel is by foot or boat. The park has 165 miles of scenic hiking trails and 36 campgrounds. Overnight accommodations also are available at Rock Harbor Lodge. The park is open mid-April to October 31, with full transportation services mid-June to Labor Day.

"I've Got a Gal in Kalamazoo"

The Glenn Miller Orchestra introduced the Mack Gordon-Harry Warren song in the 1942 film *Orchestra Wives*. In swing tempo, the song tells of a soldier dreaming of his girl back home. It was nominated for the 1943 Best Original Song Oscar but lost to Irving Berlin's "White Christmas."

Isle Royale National Park has 165 miles of scenic hiking trails.

J

Jeffrey, Mildred McWilliams "Millie" (1910–2004)

Union activist. She moved to **Detroit** in 1944 to become the first director of the **United Auto Workers** Women's Bureau. She organized the first UAW women's conference, ran the union's radio station and community relations department, and directed its consumer affairs department. She was a Presidential Medal of Honor recipient and **Michigan Woman's Hall of Fame** inductee.

Jeter, Derek (1974–)

Baseball player. As a teenager in **Kalamazoo**, Jeter was named National High School Player of the Year. Pursued by the **University of Michigan**, he decided to sign with the New York Yankees. In the Yankees' farm system, Jeter became Minor League Player of the Year. Alternating between AAA Columbus and the Yankees in 1995, he was called up to become the Yankees' starting shortstop in 1996. In 2000, Jeter was named All Star game MVP. Later that year, he was voted World Series Most Valuable Player, the first player in major league history to capture both awards in the same year.

Millie Jeffrey, the first director of the United Auto Workers Women's Bureau.

Johnson, Arte (1929–)

Actor. Already well-known as an actor and comedian in the 1950s, Johnson burst onto the popular scene in 1968 as a regular cast member of *Rowan and Martin's Laugh-In*. Johnson, a Benton Harbor native, often guest stars on TV shows. He is also noted for voice work.

Johnson, Earvin "Magic" (1959–)

Basketball legend. The East Lansing native led **Michigan State University** to an NCAA title over Indiana State University and ignited a rivalry with ISU's Larry Bird that continued throughout the two players' careers with the Los Angeles Lakers (Johnson) and Boston Celtics (Bird). In his rookie year with the Lakers, he led the team to the first of his five NBA championship titles. Playing all five positions, he scored 42 points and was named Finals MVP, an honor he received two more times. A 12-time NBA All-Star, he was on the All-NBA first team nine times. Following his 1991 retirement, he returned for the 1992 NBA All-Star Game and again for the 1995–96 season. He spent one season as head coach of the Lakers but quit after a disappointing season. He was co-captain of the gold-medalist U.S. Olympic Dream Team in 1992.

Through his Johnson Development Corporation, he establishes entertainment

Earvin "Magic" Johnson,
basketball legend and founder of
the Magic Johnson Foundation.

venues and businesses that employ local minority contractors and vendors in under-served areas. *Fortune* magazine has named him one of its 50 Most Powerful Black Executives in America.

In 1991, he founded the Magic Johnson Foundation to fundraise for community-based HIV/AIDS education and prevention programs. The foundation, which he chairs, has since broadened its scope to address other critical issues of inner-city youth. He chairs the annual Muscular Dystrophy Association Magic Johnson Sports Star Award Dinner and Auction and has numerous other philanthropic inter-ests, including the Make a Wish Foundation and the United Negro College Fund.

Jolliet, Louis (1645–1700)

Explorer, trader. Born in Quebec, New France (Canada), he studied as a Jesuit but left the clergy to become a fur trader. He was sent by the French to explore the Mississippi River and, with Father **Jacques Marquette**, discovered the river's mouth on June 17, 1673. After the expe-dition, Jolliet returned to trading.

Jones, James Earl (1931–)

Actor. Long noted for his impressive voice, Jones began his career in the theater, where he won the Tony award for *The Great White Hope*. His movie roles include a reprise of his character in *The Great White Hope*, for which he received an Academy Award nomination. He also starred in *Field of Dreams*, *The Hunt for Red October*, *Patriot Games*, and *Clear and Present Danger*. His voice work in films includes the voices of Mufasa in *The Lion King* and Darth Vader in the *Star Wars* movies. He is also the voice of the Cable News Network (CNN). Jones grew up in Dublin, Michigan.

Jones, Sarah Van Hoosen (1892–1972)

Animal geneticist, farmer. She was a Michigan Premier Breeder and among the first American women awarded Master Farmer status. She was the first woman to earn a doctorate in genetics from the University of Wisconsin. She served on the State Board of Agriculture, the governing board of **Michigan State University**.

J.T. Wing

Under various names, the ship carried mahogany from West Africa to Canada, ran rum during the Depression, and ferried logs across lakes Huron and Michigan. The last commercial sailing ship on the **Great Lakes**, it was on exhibit at the **Dossin Great Lakes Museum** until it was condemned in 1956 and destroyed two years later.

Comedian Lily Tomlin and singer Diana Ross both went to Cass Technical High School, designed by Albert Kahn.

Kahn, Albert (1869–1942)

Industrial architect. He became the darling of early automakers after designing a plant for the Packard Motor Co. using reinforced-concrete, an innovative technique for an industry that crammed its workers into dirty, dangerous, timber-framed plants. By designing buildings to accommodate workers' functions and materials, he increased the efficiency of the plants. During World War I, he designed the majority of U.S. army airfields. During **World War II**, he quickly converted auto plants for war production. He was lauded for his inventive designs of homes, hospitals, theaters, office buildings, and hotels. His designs include Detroit's **Fisher Building** and the Clements Library of the **University of Michigan**.

Kalamazoo

Everyone agrees the city's peculiar name was derived from an Indian word. But English-speaking settlers so distorted the pronunciation, no one today knows exactly what the word meant. The most popular translations, variations of "boiling water," derive from the legend that, to win his girl, a Potawatomi named Fleet Foot ran from the settlement to the nearby river and back before water in a heating pot boiled away.

The city originally was named by and for its first settler, **Titus Bronson**, who arrived in 1827, two years after the area was deeded to the United States by the Potawatomi. To the annoyance of the other settlers, the eccentric Bronson railed against the vices of card

Bird's eye view of Kalamazoo, 1874

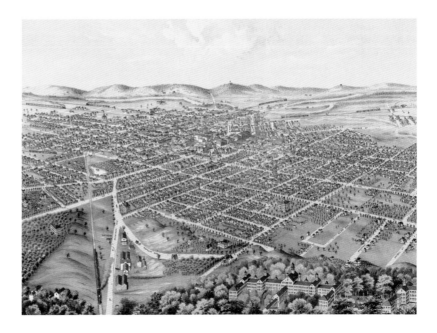

playing, dancing, and drinking. The settlers got the last laugh: Bronson was convicted of stealing a cherry tree, and they petitioned for a name change. By the time Michigan was admitted to the union, the town was called Kalamazoo. Today the city is the seat of Kalamazoo County.

Kalamazoo's railroad links to **Detroit** and Chicago made it an attractive place for industry and won it a variety of nicknames: Mall City, after the nation's first outside pedestrian mall was constructed there; Bedding Plant Capital of the World, because it's home to the world's largest bedding plant cooperative; and Paper City, for its paper and cardboard mills.

Kalamazoo also was known as Celery City, because its fertile soil was the birthplace of celery cultivation in America. A Scottish immigrant, James Taylor, was the first to farm celery, which he raised from seeds he imported from England. But the vegetable's resemblance to the poisonous hemlock plant wasn't much of a recommendation. Another celery farmer, Marinus De Bruin, sent his children door to door to sell his produce. The trick worked. By the late 1800s, Dutch immigrants were draining swamps and turning them into farmland.

The Upjohn Pill and Granule Company was founded in Kalamazoo in 1885 by **William E. Upjohn**, a physician who had invented a pill-making machine and dissolvable pills. Upjohn became the Fortune 500 company Pharmacia Corporation, which eventually was purchased by Pfizer, resulting in the world's largest pharmaceuticals company.

The city produces much of the nation's supply of peppermint oil and **checker** cabs were manufactured here. Frank Lloyd Wright built a number of his Usonian homes in and around Kalamazoo.

One of the bleakest moments in Kalamazoo history was May 13, 1980, when a tornado raced through the downtown and surrounding areas. In less than a half hour, five persons were dead and 79 were injured. The twister caused more than $50 million of

Al Kaline, right, with fellow Detroit Tiger Denny McClain

damage and prompted then Governor William Milliken to compare the area to "a bombed-out city."

Kalamazoo Bach Festival

Among the oldest arts organization in **Kalamazoo**, since 1947 the festival has presented Christmas and spring concerts of J.S. Bach and his contemporaries. Other offerings include Bach-to-School education programs, BachStage master classes, and the Young Vocalists Competition.

Kalamazoo Mall

The Jimmy Dorsey Orchestra was on hand August 19, 1959, to celebrate the nation's first pedestrian shopping mall. Facing urban decay, **Kalamazoo** hoped to bring back downtown business. It worked—for nearly 40 years. When the mall was demolished, a citywide raffle determined who would drive the first car through the area.

Kaline, Al (1934–)

Hall of Fame outfielder for the **Detroit Tigers**. During his 22-season playing career with the Detroit Tigers baseball club, Al Kaline was a model of consistency with a minimum of fanfare. "Mr. Tiger" was the recipient of 10 Golden Glove titles and 15 All-Star team selections. During the 1968 World Series he batted .379, with two home runs among his 11 hits. Despite nagging injuries Kaline retired with a .297 lifetime batting average, 3,007 hits, and 399 home runs. He was inducted into the Hall of Fame in 1980, during his first year of eligibility. At the time of his retirement, he was one of only two Tigers to play 20 or more seasons in **Detroit**. The other was **Ty Cobb**.

Kasem, Casey (1932–)

Radio personality. Kasem (who grew up in **Detroit**) originally aspired to be a sports star, but his stint as a high school sports announcer was the beginning of a long career in radio. He became one of the busiest voices in

commercials and cartoons and his weekly countdown show, *American Top 40*, is the exemplar against which similar shows are measured. He is noted for "trivia teasers" and long-distance dedications.

Kasem was the youngest member ever inducted into the Radio Hall of Fame. In 1997, *Billboard Magazine* presented him with its inaugural Lifetime Achievement Award. He is also widely known for his participation in charitable causes and philanthropies.

Kellogg, John Harvey (1852–1943)

Surgeon, hygienist, food manufacturer. Interested in nutrition and health from an early age, he has been credited with developing a menthol nasal inhaler and an electric blanket. While medical superintendent of the **Battle Creek Sanitarium**, he began to experiment with nutritious food supplements. He assisted his brother Will, in perfecting a method of producing a cereal flake that could take the place of hot cereals for the patients. Their success led to the creation of the Battle Creek Toasted Corn Flake Company in 1906.

John Harvey Kellogg, along with his brother Will, helped to create the W.K. Kellogg breakfast cereal company.

Kellogg, Will Keith "W. K." (1860–1951)

Businessman, philanthropist. W. K. Kellogg was born in **Battle Creek**, where he worked as a businessman. In 1894, he and his brother John created a breakfast cereal made by rolling out cooked wheat mush into flakes, which were then baked for added crunch. Corn and other grains were later used. In 1906, Kellogg established the Battle Creek Toasted Corn Flake Company, which became the W. K. Kellogg Company.

In 1930, he established the W. K. Kellogg Foundation, one of the country's wealthiest philanthropic institutions, to advance the health and well-being of children.

Kettering, Charles F. (1876–1958)

Inventor, engineer. His inventions include the automobile self-starter that made him famous

Charles F. Kettering, inventor of the automobile self-starter.

and an incubator for premature infants. As president of General Motors Research Corporation, he worked on shock absorbers, safety glass, and coolants. With **Alfred P. Sloan**, he endowed the Sloan-Kettering Institute for Cancer Research.

Kettering University

Founded in 1919 as the School of Automotive Trades, it later became a training ground for General Motors engineers. Although the **Flint**-based school became independent of GM in 1982, it retains its close ties. On January 1, 1998, it was renamed to honor **Charles F. Kettering**, an automotive innovator and a force behind the school's establishment.

Kevorkian, Jack (1928–)

Physician. Kevorkian was a pioneer in physician-assisted suicide. In 1990, he was present at the first suicide; he helped more than 130 people kill themselves. His license to practice medicine in Michigan was revoked in 1991. He was charged with doctor-assisted suicide four times. Three trials ended in acquittals, the fourth in a mistrial.

In 1998 Kevorkian himself administered a lethal injection to a patient and videotaped the event. CBS broadcast the tape on *60 Minutes*. The state of Michigan prosecuted Kevorkian and he was convicted of second-degree murder. He was sentenced to 10 to 25 years.

King, Carolyn (n.d.)

At 12, she became the first girl to play Little League baseball when she took the field for the Ypsilanti Orioles baseball team on May 8, 1973. In response to a sex discrimination suit filed by the city of Ypsilanti, the U.S. Division of **Civil Rights** ordered the Little League to drop its boys-only policy.

King, Charles Brady (1868–1957)

Automotive pioneer. He was the first to drive a gasoline-powered car down a Michigan street. On March 6, 1896, he drove down **Detroit**'s Woodward Avenue in an auto of his own design. **Henry Ford**, driving a quadricycle he built with King's advice, was behind King by three months.

Kirby, Frank E. (1849–1929)

Naval architect. He designed the largest, most expensive of the sidewheelers that carried passengers across the **Great Lakes** as extensions of the railroad lines. Among his most famous floating palaces were the *Greater Buffalo* and the *Greater Detroit*, built for the **Detroit** and Cleveland Navigation Company.

Frank Kirby, who designed the largest passenger ships to cross the Great Lakes.

K

Kiwanis

Founded in **Detroit** and chartered by the state of Michigan in 1915, Kiwanis was established to promote business among its members. By 1919, the mission of the organization had become service to the community.

In 1916, the first Kiwanis club outside the United States was formed in Hamilton, Ontario. Kiwanis now reaches across the globe and more than 600,000 Kiwanis-family members in 91 countries are "Serving the Children of the World." A major priority is eliminating iodine deficiency disorders, the world's leading preventable cause of mental retardation. Originally a men's group, Kiwanis opened its doors to women in 1987.

William Knudsen was head of production at Ford and General Motors.

Knudsen, William (1879–1948)

Industrialist. He managed production at both Ford and General Motors, where he also served as president and was considered a production genius. During **World War II**, he directed national industrial production for the National Defense Commission and the War Department.

Kresge Foundation

S.S. Kresge celebrated the 25th anniversary of his discount store chain by giving away $1.3 million. He created the Kresge Foundation with instructions "to promote the well-being of mankind." Over his lifetime, he added more than $60 million to the fund.

The foundation supports a number of initiatives, including strategic investment in **Detroit** and Southeastern Michigan.

Kresge Company, S.S.

Sebastian Spering Kresge (1867–1966), a former traveling salesman, pooled his money with John McCrory in 1897 to open a store in Memphis that would offer everything a person could want, under one roof, for five or 10 cents. The concept was so successful, the partners opened a second store in **Detroit** in 1898. The following year, Kresge and McCrory parted

The Kresge Building, Detroit. Designed by Albert Kahn in 1914, it served as world headquarters to the Kresge Company until 1930.

ways. Kresge took the Detroit store. By 1912, he had 85 stores, and in 1916 he had 150.

S.S. Kresge opened its first Kmart store in Garden City in 1962 and officially changed the company name to the Kmart Corporation in 1977.

Ladewig, Marion (1914–)

Bowler. Voted Michigan's Woman Athlete of All Time, she was named Woman Bowler of the Year nine times, won the World International five times, and won the first women's professional tournament. She was the first Superior Performance inductee into the Women's International Bowling Congress Hall of Fame.

Lansing

Michigan's capital is the center point of three interdependent counties—Clinton, Eaton, and Ingham—with an overall population of about 450,000. Lansing is in Ingham County. The city was named for John Lansing, a late-18th century mayor of Albany, New York, and a delegate to the U.S. Constitutional Convention, by Joseph H. North, a New Yorker who settled in the city in 1841. The region is known for its economic stability, educated work force, and low cost of living; factors that contributed to five-star recognition of Lansing's excellent quality of life in a survey by a national monthly magazine for executives of companies on the move. Lansing's economy stands on three legs: state government, **Michigan State University**, and General Motors.

Lansing wasn't Michigan's first choice as capital city. That distinction goes to **Detroit**, though it was never intended to be permanent; the 1837 constitution required that state legislators choose another site within 10 years. Lansing, halfway across the state, was a more centralized location. And because it was slightly north of heavily settled areas, it was seen as a gateway to growth in the northern part of the state. In 1847 the legislature voted to move the capital to what at the time amounted to little more than a log house and a sawmill—Lansing would not incorporate as a city until 1859. Work on the **State Capitol** began in 1873. At its dedication on January 1, 1879, the "Capital in the Wilderness" had a $1.4 million, technologically cutting-edge capitol complete with a steam-powered elevator and electric light switches.

Yet another piece of legislation, also passed before Lansing was granted its charter, helped shape the city's future. Act 130 of 1855 appropriated $40,000 for the establishment of an

David Barr's sculpture Polaris Ring *graces the front grounds of the Michigan Historical Center complex in Lansing.*

Constitution Hall has the contemporary look of many of Lansing's office buildings.

Bird's eye view of Lansing, 1866

L

institution of high learning specifically for the study of scientific agriculture. The Agricultural College of the State of Michigan, now Michigan State University, was the first college in the world to offer agriculture courses for credit and served as the prototype for more than 70 land-grant schools established under the Morrill Act of 1862.

Ransom E. Olds launched the automobile industry in Lansing in the 1890s. **Henry Ford** had created a horseless carriage, but it was Olds who took it to the people. In his father's Lansing machine shop, he developed first a steam-powered engine, then one that ran on gas, both with the objective of creating a light-weight auto inexpensive enough that anyone could afford. He built the first automobile plant in **Detroit**. After a fire in 1901 slowed produc-tion, the company built an additional factory in Lansing and, in 1905, moved all operations there. Oldsmobiles continued to be manufac-tured in Lansing until the brand ceased production in April 2004.

The **R.E. Olds Transportation Museum** tells the history of auto manufacturing in Lansing. Other attractions in Lansing include the hands-on Impression 5 Science Center, **Lansing City Market**, and the Art Deco Michigan National Bank Tower. The **Lansing Lugnuts**, a minor league baseball team, play at Oldsmobile Park.

Lansing City Market

The historic market was established in 1909 as a way for local farmers and craftspersons to market their quality goods to the public. The market, still on Cedar Street, is open Tuesday, Thursday, Friday, and Saturday from 8 a.m. to 6 p.m.

Lansing Lugnuts

The Lugnuts are the farm team for the Chicago Cubs. The franchise, which arrived in **Lansing** in 1996, plays at Oldsmobile Park. Its first year in town, the team drew 538,326 people into the park.

Ring Lardner, one of America's finest short story writers.

Lardner, Ring (1885–1933)

Author. Considered to be among American's finest short story writers, the Niles native was one of nine children. From his youth, Lardner aspired to be a sports writer, and after working for two years as a reporter for the South Bend, Indiana, *Times*, he was hired by the *Chicago Examiner* to cover sports. During the next decade, he worked in Chicago and New York, becoming one of the country's best-known sportswriters. His first book, *You Know Me, Al: A Busher's Letters*, was followed a year later by *Gullible's Travels*. His most famous stories include "Haircut," "Some Like Them Cold," "The Golden Honeymoon," and "Alibi Ike."

La Salle, Robert Cavelier (1643–1687)

Explorer. La Salle came to America to explore the new land, settle it, and claim some of it for France. In 1671, he visited **Mackinac Island** with Father **Jacques Marquette**. Later, in 1679, La Salle and Father Henepin sailed to the Straits of Mackinac in the *Griffon*, a ship he built and the first commercial sailing ship on the **Great Lakes**. La Salle sailed from Lake Erie to Lake Michigan and along the Michigan

A sculpture of Robert Cavelier La Salle, second from left, stands cheek-by-jowl with other historical figures of the period, from left, Father Jacques Marquette, Father Gabriel Richard, and Antoine de la Mothe Cadillac.

coast. He erected Fort Miami on the site of the present city of St. Joseph.

Leland, Henry (1843–1937)

This automotive industry giant is best known for his invention of the Cadillac and the Lincoln. Henry Leland originally built engines for the Olds, the first mass-produced car in the world and the first to be produced in **Detroit**. He later invented a car with a smaller, more compact car engine known as the Cadillac. The Cadillac won many awards, including the first American car to win Great Britain's Royal Automobile Club's Dewar Trophy for distinguished automotive achievement. Leland sold Cadillac to General Motors and then moved on to build his second great automobile, the Lincoln. After World War I, his company fell

Henry Leland, who invented the Cadillac and the Lincoln.

L

into disarray and Ford Motor Company became the distributor of the Lincoln.

Leonard, Elmore (1925–)

Author. After service with the Seabees in **World War II**, Leonard graduated from the University of **Detroit** and went to work for the Campbell-Ewald advertising agency. Moonlighting, he wrote western-themed short stories and novels, many of which became movies. Leonard later turned to the crime genre, writing novels and adapting them for the screen. The success of films such as *Get Shorty*, *Jackie Brown*, and *Out of Sight* brought Leonard enormous popularity. His novels routinely appear on best-seller lists as soon as they are released, and Hollywood producers continue to bring his novels to the screen.

LeValley, Orlando (1848–1948)

Civil War veteran. Born in Marathon, he was the last surviving native-born Michigan veteran of the war. He first tried to enlist at age 13 but was rejected and had to wait three years. He was one of the six veterans at the Michigan chapter's last **Grand Army of the Republic** encampment, in 1940.

Orlando LeValley was the last surviving Civil War veteran from Michigan.

Lighthouses

More than 120 lighthouses dot the coast and islands along Michigan's 3,200 miles of shoreline. Michigan has more than any other state. Rendered obsolete by advanced technologies, nearly all are either listed on or eligible for the National Register of Historic Places.

Lighthouses came into use in the United States by an act of Congress on August 7, 1789, that called for the federal government to pay for placement of a lighthouse "at the entrance of, or within any bay, inlet, harbor, or port of the United States, for rendering the navigation thereof easy and safe." Provided that the state gave the federal government the land the lighthouse stood on, the government would continue to pay for maintenance. Two hundred years later, the government is selling off

lighthouses as quickly as it can. In 1998, Michigan's lighthouses, exemplified by **DeTour Reef Light**, made the list of America's 11 Most Endangered Historic Places, an annual spotlight on significant United States spots threatened by poor maintenance or lack of funding. The listing has no teeth but is meant to rally support for the endangered sites.

Nearly a third of Michigan's lighthouses are still owned by the U.S. government. In response to concerns about their disposal, the Michigan Lighthouse Project was established in 1998 to increase public awareness and identify ways to preserve the lighthouses. A year later, the state legislature established the Michigan Lighthouse Assistance Program to fund preservation projects.

Michigan, with more lighthouses
than any other state, also has
legislation to protect them.

Beaver Head Lighthouse,
Beaver Island St. James, Mich.

Beaver Head Lighthouse,
Beaver Island.

L

Lindbergh, Charles A. (1902–1974)

Aviator. **Detroit**-born Charles Lindbergh is best known for his May 1927 nonstop solo flight from New York to Paris in the Spirit of St. Louis. The successful flight to Paris earned him universal acclaim; he was awarded the Congressional Medal of Honor and the Distinguished Flying Cross.

In 1932, he and his wife, Anne Morrow Lindbergh, lost their infant son to kidnapping and murder. Bruno Hauptmann was executed for the crime.

In 1938, Lindbergh accepted military honors from Germany. When he opposed America's entry into **World War II**, he was accused of being a Nazi sympathizer.

Lipinski, Tara (1982–)

Ice skater. Taking up ice skating at the age of six, Tara Lipinski moved rapidly to dominance in the sport. She is the youngest Olympic, World, and U.S. National Ladies Figure Skating Champion in history. She won the World Championship at 14, and at 15 became the youngest individual athlete ever to win a gold medal at the Winter Olympics. In her last two years as an amateur, she was placed first in five of six competitions. Turning pro in April 1998, she became the youngest World Professional Ladies Champion, at 17, in 1999. She trained in Bloomfield Hills.

Little Traverse Bay Regatta

For more than 40 years Petoskey has played host to one of the country's oldest regattas. In late July sailing enthusiasts gather along the downtown lakefronts in Petoskey and Harbor Springs or in Petoskey State Park to watch 100 sailboats race.

Logging

During his early travels on the **Great Lakes**, French explorer **Jean Nicolet** took note of the great forests in what would later become Michigan. But in the 1630s he was interested in how the land could be exploited for the

The annual Little Traverse Bay Regatta is one of the highlights of summer in the Petoskey area.

burgeoning **fur trade** and not those virgin stands. Nearly 200 years later, when the traditional sources of white pine in Maine and New York became unable to meet a growing demand for construction lumber, the nation turned to Michigan. Here lumbermen found not only the state's abundant white pine forests, but also a system of rivers to help transport logs to the sawmills and lake shipping ports.

In the early years of the logging boom, weather played a major role in when trees were cut and how they were moved to the sawmills. Cutting was done during the winter when timber could be placed on sleds and dragged along icy paths. Then the spring river drive hinged on a good winter snowfall that would melt and carry the logs to the mills. American folklore is filled with logging camp legends of the strapping lumberjacks in red flannel shirts who felled the trees in the winter

Excursion logging train—Harbor Springs, Michigan, 1906

months and then drove the huge pine logs to the sawmills via churning spring-fed rivers.

Two Michigan-bred innovations in the 1870s would free lumbermen from their dependence on the weather. Silas Overpack of Manistee invented the "big wheels," in which logs were chained under the axle of an enormous set of wheels drawn by a team of horses. Then, in Clare County, **Winfield Scott Gerrish** showed how temporary narrow-gauge railroads could also supplement the use of logging sleds. These innovations helped Michigan lumber production increase dramatically during the middle decades of the 19th century.

The Saginaw Valley was the leading lumbering area between 1840 and 1860, when the number of mills in the state doubled. While early mills were water-powered, steam saws began to replace them. In 1834 Harvey Williams installed the valley's first steam-powered mill, using the engine that had once powered *Walk-in-the-Water*, the first steamboat to ply the upper Great Lakes. Muskegon, at the mouth of one of the state's longest rivers, became the leading lumber center on the western side of the state but never surpassed Saginaw's output. The lumber would be shipped east through the **Erie Canal** and southwest to Chicago and an exploding Midwest market.

By 1869, Michigan was producing more lumber than any other state, a distinction it would hold for 30 years. The year of greatest production was in 1889, when Michigan forests

Michigan's plentiful virgin forests attracted lumbermen who decimated them.

yielded 5.5 billion board feet of lumber. By the end of the century the great forests in the Lower Peninsula were nearly gone, and Michigan had slipped to second place in lumber production. The logging bonanza would feed other industries in the state, most notably **carriage** making, paper, and **furniture**.

The **Harwick Pines Logging Museum** in Grayling is a must-see for visitors interested in learning more about Michigan's logging heritage. The museum features representations of an early logging camp and sawmill. In Manistee, one of the sites of the industry boom, relics of the logging era may be seen in the ornate Victorian mansions of the lumber barons and in the town's refurbished commercial buildings.

Louis, Joe (1914–1981)

Boxer. The legendary heavyweight champion fought 71 bouts and won 68 of them, 54 by knockout. He held the world title from 1937 to 1948, with 25 successful defenses of his title. He won the title in 1937, becoming the first African American to earn it since Jack Johnson in 1908. Louis, who grew up in **Detroit**, served in the United States Army during **World War II**. He continued to box until 1951; when he was defeated by Rocky Marciano, he retired at the age of 37. He was inducted into the International Boxing Hall of Fame in 1990.

Lousma, Colonel Jack (1936–)

Astronaut, businessman. He piloted the Skylab 3 mission, from July 28 to September 25, 1973, and spent 11 hours on two space walks. After logging more than 1,600 hours in space, he retired from NASA and returned to his hometown, **Ann Arbor**, where he is chairman and vice president of marketing and sales for AeroSport Incorporated.

Love, Nancy Harkness (1914–1976)

Aviator. During **World War II**, Love was director of the **Women's Airforce Service Pilots** (WASP) aircraft ferrying operations. WASP squadrons flew 77 different types of military planes, piloting 12,650 aircraft between factories, modification facilities, and operational units. The first woman to fly the B-25, Love received the Air Medal after the war. Love was born in Houghton.

A group of boys are awestruck at meeting Joe Louis.

M

The main cables that hold the Mackinac Bridge, 24 inches in diameter, are made up of 12,580 wires each. It took 42,000 miles of wire to complete the bridge.

Mackinac Bridge

The 1957 completion of the suspension bridge made an easy connection between the Upper and Lower peninsulas and ended the lines, as long as 23 miles, that waited for ferry crossings over the Straits of Mackinac.

Each Labor Day morning, two lanes on the five-mile-long Mighty Mac close for the Mackinac Bridge Walk from **St. Ignace** to Mackinaw City.

Mackinac Island

Mackinac Island became one of the nation's favored summer resorts during the Victorian era. Boat and railroad companies financed the building of the **Grand Hotel**, which became the principal meeting place for all of Mackinac Island. Then, as now, tourists played tennis, hiked, rode bicycles, and examined the natural wonders.

Transportation on the island is limited to horse and buggy, bicycle, and foot. State Rt. 185, which rims the island, is touted as the only state highway in the nation on which there has never been a motor vehicle accident.

A ferry service runs from the mainland between May and November. During the winter, even for residents, the only way off the island is by plane.

Madonna (1958–)

Singer. Born Madonna Louise Ciccone in Bay City, she stood out in dance and drama,

excelling in both in high school and at the **University of Michigan** in **Ann Arbor**, where she attended college. In 1977, she moved to New York, studied with choreographer Alvin Ailey, and modeled.

In her first band, the Breakfast Club, she played drums and sang. In 1980 she formed the group Emmy, which led to a recording contract with Sire Records. Her first single, "Everybody," in 1982, became a hit in clubs, and her career took off. With her innovative style and sharp business sense, Madonna has continued to be successful.

Malcolm X (1925–1965)

Malcolm X was born Malcolm Little in Omaha, Nebraska. His father, a Baptist minister, moved the family to **Lansing** in 1929. Two years later, Malcolm's father, an outspoken follower of black nationalist Marcus Garvey, was found dead; the family suspected he'd been murdered for his views, but the police called the death an accident. Soon after, Malcolm's mother was committed to a mental institution.

Mackinac Island has lovely warm summer days, with cool evenings. Winters are for cold-lovers only: the Straits of Mackinac and Lake Huron both freeze.

Madonna has appeared in several movies, including Evita, Desperately Seeking Susan, A League of Their Own, *and* Dick Tracy.

Malcolm X, the civil-rights activist, was assassinated in 1965.

M

Malcolm left school after the eighth grade, moved to New York, quickly got into trouble, and was sentenced to a 10-year jail term on burglary charges. In 1946, while in prison, he began to follow the teachings of Black Muslim leader Elijah Muhammad, whose philosophy

Mann House, Michigan. This well preserved Victorian house is open to the public.

held that blacks must separate themselves from the "devil race" of whites. Malcolm dropped his "slave name" and took the Muslim surname "X." After his release from prison in 1962, Malcolm became a Muslim minister.

The charismatic Malcolm advocated separatism and the use of violence for self-protection, the opposite of what Rev. Martin Luther King and other mainstream **civil rights** leaders stated. While his eloquence won him a large and dedicated following, he was rejected as a fanatic by many leaders, both black and white. After an inflammatory statement about President John F. Kennedy in 1963, Malcolm was suspended from the Black Muslim movement. He formed his own organizations, the Organization of Afro-American Unity and the Muslim Mosques Incorporated.

During a pilgrimage to Mecca in 1964, he was impressed with the way races joined forces in the name of Islam and modified his views to accept the possibility of world brotherhood.

Memorial to Father Jacques Marquette. He died before he could return from exploring the Mississippi River.

Hostilities continued to grow between Black Muslims and Malcolm's followers. On February 21, 1965, Malcolm was shot and killed at a rally of his followers.

Mann House

A late-Victorian period piece, the house provides a window into Michigan life of the late 19th and early 20th centuries. The eight-room house includes furniture dating back to the 1840s. Outside are restored herb and flower gardens and a carriage house complete with carriages and sleighs. The house, at 205 Hanover Street, Concord, is open daily, 10 a.m. to 4 p.m., June 1 through Labor Day.

Marquette, Father Jacques (1637–1675)

Missionary, explorer. He founded the first permanent settlement in Michigan, at Sault Ste.

Marie, in 1668. Three years later, he established a mission at **St. Ignace**. With **Louis Jolliet**, he explored and mapped the Mississippi River. He is considered one of the great explorers of North America. The Father Marquette National Memorial and Museum tells his story. The museum, at Straits State Park in St. Ignace, is open daily, Memorial Day through Labor Day, 9:30 a.m. to 5 p.m., with evening hours mid-June through mid-August.

Marshall Historic District

The district comprises a unique collection of 19th- and early 20th-century architectural styles that has won it status as a National Historic Landmark District. Greek Revival and Art Deco homes stand cheek-by-jowl with Gothic Revivals, Beaux-Arts Classicals, and Italian Villas. The Honolulu House—Italianate, Gothic Revival, and Polynesian all wrapped into one—has been home to the Marshall Historical Society since 1962 and is on the National Register of Historic Places.

The area also boasts museums, including the **American Museum of Magic** and the two-room **Capitol Hill School**.

Martin, Homer (n.d.)

Minister, union activist. After serving in Baptist churches, he went to work in an auto plant and became active in the union movement. In 1936, he was elected first president of the **United Auto Workers**. He helped negotiate the union's contract with Chrysler Corporation.

Mason, Stevens T. (1811–1843)

Governor. He was born in Virginia to a politically powerful family that included state and federal legislators, a Virginia Supreme Court chief justice, and a participant in the U.S. Constitutional Convention. The Masons moved to Michigan when his father, through family connections, was appointed territorial secretary in 1830. After his father was sent on a mission to Mexico, 19-year-old Mason, still too young to

vote, took over the appointment. When Territorial Governor **Lewis Cass** left office to become President Andrew Jackson's secretary of war, Cass was replaced by George B. Porter, who spent so much time away that Mason essentially became the territory's acting governor.

The 22-year-old Mason, nicknamed the Boy Governor, was a driving force in petitioning for Michigan statehood. After an 1832 petition was ignored, he commissioned a census of the territory that determined a population of 86,000, far more than the 60,000 required for statehood by the **Northwest Ordinance**.

Michigan's dispute with Ohio over the Toledo Strip blocked its statehood and led to the **Toledo War**. Mason, adamant about keeping the area, took a force into Ohio to rattle some swords and, returning to Michigan, found himself out of a job—Jackson had fired him. In 1835 voters approved a constitution and voted him back into office. Once the Toledo dispute was resolved, Michigan entered the union and Mason became the state's first governor.

Stripped of his governorship by President Andrew Jackson, Stevens Mason was re-elected by the people of Michigan.

Stevens Mason signed legislation to create the University of Michigan and to move the state capital to Lansing.

His accomplishments as governor included creating an educational system and relocating the **University of Michigan** from **Detroit** to **Ann Arbor**.

McCoy, Elijah (1844–1929)

Inventor. He was born in Canada, the son of former slaves who escaped before the **Civil War**. He grew up in Ypsilanti and was educated as an engineer in Scotland before returning to settle in **Detroit**. He patented 57 inventions, including an ironing board and sprinkler, but is best known for his first invention, an automatic lubricator for steam engines. The device, which allowed machines to be lubricated as they were still in motion, revolutionized the industrial machinery industry. Imitation lubricators were hard to sell; everyone wanted "the real McCoy," and his name became synonymous with the genuine article.

Elijah McCoy, whose unique invention gave way to the popular phrase "the real McCoy."

McDivitt, James (1929–)

Astronaut. The 1959 **University of Michigan** graduate was commander of *Gemini 4*, his first space flight, in 1965. Four years later, he commanded *Apollo 9*, which tested the Apollo lunar module. He left NASA in 1972.

McMahon, Ed (1923–)

Entertainer. For 30 years, McMahon was Johnny Carson's sidekick on *The Tonight Show*. His association with Carson began in the 1950s, when he was the announcer for Carson's TV game show *Who Do You Trust?* McMahon, a native of **Detroit**, hosted *Star Search* and *Next Big Star* and was spokesman for the American Family Publishers sweepstakes.

McMillan, Terry (1951–)

Author. After graduating from the University of California at Berkeley, the Port Huron native moved to New York, where she earned a master's degree in film from Columbia University.

McMillan's first book, *Mama*, was published in 1987. Her second, *Disappearing Acts*, was published in 1989, and her third book,

Waiting to Exhale, was a runaway success, selling nearly four million copies. The book was made into a blockbuster movie. Her next novel, *How Stella Got Her Groove Back*, an immediate best-seller, also was adapted for the screen.

McMillan also was the editor of *Breaking Ice: An Anthology of Contemporary African-American Fiction*.

Meadow Brook Hall

The 110-room Tudor-revival castle was the home of Alfred G. and Matilda Dodge Wilson, founders of Oakland University in Rochester. In the mid-1920s, it cost $4 million to build. Tours of the house are conducted Monday through Friday at 1:30 p.m. and several times on Saturday and Sunday.

Meijer Gardens and Sculpture Park, Frederik

The 125-acre attraction contains gardens, nature trails, and a five-story conservatory. More than 30 bronze sculptures are featured, most notably a 24-foot-tall Leonardo da Vinci-inspired horse by Nina Akamu. The gardens and park, on East Beltline N.E. in **Grand Rapids**, are open daily except Christmas and New Year's Day. Hours vary.

Mesta, Perle (1889–1975)

Socialite, diplomat. Accompanying her husband on extensive European travels, Mesta developed relationships with many business and political leaders. After her husband's death, she switched her allegiance from the **Republican Party** to the Democratic Party and became an active lobbyist on behalf of the Equal Rights Amendment. During 1948, she served on the finance committee of the Democratic Party. Upon Truman's re-election, she was appointed U.S. Minister to Luxembourg, the first to hold this diplomatic post. She was noted for her skills as a hostess and was the model for Irving Berlin's long-running musical *Call Me Madam*.

Michigan Freedom Trail. Sojourner Truth, depicted here with President Abraham Lincoln, told her own story of emancipation in her book The Narrative of Sojourner Truth.

Michigan Female School

Established in **Lansing** in 1855, it was a preparatory school for the **University of Michigan**. For 15 years, the best families in Lansing, Jackson, and **Detroit** sent their daughters to the school, run by Abigail and Delia Rogers. The building later became the Michigan School for the Blind.

Michigan Freedom Trail

Battle Creek was a major stop on the **Underground Railroad** from 1840 to about 1855. Between 1,000 and 1,500 fugitive slaves went through Battle Creek on their way to Canada. Battle Creek was a stop on the Michigan Central Line. The Michigan Freedom Trail preserves, promotes, and protects this legacy.

M

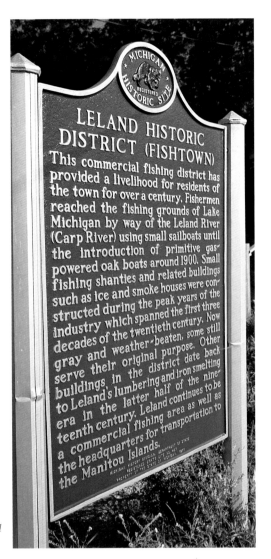

Michigan has the largest historical markers program in the country.

Michigan Historical Markers Program

Established by the Michigan Legislature in 1955, the program has five purposes: to locate Michigan historical sites and subjects, educate the public about Michigan history, encourage the preservation of historic resources, enhance tourism, and unite the people of Michigan through dissemination of information about their state. It is the largest privately funded historical marker program in the nation, with more than 2,500 sites listed. A dedication ceremony accompanies the placement of each marker, to call attention to the state's preservation efforts. The first of more than 1,500 markers was dedicated at **Michigan State University** in East **Lansing**, October 22, 1955.

Michigan Historical Museum

This flagship of the 10 sites of the Michigan Historical Museum System is located in the Michigan Historical Center in **Lansing**. The museum covers Michigan history from prehistoric times through the late 20th century.

Major museum features include a three-story relief map of Michigan, walk-through **Upper Peninsula** copper mine, one-room schoolhouse, 1920s street scene, 1957 **Detroit** auto show, and a diorama complete with a rustic cabin and lighthouse.

The State Archives of Michigan and Library of Michigan also are located in the complex.

The museum is at 717 West Allegan, Lansing. Hours vary.

Michiganian or Michigander?

What do you call a Michigan resident? *Michiganian* first appeared in 1813 in writings of the time. In 1848, Abraham Lincoln is credited with popularizing *Michigander* while making a speech on behalf of Whig presidential candidate Zachary Taylor. Lincoln called Democratic contender **Lewis Cass** "the great Michigander." Because Lincoln's intent was not a complimentary one, and because it has a somewhat silly ring to it, many have opposed its use. Nevertheless, both terms are heard in the state.

Michigan Iron Industry Museum

From 1848 to 1855, the Jackson Iron Company and others manufactured wrought iron from local ore and pioneered the Michigan iron industry that flourished for 125 years. The Michigan Iron Industry Museum, in the ravines of the Marquette Iron Range, overlooks the Carp River and the site of the first iron forge in the Lake Superior region. It features exhibits, audiovisual programs, and outdoor interpretive paths that depict the large-scale capital and human investment that made Michigan an industrial leader. The museum, at 73 Forge Road in Negaunee, is open daily,

9:30 a.m. to 4:30 p.m. from May 1 through October 31.

Michigan Liberty Bell

In 1950, the U.S. Treasury Department gave each state a full-sized replica of the Liberty Bell. Michigan's went into the **Michigan State Capitol**, where children rang it so often, legislators and staff members complained of the noise. The bell now resides at the **Michigan Historical Museum**.

Michigan Maritime Museum

The Michigan Maritime Museum offers collections and hands-on education about **Great Lakes** history and culture. Unique collections include personal possessions of maritime persons of the lakes. The museum, located at 260 Dyckman Avenue, South Haven, is open every day but Tuesday. Hours vary.

Michigan Quarter

The Michigan quarter, released at the beginning of 2004, spotlights the state's unique shape. The quarter depicts the border of Michigan surrounded by the **Great Lakes**, with the text "Great Lakes State."

Michigan Soldier's Relief Association

Located both in **Detroit** and Washington, D.C., it collected supplies to send to **Civil War** soldiers at the front and sent female volunteers to tend to the wounded and dying. **Julia Wheelock**, the Florence Nightingale of Michigan, published a journal of her experiences with the organization.

Michigan State Capitol

It was the first of three state capitols designed by **Elijah E. Myers** after the **Civil War** and one of the first to resemble the U.S. Capitol. Dedicated in 1879, it was Michigan's third seat of state government. When Michigan became a state in 1837, the capitol was the Michigan Territorial Courthouse in **Detroit**, at that time

The Michigan Liberty Bell sits just off the main lobby of the Michigan Historical Museum.

the state capital. A capitol was built in **Lansing** when the state government was moved there 12 years later, but it was quickly outgrown. The current capitol, begun in 1871, was completed at a cost of $1,500,000.

Intended not only to house a growing government but also to be a repository of mementoes of the Civil War, the design inspired a trend toward fireproof buildings. The interior, extensively decorated with architectural painting, was created over a number of years after the building was already in use. The work was done so skillfully that the building, now restored, contains one of the nation's best surviving displays of the Victorian technique. The capitol's chandeliers feature the elk and shield from the state's coat of arms. A grandfather clock in the hallway once was the building's master clock and, after more than 120 years, still works. The rotunda, which rises 267 feet to its finial, has a floor made of 976 variously sized blocks that from the upper floors give the optical illusion that the floor is sinking; it appears to mirror the dome above it. Offices for state senators are in the south

Elijah Myers moved to Michigan to supervise the building of the State Capitol.

An early map of Michigan State University

wing of the building. House offices are in the north wing.

An extensive restoration of the capitol, completed in 1992, returned the building to its original appearance.

Michigan State University

Michigan State is a major public university, containing 14 degree-granting colleges and an affiliated private law school. More than 44,500 students attend classes on the 5,200-acre campus. The university uses an additional 15,000 acres throughout Michigan for agricultural, animal, and forestry research.

Founded in 1855 as the Agricultural College of the State of Michigan, the school was renamed Michigan State University in 1964. It was the nation's first land-grant university and served as the prototype for about 70 land-grant institutions created under the Morrill Act of 1862.

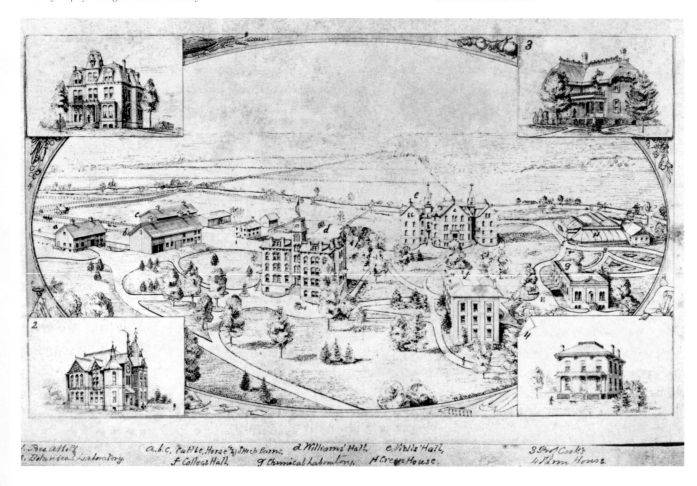

The Morrill Act, named for its proponent, Congressman Justin Morrill of Vermont, offered states a way to establish institutions of higher education that built on the basic education that had always been central to American democratic thought. The legislation granted states 30,000 acres of public land for each senator and congressman—a minimum of 90,000 acres, as each state had two senators and at least one congressman. The lands were to be sold and the proceeds used to establish colleges in such practical professions as **agriculture**, home economics, and technical skills. As the South had already seceded, the bill applied only to the states that remained in the Union; in 1890, a second act extended the provision to the southern states.

Michigan enacted land-grant legislation long before the Morrill Act. State Act 130 of 1855 appropriated about 14,000 acres to establish what is now MSU and provided $40,000 to maintain the college for its first two years.

The money was well spent, with the college quickly emerging as an important agricultural research institution. As early as the 1870s, the college had racked up important research on cross-fertilizing corn. It has continued to make research breakthroughs, including homogenization of milk in the 1930s, an early anticancer drug in the 1960s, and a faster method of detecting salmonella on fruits and vegetables in 2000. MSU shares practical information with the rest of the state through its Extension program.

The campus hosts the National Science Foundation's Center for Microbial Ecology and Food Safety and Toxicology Center and also is home to the top rare isotope research facility in the nation, the National Superconducting Cyclotron Laboratory.

With nearly 200 programs in more than 60 countries, MSU's study-abroad program is the largest of any single-campus university in the county. The university sends students to every continent on the planet.

Notable graduates of MSU include U.S. Secretary of Energy Spencer Abraham and **Earvin "Magic" Johnson**.

Among attractions on the campus are the Wharton Center for the Performing Arts, Kresge Art Museum, and the Abrams Planetarium. MSU's athletic teams, dressed in the school's colors of green and white, are called the Spartans. In the 1979 NCAA Basketball Championship game, the Spartans, led by Johnson, defeated an Indiana State team featuring Larry Bird.

Michigan State is located off State Route 43, three miles east of the state Capitol in **Lansing**.

Michigan Theater

The **Ann Arbor** landmark, built as "a Shrine to Art" in 1928, was a vaudeville and movie palace. By the 1950s, TV had taken much of its audience, and modernization had destroyed its elegance. Restored in 2001, the theater is now home to the Ann Arbor Symphony Orchestra.

Michigan Women's Hall of Fame

The Hall of Fame was established to give visibility to Michigan women who have made contributions as artists, politicians, scientists, community activists, photographers, lawyers, and in other areas. The Hall of Fame incorporates a Women's Historical Center.

Michigan Womyn's Music Festival

Every August for almost 30 years, thousands of women have found their way to a remote site in northern Michigan for five days of camping and concerts under the stars. Performers have included Sweet Honey in the Rock and the Indigo Girls. The festival is a celebration of women's strength and diversity. The event is held on 650 secluded acres. Participants pitch in to build stages, install temporary electrical and plumbing amenities, and cook.

Michinemackinong PowWow

Ojibwa tribe members in traditional dress perform dances and music at this annual early

September gathering in the **Hiawatha** National Forest, just north of **St. Ignace**. **Native Americans** demonstrate beading, woodcarving, and other skills, then sell their handiwork.

Miller, Arthur (1915–)

Playwright. He wrote his first play as a student at the **University of Michigan**. His *Death of a Salesman* won the Pulitzer Prize. *The Crucible*, which won a Tony, used the Salem witch trials as a metaphor for the 1950s congressional investigations into subversion. In 1957, Miller was convicted of contempt of Congress for refusing to name names when called before the House Un-American Activities Committee. His conviction was overturned the following year.

Milles, Carl (1875–1955)

Sculptor. Born in Uppsala, Sweden, he settled in Michigan to teach at **Cranbrook Academy** and became a U.S. citizen. His early work, inspired by Rodin, gave way to more abstract pieces. He was particularly renowned for his fountains. His works include the *Wedding of the Rivers* in St. Louis and statues in the Rockefeller Center, New York.

Milwaukee Clipper

Originally named the *Juniata*, the S.S. *Milwaukee Clipper* was built in 1904 as a first-class passenger and package freight steamer. The ship was built to travel the **Great Lakes**, beginning in Buffalo and sailing to Duluth, Minnesota. The **Detroit** Shipbuilding Company crafted the 3,000-horsepower quadruple-expansion steam engine, which allowed the ship to carry 350 passengers. The ship aided in **World War II** by carrying defense materials from Muskegon to Milwaukee. The queen of the Great Lakes, on the Muskegon waterfront, recently reopened and offers a living museum, banquet facilities, and a bed and breakfast.

Mining

"There! On the riverbank, sir! The great copper boulder before our very eyes… The tales we have heard all these years bore the truth!" Surveyor **Douglass Houghton** (the first State Geologist of Michigan) must have savored the moment. The Jesuit stories were true. There, near the Lake Superior shore, the late 1830s geological expedition had discovered evidence of copper in Michigan's **Upper Peninsula**, a

huge chunk of native copper they called the **Ontonagon Boulder**.

While salt, limestone, gypsum, and even small amounts of coal, silver, and gold have been successfully mined in Michigan, the principal discoveries would be the massive copper and iron reserves of the U.P.

Copper Harbor, Eagle River, and other boomtowns quickly sprang up to accommodate the hordes that rushed north to the Keweenaw Peninsula area to seek their fortunes in Copper Country. Most notably among the **immigrants** were the Finns and Cornish miners from England. At first the copper was found close to

Carl Milles created the Orpheus *fountain at Cranbrook Academy.*

M

the surface, but later mining involved digging deep into the earth. Some of the Keweenaw shafts went down for more than a mile, with spurs running under Lake Superior. By 1860, Michigan was producing 12 million pounds of copper annually. Copper production would continue to grow, from 72 million pounds in 1872 to a peak of 267 million pounds in 1916.

The rich iron ore deposits were discovered in the Upper Peninsula in 1844, when a geological survey team headed by **William A. Burt** noticed erratic fluctuations on a magnetic compass. Not unlike the copper finds, iron ore was initially extracted close to the surface but would later involve shaft mining. The iron ore industry grew in response to an increased demand for iron and steel. Early successful production would even play a role in the Union's victory in the **Civil War**. By World

War I, Michigan was peaking at 18 million tons a year from the Marquette, Menominee, and Geogebic iron ranges. The Stock Market Crash of 1928 hit the mining country hard, with some mines closing, never to reopen. In addition, mining areas farther west had supplanted Michigan's supremacy.

In the early years of the mining boom, the rapids at Sault Ste. Marie served as a natural barrier to the efficient shipping of copper and iron ore. But business interests lobbied the government for a canal with a series of locks. In June 1855 the steamer *Illinois* became the first ship through the **Soo Locks**. In the 20th century specialized ore carriers, basically hugely overgrown canal boats, were developed to transport the minerals to southern iron and steel centers. Each spring the race was on to ship as much ore as possible until the **Great**

The discovery of copper and iron in the Upper Peninsula fueled immigration into the area, but the vast resources were tapped out by the mid-20th century.

Lakes would freeze over and the mines would have to rely solely on rail transport. In one famous incident, the *Edmund Fitzgerald* iron ore carrier sank in a November 1975 storm trying to get one last shipment to Cleveland.

The heritage of the copper and iron mining eras may be seen in many of the original structures and landscapes, in particular in Calumet at the **Calumet Historic District** and in Hancock's **Quincy Mining Company Historic District**. Exhibits at the **Michigan Iron Industry Museum** in Negaunee depict the history of the iron ranges.

Mitten

A "handy" guide to navigation, the Lower Peninsula resembles the outline of a very large mitten. This distinction has lead to interesting geographic names for parts of the state, in particular the Thumb region located northeast of **Flint** and Saginaw.

Monteith, John (1787–1868)

Pastor, educator. With Father **Gabriel Richard** and Judge **Augustus B. Woodward**, he drafted Michigan's first law about public education. He was a founder of the University of Michigania, which became the **University of Michigan**, and served as the first president.

Monument to Joe Louis

It is 24-feet long and packs an 8,000-pound punch. Sculptor Robert Graham named it *Monument to Joe Louis*, but locals call it simply *The Fist*. It is a huge bronze forearm with clenched fist, suspended from steel beams at one of **Detroit**'s most famous intersections.

The Fist was unveiled in 1986 on a boulevard at the corner of Jefferson and Woodward avenues. *Sports Illustrated* picked up the $350,000 tab, as a gift to the city and a tribute to boxing's long-time heavyweight champion of the world. Critics said it looked like the militant black power symbol.

A larger-than-life size statue of Louis' entire body, in boxing pose, sits a few blocks to the west of *The Fist*, in the lobby of **Cobo Hall**, which also houses the Joe Louis Arena.

Moore, Michael (1954–)

Filmmaker, activist. His first movie, *Roger & Me*, was a satirical documentary about the way a slumping General Motors affected his hometown of **Flint**.

He has repeated his offbeat, rabble-rousing style in other films, including *Bowling for Columbine*, about guns in America and around the world today.

MotorCities-Automobile National Heritage Area

Early in the 20th century, a small group of manufacturers started to assemble the horseless carriage and changed the industrial, cultural, and natural heritage of the country by establishing the **auto industry**. Within 20 years Michigan was home to more than 70 automotive-related companies.

In 1998, the Department of Interior authorized a collection of auto-related museums, attractions, activities, and events that exist to preserve, interpret, and promote Michigan's

Sculptor Robert Graham inscribed a tribute to Joe Louis on the arm of Monument to Joe Louis.

rich automotive and labor history as a national heritage area. This area consists of six significant corridors including almost 10 square miles; portions of 13 counties; nearly 250 municipalities and townships; over 1,000 diverse cultural, historic, and national resources; 15 watersheds; and approximately six million residents in southeastern and central Michigan. Included in the area are the motor cities of **Detroit**, Dearborn, **Flint**, **Lansing**, Jackson, Pontiac, and Warren.

The MotorCities-ANHA is nationally significant as the story of the region that invented the 20th century and became the center of the global automobile industry. It is there that the assembly line and mass production were perfected. The American middle class, the modern labor movement, and numerous wage and benefit advancements started there. The economic strength of the nation is connected integrally to the vitality of the automobile industry and this area.

ANHA is headquartered in Detroit at **Stroh**'s River Place. Nine institutions, including the **Michigan Historical Center**, **Alfred P. Sloan Museum**, and **Detroit Historical Museum** serve as gateway museums to the Automotive National Heritage Area.

Motorsports Museum and Hall of Fame

Tucked inside the Expo Center in Novi, the Motorsports Museum and Hall of Fame houses over 40 racing and high-performance vehicles. The Hall of Fame honors the Heroes of Horsepower, the greatest legends of

Nearly half of Michigan's $11 billion tourist industry is generated in the motor cities, where the 20th century was born.

motorsports on land, sea, and air, such as pilot Amelia Earhart and auto racer Don Prudomme.

Motown

Established by **Berry Gordy Jr.** in **Detroit** in 1959, Motown Records was named for the city's principal industry. Motown, short for "Motortown," quickly came to refer to not just a record company but a distinct genre of music. The Motown sound was characterized by its distinctive use of orchestration, carefully arranged harmonies, and gospel-style call-and-response vocals.

Gordy assembled an industrious staff of songwriters, producers, and musicians and created one of the most impressive rosters of artists in the history of pop music. By 1964, Motown was the largest, most successful independent record company in the United States.

During the mid-1960s, Gordy established a music empire, with eight record labels, a management service, and a publishing company that grossed millions of dollars a year. Between 1964 and 1967, Motown had 87 Top 15 pop and rhythm-and-blues singles, including 34 number one hits. In 1966 alone, 75 percent of Motown releases made the charts. Until the advent of hip-hop, Motown was the most consistently chart-topping machine of all time.

Berry Gordy was born into an ambitious middle-class family with roots in Georgia farming and in retailing. He learned to work hard and to take pride in what he did. He dropped out of high school in the 11th grade to become a professional fighter but earned a GED later, while serving in the army. Back in Detroit, he opened the 3-D Record Mart-House of Jazz. Unbending in his love of jazz, he refused to stock the more popular and profitable rhythm and blues, and his store went bankrupt in 1955. Married, with three children to raise, he went to work at Ford's Lincoln/Mercury plant in Detroit, but he quit in 1957 to devote his time to songwriting.

During the 1950s, the Flame Show Bar was the showplace for Detroit's top black talent.

Club owner Al Green invited Gordy to write songs for the artists he managed, including Jackie Wilson. Gordy teamed with his sister Gwen and Wilson's cousin, Billy Davis, to write such successful songs as "To Be Loved," "That's Why I Love You So," and "Lonely Teardrops," which Wilson recorded.

He also began to produce records. Divorced from his first wife, Thelma Coleman, he formed the Rayber Music Company with his second wife and writing partner, Raynoma Liles. His first success was "Reet Petite," recorded by Wilson in late 1957. He used his royalty checks to form Tamla Records and, in 1959, established his own publishing company, Jobete, which became one of the most powerful companies in the industry.

Also during that time, Gordy heard a group called the Matadors sing in a local contest. The Matadors lost the competition but gained a friend in Gordy, who began a lasting relationship with the lead singer, **Smokey Robinson**. The group changed its name to the Miracles and in 1960 recorded "Shop Around" for Gordy's newly formed Motown Records. The song hit big, establishing Motown as an important independent record company.

Over the next four years, capitalizing on the popularity of "girl groups" such as the **Supremes**, Gordy continued to produce hits. He even tried the singing end of the business. "Do You Love Me? (Now That I Can Dance)" by Berry Gordy and the Contours was a hit, the only one the Contours ever had.

Gordy preferred to produce. By the mid-1960s, he had put together a team of coaches to take poor, talented black youths and teach them to talk, walk, and dress as successful debutantes and debonair gentlemen. They were told that by breaking into the white popular music market they became ambassadors for other African American artists seeking broad market acceptance, and that they should think, act, walk, and talk like royalty.

Motown artists were fastidiously groomed, dressed, and choreographed for

Members of two R&B groups, the Primes and the Distants, came together to form the Elgins. Renamed the Temptations by Berry Gordy Jr., they became the most successful group in black music history.

Martha and the Vandellas was fronted by a former Motown secretary.

live performances. Gordy combined his artists' polished images with gospel-based music that appealed to mainstream America. He sought to erase the image of liquor and drugs white America associated with rhythm and blues and replace it with a squeaky-clean look fathers and mothers would approve of. All over America teenagers, both black and white, joined friends in imitating the Supremes and the Four Tops. Everyone knew the Motown walk. They could imitate it.

Copying the methods of the Detroit auto factories where he had worked, Gordy ensured the continued success of his groups by assembling a hit-making machine that included standardized songwriting, an in-house rhythm section, a quality-control process, selective

promotion, and a family atmosphere reminiscent of the paternalism of **Henry Ford**'s early 20th century automobile plants.

Gordy's two major song-writing teams were **Holland-Dozier-Holland**, who wrote many of the Supremes' hits, and Ashford and Simpson, who themselves became a hit duo in the late 1980s. In addition to the Miracles, the Supremes, the Temptations, and the Four Tops, the Motown roster of artists included Martha and the Vandellas, the Isley Brothers, **Stevie Wonder**, the Jackson Five, and Lionel Ritchie. By 1966, the company virtually dominated black popular music and had attracted a significant white audience as well.

Motown's hit-making pace slowed somewhat with the departure of Holland-Dozier-Holland in 1967. At the same time, Gordy fired Florence Ballard of the Supremes and tried to replace her with an unknown artist. He did the same with David Ruffin of the Temptations. Gordy quarreled with Holland-Dozier-Holland about royalty rates and was sued by the trio and various other artists.

In 1971, Gordy moved company headquarters to Los Angeles and established Motown Industries. He began to focus on the Jacksons and on the solo career of **Diana Ross**, who had emerged from the Supremes as a headliner. Many of Gordy's former artists defected to other record companies. After dabbling in motion pictures and television, Gordy sold Motown Records to MCA and Boston Ventures for $61 million in 1988. Boston Ventures later bought out MCA's interest and sold Motown Records to the Dutch-based Polygram Conglomerate in 1993 for $325 million.

Motown's original building, Hitsville USA, is now part of the **Motown Historical Museum**, housed in two adjacent building at 2648 W. Grand Boulevard in Detroit.

Motown Historical Museum

Located in the house **Berry Gordy Jr.** called Hitsville USA, the museum tells the **Motown** story, from the $800 Gordy family savings club

M

The son of a minister, Marvin Gaye combined his spiritual beliefs with social concerns on such hits as "What's Going On" and "Mercy Mercy Me (The Ecology)."

loan that financed the first record to the label's evolution into one of the most influential entertainment ventures in the world. Included are photographs, artifacts, musical instruments, and the original Studio A, where all the hits were made. The museum, at 2648 W. Grand Boulevard, **Detroit**, is open Sunday and Monday, noon to 5 p.m. and Tuesday through Saturday, 10 a.m. to 5 p.m.

Mott, Charles Stewart (1875–1973)

He was born in Newark, New Jersey, where his father owned a successful beverage business that later became Mott's Applesauce. Mott began a bicycle wheel manufacturing company, the Weston-Mott Company, and in 1905 moved to **Flint**, where he joined forces with Buick. He served as mayor of Flint and vice president of General Motors. Deeply committed to his community, Mott helped to rebuild Flint in 1953

after the Beecher Tornado leveled part of the town. In 1954, Mott was awarded the Big Brother award by President Dwight D. Eisenhower.

Mott is best known for his philanthropy and the many educational programs that have been funded by the Charles Stewart Mott Foundation.

Murphy, Frank (1890–1949)

Governor, jurist. As governor of Michigan from 1937 to 1938, he mediated a settlement between the **United Auto Workers** and General Motors. After leaving office, he served as U.S. attorney general from 1939 to 1940. In 1940, he was appointed to the U.S. Supreme Court.

Myers, Elijah E. (n.d.)

Architect. He designed the **Michigan State Capitol**, the first of three capitol designs that clinched his reputation as a designer of public buildings. He was among the first to model state capitols after the U.S. capitol.

Charles Stewart Mott helped to rebuild Flint after it was struck by the Beecher Tornado in 1953.

Former Governor Frank Murphy uses a quill pen to sign a piece of legislation.

N

Nash, Charles (1864–1948)

Charles Nash began his career working on farms in his Illinois hometown. He moved on to automotives in 1890 as a cushion stuffer for **Flint** Road Cart Company, making $1 a day. He took his knowledge and his interest in cars to **Durant-Dort Carriage Company**, where he became the general manager and vice president. In 1910, Nash's leadership and know-how helped him successfully lead Buick and General Motors as president. Later he branched out to form Nash Motor Company. That company merged with Kelvinator to become the Nash-Kelvinator Company, which produced the Nash-designed car in 1914.

Charles Nash, founder of the Nash Motor Company.

National Association for the Advancement of Colored People

The **Detroit** chapter of the National Association for the Advancement of Colored People has been thriving for almost a century. Established in 1912, it has been at the forefront of **civil rights** triumphs in the city.

In the 1940s, the organization helped secure a victory over segregation that had national repercussions. A black man purchased a house in a white Detroit neighborhood. The property's deed

The Detroit offices of the National Association for the Advancement of Colored People.

contained a covenant that restricted sales to Caucasians, and the white neighbors sued to negate the sale. With the backing of the NAACP, the case went to the U.S. Supreme Court. The court ruled that such restrictions violate the 14th Amendment to the Constitution, thus outlawing the practice nationwide.

The organization was also at the forefront of a major lawsuit to end school segregation in the 1970s, and over the years it worked with the United Auto Workers to secure civil rights for blacks who worked in auto plants.

The NAACP also has led the charge to end police brutality. African-Americans complained for years that police stopped their cars simply because they were "driving while black." Allegations of racial profiling, and pressure from the NAACP, led the U.S. Department of Justice in recent years to begin monitoring the police department.

National Baby Food Festival

Fremont, the hometown of **Gerber** baby foods, is the stage in late July for a festival that celebrates… baby food. Folks can enter an adult baby-food eating contest or cook up a dish in the baby-food cook-off. Concerts, carnivals, and a hands-on Kids Zone are also featured.

National Blueberry Festival

It's blue heaven at this annual festival held in South Haven in mid-August. Blueberry pie, chocolate-covered blueberries, blueberry popcorn—you name it, and it'll have blueberries in it. An arts festival, concerts, and sand-sculpting contest on the Lake Michigan shore round out the activities.

Michigan is the world's leading producer of cultivated blueberries.

The Food Network named the National Cherry Festival its number one Top Amazing Celebration of 2003.

National Cherry Festival

Traverse City, the Cherry Capital of the World, celebrates its harvest every year during this early July event. Orchard tours, pie-eating contests, parades, and fireworks fill the days. Folks can eat their fill of the area's bounty at the Taste of Cherries and Grand Cherry Buffet.

National Lilac Festival

Mackinac Island celebrates the nation's oldest living lilacs at this aromatic event every June. Horses pull flower-themed floats in the Grand Lilac Parade. Garden tours, sunset cruises, and dancing also are offered. Island chefs dish up specialties at the Taste of Mackinac.

The National Lilac Festival is on the American Bus Association's list of the most recommended U.S. events for tourists.

National Morel Mushroom Festival

Persons interested in honing their mushroom-hunting skills go to this festival in Boyne City in mid-May. A practice hunt happens on a Friday, with the real deal—heading out to the hunting grounds—on Saturday. Whoever bags the most morels wins a prize. Visitors can sample the tasty morsels at the Taste of Boyne.

National Trout Festival

Kalkaska, the nation's trout capital, celebrates the opening of trout season in late April. Fishing contests, parades, 5K and 10K runs, plus a car show and arts fair are featured.

Native Americans

Michigan's first prehistoric inhabitants advanced into the area soon after melting glaciers created deep gashes in the earth and filled them with water. The **Great Lakes** and other streams and lakes in this part of North America attracted wildlife as well as human life. The earliest dwellers hunted, fished, and farmed in this fertile, densely tree populated environment for centuries.

From around 200 B.C. to A.D. 500, the Hopewell Indians were the primary tribe who occupied this area. Hopewell settlements also existed throughout southern Ohio, Wisconsin, Indiana, Illinois, Iowa, Kansas, Pennsylvania, and New York. The name Hopewell comes from the Hopewell farm in Ross County, Ohio, where the first group of burial grounds was uncovered. Hopewell Indians were called Mound Builders before scientists discovered the mound-building practice was characteristic of other Native American cultures, not just the Hopewell.

The Hopewell placed their communities along the state's rivers and streams. Hopewell villagers planted maize and beans but still depended on hunting, fishing, and berry and nut gathering. **Fur trading** also was a part of the Hopewell culture. Intricate and ornate stonework, pottery, and metalwork left by the Hopewell suggest a sophisticated people with a

An Upper Peninsula Chippewa chief, photographed in 1894

N

Caa-Ton-See, an Ojibwa warrior.

Shin-Ga-Ba-Wossin, Chippewa chief, shown in European clothes

division of labor and maybe even forced labor. Pottery remnants are well-made and show stamped lines. Effigy pipes in the shapes of birds, fish, and other animals were carved from stone and polished. In addition, copper, silver, meteoric iron, mica, and gold were used for jewelry and ornaments.

Artifacts recovered from Hopewell burial mounds include decorations and jewelry made from Michigan copper and North Carolina mica, shells and pearls from the Gulf of Mexico, carved obsidian rock from the Rocky Mountains, and shark teeth from Virginia's Chesapeake Bay. The relics from different areas indicate well-developed trade routes.

While the Hopewell tribes may have been the first Native Americans in Michigan, they were by no means the only tribe. Other tribes found Michigan's valleys, forests, and abundant bodies of water a perfect environment in which to live and hunt. By the time the first European explorers ventured into the area in the 1600s, approximately 100,000 Native Americans, mainly Algonquin, were settled in Michigan.

Three main tribes known as the People of the Fires dominated the area: the Odawa or Ottawa, in the western Lower Peninsula; the Potawatomi in the southern part of the state; and the Ojibwe or Chippewa, who lived in the eastern portion of the Lower Peninsula and most of the **Upper Peninsula**. Three Fires tribe members embraced a family-centered lifestyle. Family clans were given animal names such as Elk, Bear, and Deer.

Fishing, hunting, and trapping were a way of life for the People of the Fires, just as they were for the Hopewell. The Ottawa in particular were great hunters and traders. They netted fish, trapped small game, and hunted large animals such as moose, deer, and caribou. A trademark of the Ottawa culture is the birch bark canoe. Because water was essential to their way of life, water travel became a natural transportation mode. The Ottawa also used birch for baskets, roof tiles, and other useful items. European settlers quickly copied their techniques to make items for themselves.

While those activities occurred all year long, planting and harvesting were seasonal. In the spring, tribes harvested maple sugar, which was used to season their food. A period of **agriculture** followed in the summer times. Their diet was supplemented by the wild nuts, berries, and wild rice they picked. Like the other tribes, the Potawatomi farmed. Less nomadic than the others, these Great Lakes Indians depended on corn, beans, and squash, but were especially known for the herbal gardens they grew for medicine.

The Chippewa name came from a reference to the puckered seam on the moccasins they wore. Chippewa means "to roast till puckered up." The Chippewa shared many of the same characteristics as the Potawatomi and the Ottawa, changing village sites as they pursued fish and game, their primary food source. The Chippewa were adept at using herbs to treat illnesses. Fur trading was also an important part of the Chippewa way of life. According to custom, when a Chippewa died, the body was placed in a sitting position in a grave facing west. The body was covered with enough earth to form a small mound covered with boards, pokes, or birch bark. Unless interrupted by war, the mourning period lasted for a year.

Named by the French, the Huron Indians were part of the Iroquoian group of Native Americans. Huron, which means "boar's head," came from the Old French and referred to how the male Huron heads' appeared. The Huron preferred to be called by the name they gave themselves, Wyandot, which mean "islanders" or "peninsula dwellers." The Huron tribe members were the first to meet French explorer Jacques Cartier. The meeting led to a long and friendly relationship that benefited the Huron and the French.

The Huron tribe divided itself into clans, going by the names of the Rock Clan, Bear Clan, Cord Clan, and Deer Clan. Like the other Native American tribes, the Huron grew corn, beans, and squash. They also built dwellings of bark and placed them near water so they could travel and fish for food.

Huron men excelled at hunting, using bows and arrows to kill deer and moose, but they also used harpoons and tomahawks. After trapping bears, they would feed them and fatten them up so the bears would provide more meat for the tribe members.

Animals were hunted for clothing as well as food. The Huron people wore deerskin shirts, pants, breechcloths, skirts, and moccasins. They wore animal furs to keep warm during the cold winter months. Their flamboyant, decorative clothing reflected their culture. They used mineral and vegetable dyes for their vivid red, black, violet, and green face paints. The Hurons believed in children as the future and went to great lengths to educate them.

Shin-Ga-Ba-Wossin, a Chippewa warrior.

Death celebrations were unique in the Huron culture. Following the death of a tribe member, the Huron held a feast for friends and relatives. After wrapping the body in furs, the surviving tribe members placed the deceased on a litter inside the village. Then they placed the litter in a cemetery and built a small cabin over the body. To help the body on its journey to the spiritual world, they left food and other presents for the departing person.

The Miami people lived in and around Lake Michigan around the time the first Europeans came to the New World. By 1750, many of the Miami Indians lived near Fort Wayne, Lafayette, and Vincennes. Around the 1800s, most of the Miami tribe people had moved to Oklahoma.

Much like the other Native American tribes that inhabited Michigan, the Miami tribes hunted and farmed. Not only did they grow and harvest maize and beans, they cultivated tobacco and melons. At the beginning of each summer, the Miami Indian men went on a five-week buffalo hunt. They kept dogs, not just as pets but for sacrifice.

During the American Revolution, the Miami Indians allied with the English. Even after the American Revolution, they continued to fight the Americans.

A number of subtribes such as the Wea, Menominee, and the Piankashaw inhabited the state in addition to the Chippewa, Ottawa, Potawatomi, Huron, and Miami.

As the European settlers advanced into the state and the rest of the surrounding areas, the Native Americans were pushed farther and farther west. Eventually, the clash of cultures overwhelmed the Native American culture, and the Indian population dwindled.

Nicolet, Jean (*c.* 1598–1642)

Fur trader. He lived among **Native Americans** to learn their customs and languages and served as an interpreter for missionaries. He dreamed of finding the Northwest Passage and carried a silk robe on his travels, to be properly dressed for Chinese dignitaries, but he only got as far as the Mississippi River.

Nineteenth Amendment

On June 10, 1919, Michigan became one of the first three states to ratify the Nineteenth Amendment, which gave American women the vote. Illinois and Wisconsin ratified the amendment the same day.

In 1787, the Constitutional Convention gave states the right to determine voting qualifications, and women lost the right to vote in all states except New Jersey, which revoked woman suffrage in 1804. Beginning in the mid-19th century, American women began to march, lobby, write, and lecture for the right of women to vote. In July 1890, the Territory of Wyoming, which allowed women to vote, was admitted as a state. By 1900, Utah, Colorado, and Idaho joined Wyoming in extending the vote to women, and the right to vote was constitutionally guaranteed in 1920.

Nolde, Lt. Col. William (1929–1973)

Soldier. The Menominee native, shot January 27, 1973, was the last American soldier to die in combat in Vietnam. In his last letter home, he had written, "We tend to think only in terms of what war has cost us, but by comparison, to what it has cost so many people, our price pales."

North American International Auto Show

Car lovers and **auto industry** executives agree, the North American International Auto Show is one of the world's top auto shows. Each January in **Detroit** is the scene for splashy industry unveilings of new models. Concept cars of the future also are displayed, along with vehicles for the new year.

North American Snowmobile Festival

Each year in early February snowmobilers gather in **Cadillac** for the state's largest snowmobile event. Snowmobile races through the forests, fireworks over Lake Cadillac, and a gleaming nighttime Parade of Lights are some of the attractions.

North Manitou Island Lifesaving Station

The lifesaving station has been operated by the National Park Service since 1984 and was made a National Historic Landmark in 1998. North Manitou Island is located in Lake Michigan and in the mid-1800s was an important stopping ground for ships to gather wood, ice, and food.

Many times ships would encounter severe storms, and many perished. The need for a station to aid these victims was enormous. Volunteers began the North Manitou Island Lifesaving Station in 1854. The U.S. Coast Guard acquired the station in 1915 and operated it until 1938. It has served as housing to employees and is currently used as a ranger station.

Northwest Ordinance

Thomas Jefferson proposed in 1784 that the states relinquish their claims to all the territory west of the Appalachians and that the area be divided into new states. His proposal laid the groundwork for the Northwest Ordinance, which was approved by Congress on July 13, 1787. The Northwest Ordinance laid out the rules for governing the Northwest Territory, the area north of the Ohio River and east of the Mississippi. One of the most important acts passed by Congress under the Articles of Confederation, the Northwest Ordinance defined the process for a territory to move to statehood. It also established the precedents by which the United States would expand westward across North America through the admission of new states rather than the expansion of existing states.

The Northwest Ordinance established that governors and judges appointed by Congress would rule a territory until it contained 5,000

free male inhabitants of voting age. The inhabitants could then elect a territorial legislature, which would send a nonvoting delegate to Congress. When the population reached 60,000, the district would be eligible for statehood. Freedom of religion, trial by jury, and public support of education were guaranteed by the ordinance, and slavery was prohibited. New states would be equal to the old; there would be no inferior or superior states in the union. Settlers of the territories would be equal citizens of the United States and would participate in all of the rights that had been fought for in the revolution. The Northwest Ordinance, with minor adjustments, remained the guiding policy for admission of future states into the union.

The legislation was revolutionary in establishing that lands in territories be administered by the central government rather than fall under the jurisdiction of a particular state. The establishment of a territorial government supported the westward expansion of the United States.

The most important purpose of the ordinance was the admission of new states. The actual legal mechanism of admission was established later, in the Enabling Act of 1802. Ohio was the first state admitted under the act, in 1803.

North Manitou Island Lifesaving Station is now a part of Sleeping Bear Dunes National Seashore.

Map of the Northwest Territory (north of the Ohio River and east of the Mississippi).

Many of the concepts and guaranties of the Northwest Ordinance foreshadowed those of the U.S. Constitution and the Bill of Rights. Various legal and property rights were enshrined in the Northwest Territory, religious tolerance was proclaimed, and free and public education was encouraged. The right of *habeas corpus*, freedom of religious worship, and bans on excessive fines and cruel and unusual punishment also were written into the charter.

While some northeastern states, such as New York and New Jersey, still permitted slavery, the ordinance prohibited slavery in the Northwest Territory. That provision had the effect of establishing the Ohio River as the North-South boundary between free and slave territory all the way to the Mississippi river and set the stage for the balancing act between free and slave states that became the most critical political question in American politics in the 19th century.

Norton Mound Group

The Norton Mound Group dates back approximately 2,000 years. Located on the east bank of the Grand River in **Grand Rapids**, the site is the most important and best preserved of the Hopewell mounds in the western **Great Lakes** region. Today the site consists of 17 mounds, with 11 mounds that retain their basic form. The site once consisted of a much more extensive system of well over 30 mounds.

This mound group was the center of Hopewellian culture in the Michigan area from about 400 B.C. to A.D. 400. The first excavation of the mounds took place in 1874 by W .L. Coffinberry under the auspices of the Kent County Scientific Institute, now the Public Museum of Grand Rapids, and revealed numerous burials rich in grave offerings. Excavations in 1963–1964 provided information on mound-builder construction methods.

Hopewell culture probably originated in Illinois and spread to Ohio. From this core, the Hopewell influence extended as far west as Kansas and Missouri, as far south as Louisiana, and as far east as New York.

The Norton Mound Group is listed on the State Register and National Register of Historic Places and is a National Historic Landmark.

The Public Museum of Grand Rapids operates the Norton Indian Mounds National Historic Landmark, a 55-acre Hopewell Indian site. Artifacts from the mounds are on display at the Van Andel Museum Center.

Nugent, Ted (1948–)

Musician. The **Detroit** native rose to prominence as front man for the Amboy Dukes, then went solo. His most successful album was *Cat Scratch Fever*, in 1977. He is an outspoken advocate of gun ownership and sits on the board of the National Rifle Association, among other organizations.

O

Oates, Joyce Carol (1938–)

Writer. Joyce Carol Oates settled in **Detroit** in 1962. A stream of novels and short stories erupted from her Detroit experience, earning her a number of literary awards, including the O. Henry Award and the Pushcart Prize. She is best known for her novels *Them*, *American Appetites*, *The Rise of Life on Earth*, and *We Were the Mulvaneys*.

Oldest State Fair

Michigan held the nation's first state fair, in **Detroit**, September 25–27, 1849. The fair was a moveable feast for 55 years, held in **Ann Arbor**, **Kalamazoo**, **Lansing**, and Adrian, among other places. The rounds stopped permanently in Detroit in 1905 at what is now the Michigan State Fairgrounds and Exposition Center.

Oldfield, Barney (1878–1946)

Racecar driver. One of the pioneers of racing, he began as a bicycle racer. Driving **Henry Ford**'s

Barney Oldfield, seen on the racetrack, set a land speed record.

famous 999 racer in 1903, he set a speed record: a mile a minute. He established a land speed record at more than 131mph in 1910.

Old Mackinac Point Lighthouse

The lighthouse was built in Mackinaw City in 1892. Its light was turned off in 1957, when the **Mackinac Bridge** opened with lights that provided better navigational assistance and,

ironically, a great view of the lighthouse when crossing the bridge. Nearly 50 years later, on June 12, 2004, the lighthouse was opened to the public as a restoration in progress.

Olds, Ransom E. (1864–1950)

Automotive pioneer. In 1897, Olds opened the Olds Motor Works, the first auto factory in the United States. Fire destroyed most of the

Old Mackinac Point Lighthouse is now open to the public.

Ransom E. Olds, front left, drives a Reo. Behind him is Theodore Roosevelt.

factory in March 1901. Of the 11 models Olds had in prototype in the factory, the only car saved was one called the Curved Dash Olds. It was a small, inexpensive car, but Olds threw production dollars behind its manufacture; it became known as the Merry Oldsmobile. Olds sold his interest in the company in 1904 and became president, and later chairman of the board, of the Reo Motor Car Company.

Olds Transportation Museum, R.E.

The museum focuses on **Lansing**'s part in the development of the **auto industry**. Its holdings include the oldest Oldsmobile and rare Reo, Durant, and Viking cars. The museum, at 240 Museum Drive, is open Tuesday through Saturday, 10 a.m. to 5 p.m. and Sunday, noon to 5 p.m.

Ontonogan Boulder

As proof of Michigan's mineral wealth, hardware merchant Julius Eldred bought the two-ton mass of copper from the Chippewa, intending to take it on tour of eastern cities. Neither the largest nor the purest chunk of copper ever found in Michigan, the boulder is in the Smithsonian Institution.

Orchestra Hall

Built quickly in 1919 to accommodate the demands of the **Detroit Symphony Orchestra**'s new music director, **Ossip Gabrilowitsch**, the hall was renowned for its acoustic properties. The orchestra stayed 20 years, then left for a more economical home. Renamed the Paradise Theater in 1941, the hall became an important jazz venue, drawing artists such as Billie Holiday and Count Basie. The building, abandoned after the Paradise closed in 1951, was scheduled for demolition when DSO musicians and friends spurred the community to restore it. DSO returned to the renovated hall in 1989. Considered an acoustic peer to Carnegie Hall, Orchestra Hall is on the National Register of Historic Places.

Owen, Marie (n.d.)

Police officer. The widow of a patrolman, she became the first female police officer in the United States when she entered the **Detroit** Bureau of Police in 1893.

Orchestra Hall, Detroit, has played host to artists such as Billie Holiday and Count Basie.

P

Packard, William (1861–1923) and James (1863–1928)

Auto makers. William and James Packard founded the Packard Electric Company in Warren, Ohio, in 1890, and later traveled north to start the Packard Motor Company in **Detroit**. Packard trucks were used to transport soldiers in World War I and **World War II**. Before merging with Studebaker Motors in 1956, Packard was the largest independent automaker in Detroit.

Palmer Raids

The rise of Russian Communism led to fear of "foreign radicals" in the United States. U.S. Attorney General A. Mitchell Palmer ordered a nationwide roundup of suspected radicals on January 2, 1920. The largest raid, in **Detroit**, netted 800 individuals, who were held in filthy conditions, with a single toilet, for six days. No evidence tied them to radical groups.

Paradise Valley

In the 1920s, a rapidly expanding **auto industry** lured blacks, many of them from the South, to seek employment in **Detroit**. While jobs were plentiful, housing was more difficult to obtain. One of the few areas where families could settle was on the near east side, a 60-square-block neighborhood called Black Bottom. Initially inhabited by European **immigrants**, the area was named after the dark soil farmed by early settlers. Long-time Detroit Mayor **Coleman Young** and boxer **Joe Louis** were residents.

In the 1930s, the 606 Horseshoe Bar was an active part of the neighborhood known as Paradise Valley.

Paradise Valley was the community's business and entertainment district. It contained beauty parlors, music stores, groceries, bowling alleys, and numerous restaurants and nightclubs—all owned and patronized by African Americans. Throughout the 1930s and into the 1940s, blacks and whites drank and danced side by side in an easy, relaxed atmosphere.

Top black entertainers played at the Valley's nightspots, among them, Billie Holiday, Earl Hines, and the Inkspots. Headliners such as Duke Ellington, Lena Horne, and Cab Calloway performed at such mainstream entertainment centers as the **Michigan Theater** and then jammed the night away in Paradise Valley. At that time, downtown hotels would not accept black guests, so the entertainers stayed in Valley hotels.

Increased racial tensions in the 1940s resulted in fewer white visitors to the community, and opportunities for housing elsewhere drew blacks away from the area. Black Bottom and Paradise Valley survived until the 1950s, when urban renewal projects and expressway construction destroyed the neighborhood.

Parke-Davis Research Laboratories

The company moved to its location on **Detroit**'s Joseph Campau Street in the 1870s, attracted by the **Detroit River** and a rail line that offered convenient transportation. Among the 26 buildings erected during 1891 and 1955 was the first building designed specifically as a pharmaceutical research laboratory. In 1982, Parke-Davis sold the site to a real estate developer, which turned it into River Place, a complex of offices, shops, and homes. The site became a National Historic Landmark on May 11, 1976, and was listed on the National Register of Historic Places on the same day.

Parks, Rosa (1913–)

Civil rights activist. On December 1, 1955, the "mother of the civil rights movement" refused to give up her seat in the colored section of a Montgomery, Alabama, bus to a white man. The bus driver had her arrested and, four days later, she was tried and convicted of violating a local ordinance. Her conviction sparked a year-long black boycott of the Montgomery bus system, until a U.S. Supreme Court decision that ended segregation on city buses. It also irrevocably brought to the fore the racial inequality that divided the United States.

Rosa Parks, the civil rights activist, who famously refused to give up her bus seat to a white male passenger.

Parke-Davis Research Laboratories, Detroit, is now listed on the National Register of Historic Places.

Although Parks had won the right to board a bus and sit anywhere she chose, she had lost her job as a department store seamstress and no one in Montgomery would hire her. She was threatened, and her family was harassed. She moved to **Detroit** in 1957.

After 23 years on the staff of U.S. Representative John Conyers, Parks retired and began to lecture on civil rights throughout the country. In 1987 she co-founded the Rosa and Raymond Parks Institute for Self-Development, a nonprofit organization dedicated to helping young people achieve their highest potential. She has received countless honors, including honorary degrees from 10 colleges and universities, the Martin Luther King Jr. Nonviolent Peace Prize, and a Congressional Gold Medal, the nation's highest civilian award. On the spot where she was arrested now stands the Troy State University Montgomery Rosa Parks Library and Museum, an interactive tribute to the early civil rights movement.

Petroskey, Dale A. (1956–)

President of the National Baseball Hall of Fame and Museum and political advisor. Born in **Detroit**, he graduated from **Michigan State University** and joined the Republican press corps of the Michigan House of Representatives. He also served as senior vice president of the National Geographic Society and assistant White House press secretary under President Ronald Reagan.

Pewabic Pottery

The pottery was designed and built for ceramicist Mary Chase Perry by William B. Stratton, one of the most influential architects of early 20th century **Detroit**. A decade later, Perry and Stratton were married.

Mary Chase Perry Stratton developed a national reputation for her unique ceramic glazes. Founded at the height of the Arts and Craft Movement, her pottery continues as a design and fabrication center.

The Pewabic Pottery building was designed especially for the ceramicist Mary Chase Perry.

In 1906, the pottery moved to its new home from its original location at the corner of John R and Alfred streets and immediately became an important Detroit landmark. At the new location, Pewabic became nationally renowned for its tiles, vessels, and architectural ornamentation. During the Depression, when such luxuries were prohibitive, the pottery began to produce ceramic jewelry that featured its signature iridescent glazes.

In 1966, after Stratton's death, the pottery was transferred to **Michigan State University** for a continuing education program. Fifteen years later it was turned over to the nonprofit Pewabic Society, which serves as its governing body.

Pewabic installs more than 100 custom tile designs each year. In more recent years, the pottery installed 45,000 glazed tiles in the new Edward H. McNamara Terminal at Detroit Metropolitan Wayne County Airport and created murals at **Comerica Park**.

The pottery has changed little over the years. The original clay-making machine, tables, and cabinets are still in use. The building is on both the State Register and National Register of Historic Places. It was listed as a National Historic Landmark in December 1991.

Pictured Rocks National Lakeshore

Towering above the south shore of Lake Superior are the Pictured Rocks, striking multicolored cliffs of eroded sandstone reaching 200 feet above the water. The cliffs cover 12 of the 42 miles of shoreline included within the Pictured Rocks National Lakeshore. The lofty Grand Sable Dunes, unspoiled beaches, waterfalls, wildlife, and North Woods forest also attract visitors to this 73,000-acre park on Michigan's **Upper Peninsula**. Other park features include former logging trails, deserted farmsteads, and the Au Sable Lighthouse. The park is open year round, providing four-season

Pictured Rocks National Lakeshore and the Au Sable Lighthouse

P

Hazen Pingree, "The Idol of the People"

recreation ranging from backpacking, fishing, hunting, to cross-country skiing, snowshoeing, snowmobiling, and ice fishing. Park headquarters are on Sand Point Road near Munising.

Pine Mountain Ski Jump

One of the world's best freestanding 90-meter ski jumps is found near Iron Mountain in the **Upper Peninsula**. Every February since 1939, a ski jumping tournament has been held at this tower. At a 1996 World Cup event, a Japanese skier tied the North American Ski Jumping record with a jump of 459 feet.

Pingree, Hazen (1840–1901)

Mayor and governor. Rated one of the 10 best mayors in U.S. history by historians and social scientists, he was a champion of social reform. When gas and light prices rose too high, he took control from the private utilities companies and gave it to the city. He urged arbitration during labor strikes when common practice was to use the state militia as strike-breakers. During the 1890s depression, he initiated work-relief programs and set aside areas for city residents to plant vegetable gardens. When wealthy citizens refused to donate to a relief program, he sold his prize horse at auction and donated the money himself.

A Maine native, he had arrived in **Detroit** after the **Civil War** and become wealthy selling shoes. He was nominated as Republican candidate for mayor in 1889 by a group of influential businessmen who hoped to wrest Detroit from Democratic control. After his election, when it became clear where his loyalties lay, his former supporters, expecting a wealthy man to favor business interests, shunned him. But the people loved him; he was elected to two more terms.

Despite the hostility of Republican party leaders, he was elected governor of the state in 1896, while still mayor of Detroit. For a short time, he held both positions, until the state supreme court ruled that he must resign as mayor. As governor, with an oppositional legislature, he was less successful in his reform efforts.

Plymouth Art Fair

The streets surrounding **Kellogg** Park, in the heart of downtown Plymouth, are lined with over 400 artists one weekend each July. AAA has called the Plymouth Art Fair, founded in 1980, the Gem of the **Great Lakes**. The fair features local, American, and international artists, and hands-on art opportunities for children.

Polacco, Patricia (1944–)

Writer, illustrator. Born and raised in Michigan, the award-winning author takes pride in her roots. She resides in Union City at Meteor Ridge Farms, a home built in 1859 that was once visited by Abraham Lincoln. She uses the Michigan folk she grew up with as the subjects of her beloved children's books. Her works include *The Calhoun Club*, *Chicken Sunday*, and *Picnic at Mudsock Meadow*.

Pontiac, Chief (1720–1769)

Leader of Ottawa tribe. Shortly after becoming chief in 1755, he also became head of the Council of Three Tribes, which included the Potawatomi and Ojibwa. The tribes lived peacefully with the French traders, exchanging furs for food, guns, and tobacco. The British defeated the French in 1760 and took over forts

Above: Chief Pontiac

Right: Patricia Polacco has written dozens of children's books, including The Keeping Quilt, *which won the 1989 International Reading Association Award.*

P

throughout the **Great Lakes** region. They did not welcome the Indians at the forts. An angry Pontiac, foreseeing that the British also would deprive the Indians of their hunting grounds, plotted to overthrow the new administration. He enlisted 18 local tribes, planning to have them attack the forts nearest to them in May 1763 and drive out the settlers. His own target was Fort Detroit.

Betrayed to the British, he did not attack the fort but rather laid siege to it, blocking supplies and reinforcements. At the height of the siege, he attacked 260 British troops at Parent's Creek, killing 60, including their captain, James Dalyell; thereafter the creek became known as Bloody Run. In spite of his victory there, and though the tribes captured eight of the 12 forts they attacked, Pontiac was

forced to retreat when reinforcements were able to get through.

By 1764, the French had taken sides against the Indians. The British retook much of the area the tribes had captured the previous year. Pontiac signed a peace treaty in July 1766. Three years later, he was murdered by a Peoria Indian.

Post, Charles W. (1854–1914)

Cereal maker. Inspired by a drink served at the **Battle Creek Sanitarium**, Charles William Post made his first batch of Postum— a cereal beverage—in a **Battle Creek** barn in 1895. By 1897, he had introduced Grape-Nuts, one of the first ready-to-eat cold cereals. Bran flakes and many other varieties followed.

Post played a pivotal role in the development of the cereal market. An innovative businessman, he was among the first to use now-standard marketing techniques such as extensive advertising, coupons, free samples, and recipe booklets.

Today, the factory complex covers 40 acres. C. W. Post's original white barn is still on the factory grounds.

Pritchard, Colonel Benjamin (n.d.)

Civil War hero. Pritchard led the Fourth Michigan Cavalry, which captured Confederate President Jefferson Davis on May 10, 1865. An Allegan native, he graduated from the **University of Michigan**.

Prohibition

Prohibition, the social experiment that banned the manufacture and sale of beer, liquor, and wine, was a boon to Michigan's economy during the Roaring Twenties. The state's proximity to Ontario, Canada, just across the border, made **Detroit** a convenient gateway for smugglers and rumrunners. It is estimated that 75 to 85 percent of the liquor supplied to the United States during Prohibition entered the country via Ontario-to-Detroit crossings of Lake St. Clair and the St. Clair and Detroit rivers.

Charles W. Post, who introduced Grape-Nuts (one of the first ready-to-eat cold cereals) in 1897.

Despite the 18th Amendment, bootleggers kept a steady flow of liquor in the United States.

State police with confiscated illegal liquor.

P

Michigan had preceded the rest of the country when it passed a statewide prohibition law that went into effect in May 1918. Until the federal Volstead Act of October 1919, a lively trade in bootleg booze had run between Detroit and Toledo. That ended in April 1919, when Ohio passed its own law.

Open rejection of the unpopular law through both smuggling and illegal still operations soon became widespread. In 1929 illegal liquor was one of the biggest businesses in Detroit, in fact it was second only to the **auto industry**. During that year there were as many as 25,000 speakeasies, called blind pigs, in the city.

Organized crime took advantage of the opportunities presented by Prohibition. The most notorious were the **Purple Gang** and the Licavoli Gang. Public outrage at the violence would play a role in the repeal of the 18th Amendment. In 1932 Michigan repealed its state prohibition statues, and in 1933 it became the first state to ratify the 21st Amendment to the U.S. Constitution, repealing the 18th Amendment. By the spring of 1933 the sale of beer and wine was again legal in Michigan.

Purple Gang

What the Mafia was to New York, the Purple Gang was to **Detroit** during Prohibition. A group of mostly Jewish mobsters ran bootlegging operations and dealt violently with anyone who crossed them.

In 1931, three renegade Purples dared to do business outside of their allotted venues. The bosses found out and invited the traitors to a meeting that was supposed to start a truce. It turned out to be a bloody ambush. A surviving witness testified against the shooters, and the Purple Gang's reign of terror faded.

Harry Fleischer, the leader of Detroit's Purple Gang is shown under FBI guard after being arrested in January 1950.

Quimby, Harriet (1875–1912)

Aviator. The first American woman to become a licensed pilot, she was also the first woman to fly across the English Channel. She died in an accident three months later at an air show in Massachusetts. Flying around the Boston Lighthouse, her plane nosedived, and she was thrown to her death.

Quincy Mining Company Historic District

The Quincy Mining Company is the sole surviving example of the hundreds of mines opened during the nation's first copper boom. Operators here were the first to switch from mining mass copper to mining the almond-shaped amygdaloid lodes that made Quincy one of the premier commercially successful mines on the Keweenaw Peninsula and helped clinch the district's place in the copper industry. As other mines closed during economic downturns, Quincy continued to produce. It earned its stockholders dividends 54 years straight, earning itself the nickname Old Reliable. It shut down in 1920.

The mining company properties are now part of Keweenaw National Historical Park. Only one shaft rockhouse remains, but the shafts themselves still exist. Visitors can explore the surface of the

Harriet Quimby was the first American woman to become a licensed pilot.

Q

mine, then take an underground tour via tram. There is also a cross-sectional plan of the 57-level mine that shows the labyrinthine shafts, passageways, and excavation routes that extended more than a mile below the surface. Quincy is home to the largest steam hoist in the world.

The mining company, north of Hancock along U.S. Route 41, is open Monday through Saturday 8:30 a.m. to 7 p.m. and Sunday 12:30 to 7 p.m. from the end of April through the beginning of November.

Quincy Mining Company is the oldest surviving copper mine.

Quincy Shaft No. 2, Calumet, Mich.

Radner, Gilda (1946–1989)

Actor, comedian. Gilda Radner was one of the original cast members of *Saturday Night Live*, where she created such characters as Roseanne Roseannadana, Emily Litella, and Lisa Lupner. Leaving the **University of Michigan** prior to graduation, Radner moved to Toronto and became a member of Second City, where she met John Candy, John Belushi, and Dan Ackroyd, who later joined her as part of *Saturday Night Live*. Diagnosed with ovarian cancer in 1986, Radner died in 1989. In response to her death, her husband, actor Gene Wilder, and friends established Gilda Clubs throughout the United States. The centers offer free support for cancer patients and their families.

Gilda Radner's own experience inspired Gilda Clubs, which offer support to cancer patients.

Reese, Della (1931–)

Singer, actress. As a young gospel singer, **Detroit** native Reese toured with Mahalia Jackson. During the 1950s and '60s, she recorded pop albums, her singles often landing on the Billboard charts. In 1969, Reese became the first black woman to have her own prime-time television show, called *Della*. Her most successful television role was as the angel Tess on *Touched by an Angel*, from 1994 to 2003, for which she won several NAACP Image awards and Emmy and Golden Globe nominations.

In 1987 Reese was ordained as a minister by the Universal Foundation for Better Living. She then founded Understanding Principles for Better Living Church in Los Angeles, where she continues to preach.

Renaissance Center

Years after the 1967 riots in **Detroit**, the city was still desperately trying to recover economically. In 1970, 26 business, civic, and industrial leaders came together to rebuild and revitalize the local economy, and the Detroit Renaissance was born.

In 1971, **Henry Ford II**, head of the Detroit Renaissance, presented plans to Mayor Roman Gribbs and the Detroit City Council to build a hotel, offices, and residential buildings along the **Detroit River**. John Portman, who also created the Embarcadero Center in San Francisco, was brought in as architect for the $500 million, privately funded project.

General Motors and Chrysler, among others, provided the initial $33 million down payment for Phase 1 of the Renaissance Center, which included the Western International

R

Detroit Plaza Hotel. By the end of 1973, the hotel had booked its first large convention and over 100 blocks of space before the foundation had been dug. Property values surrounding the Renaissance Center soared, and demand was high for nearby real estate.

On April 15, 1977 a plaque was unveiled honoring the private investors who funded the project. Henry Ford II, Mayor **Coleman Young**, and Elio Gabbuggiani, mayor of Florence, attended the gala.

Two more office towers opened in 1981 as Phase 2, but Phase 3, a residential development, was never initiated because of the emigration of the city's population throughout the 1980s.

In 1996, General Motors bought the Renaissance Center and announced it would spend nearly $500 million in renovations. The hotel tower is currently owned by Marriott.

The Renaissance Center dominates Detroit's skyline.

R.E. Olds Transportation Museum (*see* Olds Transportation Museum, R.E.)

Republican Party

According to the **Northwest Ordinance**, slavery was prohibited in the northern states carved out of the Northwest Territory. But when the ordinance was passed in 1787, Congress could not foresee the extent of expansion to the west that became a certainty with the outbreak of the Mexican War in 1846. During debates over the annexing of Texas, the expansion of slavery was once again a contentious issue. **Lewis Cass**, a leader of the Democratic Party and forerunner for the party's presidential nomination in 1848, declared that new states should make decisions on the issue without intervention from Congress. The Compromise of 1850 applied Cass's "squatter sovereignty" doctrine to the territory won from Mexico.

Backed by another high-ranking Democrat, Stephen A. Douglas, Congress again backtracked on slavery in 1854 with the Kansas-Nebraska bill, which repealed an earlier prohibition on slavery in the Missouri Compromise of 1820.

The antislavery North had had enough. Dissatisfied with the ideology of the political parties currently in power, northern abolitionist leaders such as Salmon P. Chase, Charles Sumner, and *New York Tribune* editor Horace Greeley called for a new one. Protests held throughout the North ultimately gave birth to the Republican Party. The name came from an editorial by Greeley, who wrote in June 1854 that a new party should have "some simple name like 'Republican' [that] would designate those who had united to restore the Union to its true missions of champion and promulgator of Liberty rather than propagandist of slavery."

The party was formed at a meeting in Jackson on July 6, 1854, by representatives of various splinter parties, including the antislavery Whigs, the Wilmot-Proviso Democrats, and the Free Soilers. Like many of today's high-level politicians, they were among the social elite of their time, men who had worked their way into the good life. Although they came from different backgrounds, they shared a common discontent with the direction they saw the nation taking.

Prominent Michigan men at the convention included **David S. Walbridge**, a successful **Kalamazoo** businessman and an active Whig, who chaired the meeting. The newly formed party sent him to Congress the following year. **Austin Blair**, who had left the Whig party six years earlier because of its refusal to endorse his antislavery views, was a member of the platform committee. In 1860 he would represent the party at the national convention in Chicago during which Abraham Lincoln was nominated for president. He served as governor during the **Civil War**.

At the meeting, the party adopted its first party platform, which took a decisive stand against slavery, denouncing the Missouri

Salmon P. Chase was among the founders of the Republican Party.

R

Compromise and calling for repeal of the Fugitive Slave Act. The party also nominated candidates for state office, choosing **Kinsley Bingham** as governor of Michigan. Six months after the convention Bingham was sworn in as the nation's first Republican governor.

The meeting, held outside because there was no building in town that could hold the group, came to be known as the Convention under the Oaks.

Reuther, Walter (1907–1970)

Union organizer. During his tenure as its president, the **United Auto Workers** became one of the largest unions in the country, with more than 1.5 million members.

Reuther learned politics from his socialist father. Fired from a tool-and-die apprenticeship for trying to organize a union, he was lured to **Detroit** by the promise of high wages at Ford Motor Company. While working at the River Rouge plant, he took classes at what is now Wayne State University, where he organized protests against establishment of a Reserve Officer Training Corps unit.

In the mid-1930s he went to the Soviet Union and worked two years at an auto plant. Back in the United States he began organizing for the fledgling UAW. Elected local president, he quickly organized 76 shops representing 30,000 workers. He was key in a successful 1937 sit-down strike against General Motors, then turned to organizing Ford.

He became director of the UAW's GM division in 1939, respected by executives as well as the rank and file, and successfully guided the union through wildcat strikes without losing the faith of the company. In 1946, he was elected UAW president, a position he held until his death in a 1970 plane crash. At his insistence, GM agreed to a historic contract that tied wage increases to cost-of-living and productivity increases.

Reuther championed national health care and job security. He fought tirelessly for **civil rights** and stood beside the Rev. Martin Luther

King Jr. during King's "I Have a Dream" speech at the 1963 March on Washington.

At the time of his death, he was working on an alliance with the Teamsters, which proved short lived.

Richard, Father Gabriel (1767–1832)

He left France during the Revolution, carrying with him the ideals of the Enlightenment. After assignments in Baltimore and what is now Illinois, he was assigned to **Detroit** in 1798 and became pastor of **Ste. Anne's Church** in 1802. Working with Judge **Augustus Woodward**, appointed by President Jefferson to prepare Michigan for statehood, he helped create a burgeoning town from what, under the French, had been a small village.

He brought the first printing press to Michigan, printing first a grammar textbook and then, in 1809, a short-lived newspaper, *The Michigan Essay or Impartial Observer.*

A firm believer in public education, he was instrumental in legislation that called for nonsectarian tax-supported schools and in the

A bucket brigade failed to keep Detroit from burning. Father Richard led rebuilding efforts.

In 1871 Fannie Richards became the first black teacher in Detroit's newly integrated schools.

establishment of the Catholepistemiad, which evolved into the **University of Michigan**. He was one of the two original professors and recruited the other, the Reverend **John Monteith**, who served as the university's first president. He also established schools for girls and Indian children.

As the territory's representative to Congress, from 1823 to 1825, he gained federal support for the Territorial Road, which linked Detroit and Chicago and opened Michigan to settlement. During a cholera epidemic that killed many Detroit residents in 1832, he ministered to the sick before he too contracted cholera and died.

A statute of Father Richard, created by Leonard Jongwirth for the Federal Arts Project of the Works Project Administration, stands at East Jefferson and Sheridan streets, Detroit.

Richards, Fannie (n.d.)

Teacher. The Virginia native moved to **Detroit** as a young child and studied in Detroit and Toronto. After attending the Teachers Training School in Detroit, she opened a private school for black children in 1863. She helped finance a

R

lawsuit against Detroit's racially segregated school system and in 1871 she became the first black teacher in Detroit's newly integrated schools.

River Raisin Battlefield Visitor Center

Dioramas and a fiber-optic map present the story of one of the most vicious battles of the **War of 1812**. The visitor center is at 1403 East Elm Street, Monroe. Open days vary by season. The grounds are open all year round.

Robinson, Smokey (1940–)

Singer, record producer. One of the founding members of the Miracles, while still in high school in 1955, Robinson teamed with **Berry Gordy Jr.** to produce a series of singles for the group in 1958–1959. In 1960, Gordy's **Motown** Records signed the Miracles, and Robinson became involved in the company, writing and producing for many Motown stars, notably Mary Wells, the Temptations, and Marvin Gaye, while continuing to record with the Miracles. In 1971, he left the Miracles to

Smokey Robinson's hits with the Miracles include "The Tears of a Clown."

concentrate on business, and in 1972 set off on a solo career. He was voted into the Rock and Roll Hall of Fame in 1988.

Robinson, Sugar Ray (1921–1989)

Boxer. Sugar Ray Robinson's career encompassed three decades. He was a world welterweight champion, and he held the middleweight title five times. Robinson turned pro in 1940. He won 40 fights before being beaten by Jake LaMotta, and after that defeat, Robinson remained unbeaten for an unprecedented eight years. He took the welterweight title in 1946. In 1955, he challenged LaMotta for the middleweight title, beating him in the 13th round.

Robinson's record included 202 fights, of which he won 175, 109 by knockout. He retired in 1965 and was inducted into the International Boxing Hall of Fame in 1990.

Roethke, Theodore (1908–1963)

Poet. The Pulitzer Prize winner poet was born in Saginaw. He grew up working in his family-owned greenhouse and was a serious and gifted student. After graduating from the **University of Michigan**, Roethke took courses at Harvard University. During the Great Depression, money was scarce and he dropped out of Harvard.

Roethke took opportunities to study under fellow writers and poets to sharpen his skills. He won a Pulitzer Prize in 1953 for *The Waking*. His other works include *Open House, The Lost Son, The Far Field,* and *On the Poet and His Craft: Selected Prose.*

Romney, George W. (1907–1995)

Governor, presidential candidate, automotive executive. As a three-term governor during the 1960s, Romney led Michigan through some of the biggest changes it had experienced since becoming a state. During his years as governor, a new Michigan Constitution took effect, **civil rights** and tax reform measures were introduced, and the state's economy improved.

Sugar Ray Robinson (pictured in 1951) was inducted into the Boxing Hall of Fame in 1990.

Romney, who was born in a Mormon community in Chihuahua, Mexico, was five years old when his parents moved the family back to the United States. He arrived in Michigan in the 1940s.

In 1954 he became chairman and president of the newly formed American Motors Corporation. Romney turned AMC into a profitable company largely through a 1957 decision to discontinue the company's legendary Hudson and Nash brands. He pushed AMC to exclusively produce the Rambler, one of the country's first compact economy cars. Sales of the small, fuel-efficient vehicle quadrupled in two years.

In 1959, Romney's interests turned to politics. He was among delegates selected by Michigan voters to write a new constitution. He resigned from AMC in 1962 to run for governor as the **Republican Party** candidate.

George W. Romney was made governor of the Republican Party in 1962.

R

He won, ending 14 years of Democratic gubernatorial control.

The popular, charismatic governor briefly campaigned for the U.S. presidency in 1967, but withdrew after three months, later saying it would have been difficult to wrest the nomination from the other Republican candidates, Richard Nixon and Nelson Rockefeller. From 1969 until 1973 he served in the Nixon Administration as secretary of the U.S. Department of Housing and Urban Development.

Rosie the Riveter

Rosie the Riveter helped mobilize women into the work force during World War II.

The mythical figure, meant to mobilize women into the work force during **World War II**, was based on a real-life Michigan woman. Rose Will Monroe, who worked on B-24 and B-29 bombers in **Detroit**, was tapped to star in a government film, directed by actor Walter Pidgeon, to promote war bonds. Monroe fit the image of the 1942 hit song "Rosie the Riveter," written by Redd Evans and John Jacob Loeb and recorded by Kay Kyser.

Artist J. Howard Miller created the 1943 "We Can Do It!" movie poster, the now-familiar picture of a shirt-sleeved Rosie flexing her muscle. Despite her nicely formed bicep and her don't-mess-with-me expression, Rosie is pictured as attractively feminine, with her face glowingly made up and perfectly coiffed hair peeking from beneath her red bandanna. Femininity was stylish during the 1940s; a Rosie who could maintain her beauty as she did skilled labor made industrial work socially acceptable. As men left defense plants to enlist, millions of women replaced them. Most returned home after the war. Monroe, a widow with two daughters, started her own construction company.

Norman Rockwell also created a Rosie the Riveter. His interpretation appeared on the cover of the May 29, 1943, issue of the *Saturday Evening Post.*

The image of Rosie came to epitomize women's strength. With the advent of the

women's movement, she was used as a symbol of the issues of women's rights.

Ross, Diana (1944–)

Singer, actress. She spent 10 years as lead singer of the **Supremes** before leaving in 1970 for a solo career. She earned an Oscar nomination for her portrayal as Billie Holiday in the 1972 film *Lady Sings the Blues.*

Before her singing career, she was the first black bus girl in the cafeteria at Hudson's.

Round Oak Stove Company

After Philo Beckwith created it to heat his machine shop, he was asked to make one first for the Dowagiac depot of the Michigan Central Railroad and then for other depots along the line. He patented the stove in 1873. By the 1890s, 350 employees used 40 tons of pig iron a day to turn out the stoves. Round Oak stoves are now valuable collectors items; Southwestern Michigan College has a gold-plated one in its museum.

Round Oak branched out into furnaces, still used in many Dowagiac homes, and water heaters. The company closed in 1947.

Diana Ross, left, with fellow Motown artists Marvin Gaye and Stevie Wonder.

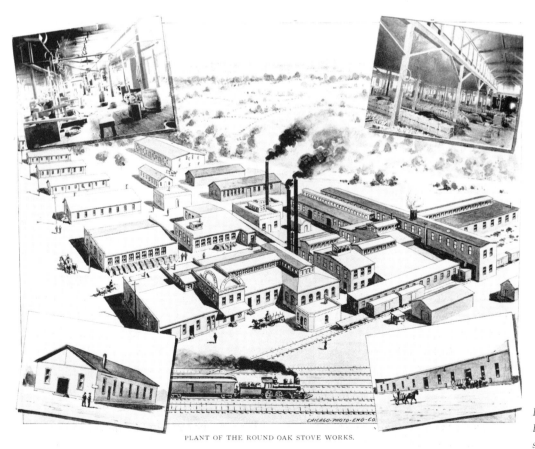

PLANT OF THE ROUND OAK STOVE WORKS.

Round Oak Stove Works. Philo Beckwith patented his famous stove in 1873.

S

Saarinen, Eliel (1873–1950)

Architect. Finland's leading architect, he immigrated to the United States, designed **Cranbrook Academy of Art**, and became president of the school. His other designs include the music shed at Tanglewood in Massachusetts. He formed a partnership with his equally renowned son, Eero Saarinen, for his later designs.

Ste. Anne de Detroit

Ste. Anne de Detroit, founded on July 26, 1701, is the second oldest Catholic parish in the United States. It was founded by French adventurers two days following the founding of Fort Ponchatrain, today's city of **Detroit**. The first child baptized in Detroit, the daughter of city founder **Antoine de la Mothe Cadillac**, was baptized at Ste. Anne. Father **Gabriel Richard** was Ste. Anne's pastor from 1802 to 1832.

The present church, built in 1886 by Leon Coquard, is an example of Gothic Revival architecture. Inside are relics from past churches, including the wooden altar at which Father Richard celebrated Mass.

St. Clair River Tunnel

Ste. Anne de Detroit is the second oldest Catholic parish in the United States.

Before the tunnel opened in 1891, no railroad had ever traveled beneath a river. To create a structure through the porous ground, engineers combined elements of tunnel construction in ways never done before. The tunnel had a diameter of 19 feet, 10 inches, and was 6,025 feet long, with 2,290 feet of it under the river bed. More than a hundred years later, though it is no longer used, it remains a technological wonder.

The tunnel provided a link from Port Huron to the Canadian city of Sarnia, Ontario. The first freight train traveled through the tunnel on October 24, 1891, and less than six weeks later, on December 7, the tunnel was opened to passenger trains. Electric locomotives replaced steam locomotives in May 1908; the railroad feared a crew might suffocate if its train stalled under the river. A new tunnel opened May 5, 1995.

The Michigan portal to the original tunnel is between Johnstone and Beard streets in Port Huron. The tunnel is on the State Register and National Register of Historic Places and is listed as a National Historic Landmark.

St. Ignace Mission

Established on **Mackinac Island** by Father **Jacques Marquette**, it was a center for the **fur trade**. Marquette, with explorer **Louis Jolliet**, left the mission to explore the Mississippi River and died before he could return. The mission is a National Historic Landmark.

A new St. Clair River Tunnel
opened in 1995. The original
tunnel (left and below) is no
longer used.

S

St. Julian Wine Company

The family-owned winery is the oldest in Michigan. Mariano Meconi opened the winery in Windsor, Ontario, during Prohibition and later moved across the **Detroit River** to the United States. The wines have won dozens of awards. St. Julian, at 716 S. Kalamazoo Street, Paw Paw, is open Monday through Saturday, 9 a.m. to 5 p.m. and Sunday, noon to 5 p.m.

St. Marys Falls Ship Canal

The largest ship canal in the world was built in 1851 on St. Marys River at Locks Park between Lake Superior and Lake Huron. The elevation between the two lakes, connected by the rapid-running St. Marys Falls, differs by 22 feet. The canal was built because the stretch of falls was treacherous to freight ships and needed to be manned for safe passage. The canal was deepened to allow the loading of larger ships.

St. Marys Falls is the largest ship canal in the world.

Sts. Peter and Paul Church

Consecrated June 29, 1848, it is Detroit's oldest operating church. Despite renovation, its original plan has been preserved and the exterior looks nearly the same as when it was built. The church, operated by the Jesuit Order, is on the State Register and the National Register of Historic Places.

Salk, Jonas (1914–1995)

Physician, microbiologist. Famed for developing the first vaccine against poliomyelitis, he began his studies of viruses as a medical student and researcher at the **University of Michigan**. While there, at the request of the U.S. Army, he worked on an influenza vaccine.

Salmon

Since the early 1800s, destructive non-native animal species have invaded the **Great Lakes**,

Sts. Peter and Paul's is Detroit's oldest operating church.

Michigan's proximity to the four Great Lakes makes it an ideal place for salmon anglers.

often via the ballast water of ocean-going vessels. The alewife, first seen in Lake Michigan in 1949, had no natural predators to control them. Fish managers at the Michigan Department of Natural Resources introduced coho salmon in 1966, followed by chinook in 1967. The salmon did well and controlled the alewife population. Anglers learned to catch the big pink fish and a new sport was born.

Sanilac Petroglyphs

The sandstone etchings were discovered in a mound near Bad Axe after widespread forest fires across the Lower Peninsula in 1881. Thought to be prehistoric, they hint at the lives of early native peoples. They are on government land, far enough from the road to be easily overlooked, and yet over the years they have been vandalized and marred with graffiti and are now protected behind a fence. The area currently is not open to the public.

Fishing at Saugatuck, Mich.

Lumber from Saugatuck helped to rebuild Chicago after the Great Fire of 1871.

Saugatuck

Saugatuck is on the shores of Lake Michigan, bordered by steep, rolling sand dunes and fruit orchards. Early settlement was due to **logging**: the area contributed much of the lumber used to rebuild Chicago after the Great Fire of 1871.

Since the early 1900s Chicagoans and others have favored the area for summer homes. Today the community is a mix of restored 19th-century architecture and modern 20th-century diversions. Art galleries, fine restaurants, plus clothing, gift, and antique shops dot the downtown. A harbor shelters sailboats, yachts, and fishing charter vessels. Nearby are highly rated state and city beaches. Visitors often stay at one of the area's many bed-and-breakfast accommodations.

Schoolcraft, Henry (1793–1864)

Henry Schoolcraft commanded an expedition that discovered the source of the Mississippi River.

Ethnologist, geologist. Born in Albany, New York, he went to Lake Superior with **Lewis Cass** as the expedition geologist, married an

Indian woman and studied her tribe, and negotiated treaties for the government. He commanded an expedition that discovered the source of the Mississippi River.

Scott, George C. (1927–1999)

Actor. Nominated for the Academy Award four times, he won in 1971 for *Patton* and created a Hollywood sensation by refusing to accept the award. Scott also was nominated for television's Emmy five times, winning twice. He received two Golden Globes and was nominated for Broadway's Tony award four times.

Second Baptist Church

Thirteen former slaves started Michigan's first African American church. Not far from the Canadian border, Second Baptist was an important stop on the **Underground Railroad**. Abolitionist leaders such as **Sojourner Truth**, John Brown, and Frederick Douglass all spoke at the church, at 441 Monroe Street, **Detroit**.

Seger, Bob (1945–)

Rock musician. The **Ann Arbor** native, relatively unknown until *Ramblin' Gamblin' Man* in 1969, has sold more than 50 million albums. *Live Bullet*, recorded with his Silver Bullet Band, was his first gold record album. His next album, *Night Moves*, shot him to superstardom. He was inducted into the Rock and Roll Hall of Fame in 2004.

Shaw, Anna Howard (1847–1919)

Social activist. She was one of the first women ordained as a Methodist minister. Also an M.D., she never practiced but instead traveled the world working for social justice. She was president of the National American Woman Suffrage Association and active in the Woman's Christian Temperance Union. She coordinated women's contributions during World War I and was the first women to receive the Distinguished Service Medal. At the request of presidents Taft and Wilson, she lectured through the United States and Europe in

Second Baptist Church, Detroit, was an important stop on the Underground Railroad.

Anna Shaw, right, with feminist activist Susan B. Anthony.

S support of the League of Nations. She was inducted into the National Women's Hall of Fame in 2000.

Sleeping Bear Dunes National Lakeshore

An Indian legend tells of a bear and her two cubs that swam across Lake Michigan to escape a forest fire. The mother bear reached the shore and climbed a cliff to wait for her children. The sleeping bear still maintains a vigil, as a dark hill on a sandy plateau, while her wayward cubs are the offshore North and South Manitou Islands.

Sleeping Bear Dunes National Lakeshore is located 26 miles west of **Traverse City** along the Lake Michigan shore. It encompasses a 35-mile stretch of the coastline with dramatic sand bluffs rising to 480 feet. Included in the park's 71,000 acres are forests, beaches, and dune formations. Educational features include an 1871 lighthouse, former coast guard stations, and a historic farm district.

The seven-mile Pierce Stocking Scenic Drive and the popular Dune Climb are favorite activities. Visitors fish and canoe on the Platt and Crystal rivers, plus hike and cross-country ski on 55 miles of trails. Ranger-led walks, campfire programs, and other activities are available in July and August. An excellent maritime museum is open Memorial Day to Labor Day. The visitor center and park headquarters, open daily, are on State Route 72 in Empire. The Manitou Islands are part of the park and may be reached via a passenger ferry in Leland.

Sloan, Alfred P. (1875–1966)

Businessman, philanthropist. After graduating from Massachusetts Institute of Technology, he worked as a draftsman at the Hyatt Roller Bearing Company in Newark, New Jersey, and rose to the company's presidency.

In 1969, Hyatt and several other automobile accessory companies merged with United Motors Corporation, and Sloan became president of the corporation. Two years later, United Motors was sold to General Motors Corporation. Sloan became a vice president and, five years later, president. He was elected chairman of the board in 1937. After retiring as CEO in 1946, he stayed on as board chairman for another 10 years, then was named honorary chairman, a position he held for the rest of his life. Under his leadership, the company gathered an increasing share of the automobile market.

Sloan had a gift for influencing the public's taste. At his urging, Hyatt began to produce anti-friction automobile bearings that became an industry standard. At GM, he convinced U.S. cities to switch from trams to buses. When unprofitable bus routes were dropped, GM persuaded citizens to become independent by buying their own automobiles. As the market approached saturation point, Sloan shifted the company's emphasis to designing dramatically different models each year and enticing buyers to keep up with the styles. He also made pointed distinctions among the various GM products, guiding buyers up the price scale from Chevrolet, the company's least expensive product, to **Cadillac**, its most expensive.

Sleeping Bear Dunes National Lakeshore encompasses a 35-mile stretch of coastline.

S

Alfred P. Sloan was made CEO of General Motors Corporation in 1937.

Sloan devoted vast energy and financial resources to philanthropy. He established the Alfred P. Sloan Foundation in 1934.

Sloan Museum, Alfred P.

One of 10 organizations that make up the **Flint Cultural Center**, the Sloan features regional history, historic automobiles, and hands-on science exhibits. The museum, at 1221 E.

Kearsley Street, is open Monday through Friday, 10 a.m. to 5 p.m., and Saturday and Sunday, noon to 5 p.m.

Slovik, Pvt. Eddie (n.d.)

Soldier. During **World War II**, Slovik was court-martialed for desertion under fire and sentenced to death by firing squad, the first member of the military executed for this crime since the **Civil War**. The execution occurred in 1945 in France. In 1987, his remains were reburied in Michigan next to those of his wife.

Soo Locks

Strategic series of locks allowing boats to travel easily between Lake Superior and the rest of the **Great Lakes**. The Soo Locks were built in the 1850s primarily to relieve a growing shipping bottleneck created by the copper and iron ore **mining** booms in the **Upper Peninsula**.

For centuries, **Native Americans** and later French and British **fur traders** had lived near the rapids on the St. Marys River, the only waterway connecting Lake Superior and the other Great Lakes. In 1688 Jesuit missionary **Jacques Marquette** named the small outpost Sault Ste. Marie. Some French translators believe the name literally means, "to jump the St. Marys." Eventually Soo became the shortened phonetic name for the area and the locks.

The St. Marys rapids involve a 21-foot-drop from Lake Superior to Lake Huron. Early travelers carried their canoes around the rapids. As the boats and their contents became larger, it became necessary to unload the boats, haul the cargoes around the rapids in wagons, and then reload the goods into other boats. The Soo Locks were constructed to bypass the rapids and eliminate this long process.

An early lock had been built in 1797 on the Canadian side of the river, but was destroyed during the **War of 1812**. The U.S. Congress approved the Sault Canal Bill in 1852, providing 750,000 acres of federal lands as compensation to the company that would build the locks. In 1853 the Michigan legislature passed a bill authorizing the hiring of a company. The Fairbanks Scale Company, which had large mining interests in the U.P., along with **Detroit** railroad officials and other investors, won the contract. Even though construction would prove difficult, a canal and

COPYRIGHT 1915
A.E. YOUNG - Soo. MICH

The Soo Locks, built to accommodate the enormous freighters that sail the Great Lakes, are the only water connection between Lake Superior and the other lakes.

Spirit of Detroit *was created by Marshall Fredericks in 1958.*

two 350-foot locks were completed within a two-year deadline set by the state of Michigan. The steamer *Illinois* was the first ship to use the locks, in June 1855.

These would be the first of a series of successively larger locks. The Poe Lock, completed in 1968, currently has the largest capacity of the four locks now operated at the Soo. Today the U.S. Army Corps of Engineers operates the locks toll free. Approximately 10,000 vessels, ranging from small passenger boats to gigantic ore carriers, travel the locks each year. More than 95 million tons of freight passes through the Soo annually.

Every year in late June the community holds a Soo Locks Festival, with historic walking tours, events, music, and entertainment. Visitors can also experience the locks through the Soo Locks Boat Tours. The two-hour narrated tours include a trip through the locks. Tours are offered daily from mid-May through October. Hours vary by season. Railroad and highway bridges connect Sault Ste. Marie with its twin city, Sault Ste. Marie, Ontario.

Spirit of Detroit

The 26-foot bronze figure, created by Marshall Fredericks in 1958, holds in one hand a rayed sphere to symbolize God and in the other small figures to symbolize human relationships. The city's best-known outdoor sculpture apparently is a **Detroit Red Wings** fan: every year during the playoffs, he's dressed in a giant Red Wings T-shirt.

S.S. Kresge Company (see Kresge Company, S.S.)

State Bird

Robin. One of Michigan's most familiar backyard birds, the robin is a member of the thrush family. Male robins are known for their red breasts, black heads, and split, white eye-rings. Females have the same white eye-ring, but they have brown heads and paler red breasts. They nest in trees or shrubs.

Male robins have a bright red breast and the females' coloring is paler.

State Children's Book

The Michigan House of Representatives adopted a resolution on May 7, 1998, to make *The Legend of the Sleeping Bear* the official children's book. Written by Kathy-jo Wargin and illustrated by Gijsbert van Frankenhuyzen, the book retells an Ojibwa legend about a mother bear that waits forever for her lost cubs.

State Fish

Brook trout. Also called speckled trout, native trout, or square rail, the brook trout lives in cold, clear waters, generally 52 to 56 degrees F, and often is found in the headwaters of spring-fed streams. The average size is seven inches. Strong for their size, and game fighters, they make an excellent meal.

State Flag

Adopted in 1911, the Michigan State Flag incorporates a blue shield on which the sun rises over a lake and peninsula. A man with raised hand and holding a gun represents both peace

S

Although Michigan's coat of arms has always been on the state flag, at one time it was back-to-back with a portrait of Gov. Stevens T. Mason.

and the ability to defend one's rights. The elk and moose are symbols of Michigan. The eagle represents the United States. The flag includes three mottos: *E Pluribus Unum* ("Out of many, one"); *Tuebor* ("I will defend"); and *Si Quaeris Peninsulum Amoenam, Circumspice* ("If you seek a pleasant peninsula, look about you").

State Flower

Apple blossom. The lovely scent and delicate beauty of pink and white apple blossoms led to a designation as the state flower in 1897. The state boasts 58,000 commercial apple orchards. Michigan produces a billion pounds of apples every year, making the state a world leader.

State Fossil

Petoskey stone is fossilized coral colonies of the Devonian period. The coral formations were plentiful during the time when Michigan was covered by a warm sea. They are found on many beaches of Lake Michigan and in rock quarries from **Traverse City** to Alpena.

State Game Mammal

White-tailed deer. Found in every county in Michigan, white-tailed deer are the smallest of the three members of the deer family found in Michigan. They range in size from 125–225 pounds and are fast runners. They have a distinctive white tail, which they raise to signal other deer in times of danger.

State Gem

Chlorastrolite. Commonly referred to as Greenstone or Isle Royale Greenstone, chlorastrolite is a variety of the mineral pumpellyite. It is found as small pebbles on the beaches of Isle Royale and also throughout the Keweenaw Peninsula; however, collecting greenstones from Isle Royale beaches is now prohibited.

State Reptile

Painted turtle. Painted turtles have bright red and yellow markings and smooth shells. They live in quiet, shallow freshwater areas with thick mud bottoms. They feed primarily on plants, small animals, and insects and often may be found in large groups basking in the sun on logs or fallen trees.

State Seal and Motto

Michigan prides itself on being a land of many splendors. The motto refers to the state's natural beauty, history, and economic opportunities: *Si Quaeris Peninsulam Amoenam Circumspice* ("If you seek a pleasant peninsula, look about you").

In the middle of the Great Seal of Michigan, adopted on June 2, 1835, is a shield that depicts a man holding a rifle. The shield is held by a moose and an elk. On top of the shield is the familiar U.S. eagle symbol with the words *E Pluribus Unum* ("Out of many, one"), and below the shield is the state motto.

State Soil

Kalkaska Sand. Found only in Michigan, Kalkaska sand covers 750,000 acres in 29 counties. It has distinctive layers and a range of colors from black to yellow-brown. Formed in sandy deposits left by the glaciers, Kalkaska sand is used for growing hardwood timbers and Christmas trees, as well as for wildlife habitat.

State Song

Actually, it's songs, not song. There's "Michigan, My Michigan," the one considered Michigan's unofficial song. And then there's "My Michigan," legislated to be not *the* official song but *an* official song.

"Michigan, My Michigan" was written by Winfred Lee Brent Lyster of **Detroit**, whose husband, Henry, was a **Civil War** surgeon. Following the Battle of Fredericksburg, a three-day bloodfest that left nearly 18,000 men dead, Lyster was inspired to pen 10 verses about the Michigan soldiers who had fallen in various battles. Apparently no musician, she set the words to the tune of "O Tannenbaum."

Major James W. Long of **Grand Rapids** rewrote Lyster's song for Michigan's semi-centennial celebration in 1886. Only six verses this time, the song celebrated the beauty of the state's natural resources but still gave a hearty nod to "thy noble sons" who "bit the dust" during the war.

The song was reworked yet again by Douglas Malloch in 1902. This version, the modern-day "unofficial" song, was commissioned by the Michigan State Federation of Woman's Clubs for a convention in Muskegon. The federation women, who didn't care much for the two blood-and-guts incarnations, continued to sing the bowdlerized version at club meetings.

Thirty years later, Giles Kavanagh wrote the lyric and H. O'Reilly Clint wrote the tune

Michiganders are so enamored of their flora, they have a state flower, a state wildflower, and a state tree. This is the state flower, apple blossom.

S

for "My Michigan." Kavanagh, a reporter for the *Detroit News*, was chummy with Governor Frank D. Fitzgerald, who designated "My Michigan" as an official song on June 18, 1936. The song has since faded into obscurity. Kavanagh is perhaps better known for another of his creations, his son Thomas Giles Kavanagh, who sat on the Michigan Supreme Court from 1969 to 1985.

State Tree

The white pine was chosen as Michigan's state tree in recognition of the state's early status in the **logging** industry. From 1870 to the early 1900s, Michigan led the nation in lumber production. White pine lumber does not swell or shrink greatly with moisture content changes and is ideal for homebuilding and millwork.

State Wildflower

Dwarf lake iris. An endangered species native to Michigan, dwarf lake iris grows near the northern shores of Lakes Huron and Michigan. It is a low-growing perennial that flowers primarily in semi-open habitats with partial sun. Although its flowers are usually blue, lilac or white flowers can sometimes be found.

Steelcase

Straw wastebaskets in the office were a fire hazard, and Steelcase received its first patent in 1913 for a steel wastebasket. Founded as the Metal Office Furniture Company in 1912, the company has always been an innovator in office furnishings. It began, and remains, in **Grand Rapids**.

Stockwell, Madelon Louisa (1845–1924)

First woman to attend the **University of Michigan**. She was admitted in 1870; she graduated with a B.A. in 1872. She also received an honorary degree from the university in 1912.

Her childhood diaries were published as *A Michigan Childhood: the Journals of Madelon Louisa Stockwell, 1856-1860*. Stockwell Hall, an all-female residence at U of M, is named for her.

Stookey, Noel Paul (1937–)

Singer and songwriter. "Stook" is one-third of the famous folk music trio Peter, Paul, and Mary. He attended **Michigan State University**.

Stroh Brewing Company

Bernhard Stroh immigrated to the United States in 1850 and began selling his lager beer first door-to-door and then as the Lion Brewery. In 1902 the brewery, by then **Detroit**'s largest, was renamed Stroh Brewing Company. The brewery survived **Prohibition** and by the mid-1980s was the third largest in America. Stroh closed in 1999.

Suomi College

Fearing a loss of identity among Finnish immigrants, J.K. Nikander established the college as a seminary in 1896. During the 1920s Suomi became a liberal arts college. Now called Finlandia University, it is the only college in the country founded by Finnish Americans.

Supremes, The

Singing group. The Supremes—Diana Ross, Mary Wilson, and Florence Ballard—were originally called the Primettes. The name was changed to the Supremes with the release of their first record. The Supremes' "Where Did Our Love Go?" went to number one, and the group went on to record five number one hits in the next year. From 1965 to 1969, seven more songs hit number one, all with Diana Ross singing lead vocals. In 1967, the name of the group was changed to Diana Ross and the Supremes; Ballard left the group, replaced by Cindy Birdsong. They gave their last performance in 1970.

A Stroh beer delivery truck, 1910

T

Tawas Point Lighthouse

The curving hook of Ottawa Point has long formed a natural shelter for Tawas Bay and in the mid-19th century frequently was used as a harbor of refuge for vessels escaping squalls out on Lake Huron. But the end of the point was difficult to discern at night or in inclement weather; in 1876 a light was added to Tawas Point.

No longer in operation, Tawas Point Lighthouse is part of Tawas Point State Park, a fascinating attraction for maritime buffs. Tawas Point is also a mecca for birdwatchers, especially in migration season. The lighthouse is at 686 Tawas Beach Road, East Tawas.

Taylor, Annie Edson (c. 1838–1924)

First over Niagara Falls. She was a Bay City schoolteacher. On October 24, 1901, she was harnessed inside a wooden barrel, towed into the rush of the Niagara River, and cut loose. She plunged over the falls, and 17 minutes later made it to the Canadian shore. Emerging from the barrel, she declared, "No one ought ever to do that again."

At the time, Edson claimed to be 43 years old, but genealogical records confirmed her to be 63. She failed to attain the fame and fortune she was hoping for and died destitute in Niagara Falls over 20 years later.

Danny Thomas, entertainer and founder of St. Jude's Children's Research Hospital.

Techno Music

The unique music mix originated in **Detroit** in the 1980s. Sometimes described as cold and dark, it is a marriage of electronics and a throbbing beat, associated with the use of the TR 808 drum machine.

Territorial Road

One of three important east-west roads, it connected the second-tier cities and followed much the same route as today's Interstate 94. Travelers could go by stagecoach from **Detroit** to St. Joseph, where they would board a steamer for Chicago. The trip took five days.

Thomas, Danny (1914–1991)

Entertainer, philanthropist. One of television's pioneers, Thomas began his career as a nightclub performer. After some early success in television, Thomas created his breakthrough role in *Make Room for Daddy*, a semi-autobiographical situation comedy, in which he played singer/comedian Danny Williams. Thomas and actor Sheldon Leonard then formed Thomas-Leonard Productions, the production company responsible for such hits as *The Real McCoys*, *The Andy Griffith Show*, *The Joey Bishop Show*, *The Bill Dana Show*, and *The Dick Van Dyke Show*.

Thomas founded St. Jude's Children's Research Hospital. For his untiring work with the institution, he received the Congressional Medal of Honor in 1983.

Thomas, Helen (1920–)

Journalist. After graduating from Wayne State University, Helen Thomas served as a copy girl for the *Washington Daily News*. Joining United Press International in 1943, she wrote radio news and articles for papers around the country.

In 1960, Thomas began to cover President-elect John F. Kennedy and became part of the UPI White House team. In 1974, she was the first female White House bureau chief of a wire service. In all, she covered nine presidents. She captured her experiences in two books, *Dateline: White House* and *Front Row at the White House: My Life and Times*.

In 2000, Thomas became a columnist for the Hearst Corporation.

Thomas House, Dr. Nathan

The Dr. Nathan Thomas House, built in 1835, still stands on Cass Street in Schoolcraft. Dr. Nathan Thomas and his wife, Pamela, hid about 1,500 fugitive slaves traveling the **Underground Railroad**. The doctor treated their wounds and illnesses before letting them continue their journey to freedom.

Thomas, Isiah (1961–)

Basketball player. He played on the **Detroit Pistons** basketball team from 1981 to 1994. The Pistons' all-time leading scorer, he averaged 19.2 points per game, for a career total of 18,822. He led **Detroit** to two NBA titles, in 1989 and 1990. He retired in 1990 and was elected to the NBA Hall of Fame in 2000.

Thompson, Ruth (1887–1970)

Legislator. A Whitehall native, she was elected as the first female State Representative in 1938. In 1950, she was the first woman elected to the U.S. House of Representatives and received the first House Judiciary Committee appointment granted to a woman. She served three terms and gained recognition for her work as a children's rights advocate.

Three Oaks Bicycle Museum and Information Center

The bicycle museum combines town history and the history of cycling. Housed in a historical 1898 Michigan Central Railroad Depot in downtown Three Oaks, the museum, at One Oak Street, is open daily, 9 a.m. to 5 p.m.

Tiger Stadium

Tiger Stadium opened in 1912, but baseball had been played on the site since 1896. Originally named after owner Frank Navin, the stadium

Ruth Thompson was the first woman elected to the U.S. House of Representatives.

A sign above the visitors' clubhouse at Tiger Stadium read, "Visitors' Clubhouse. No Visitors Allowed."

To slow down Ty Cobb's bunts, Tiger Stadium groundskeepers soaked an area in front of home plate. They called it Cobb's Lake.

was built on the old Bennett Field. It was renamed Briggs Stadium in 1938, two years after Walter Briggs took over the team. It was finally named Tiger Stadium in 1961.

The stadium was home to the **Detroit Tigers** for nearly a century. The best of the stadium's 52,400 seats put fans as close to the action as in any ballpark in the league. Some seats, however, were behind posts. And the upper deck's overhang kept fans in other seats from seeing balls that were hit into the air.

Tiger Stadium was the playground for the likes of Lou Whitaker, Alan Trammell, Kirk Gibson, **Al Kaline**, and **Ty Cobb**. There were a few modifications over the years, including various replacements of the centerfield scoreboard and a large food court called Tiger Plaza. But the features that made Tiger Stadium unique remained. Since 2000, the Tigers have played at **Comerica Park**. Many fans were saddened when the last game was played at The Corner, but Tiger Stadium remains standing. There has been talk of college or minor league baseball teams using the facility.

Todd Company, A.M.

Founded in 1869 by Peppermint King Albert M. Todd (1850–1931), it is the world's largest supplier of natural peppermint and spearmint oils. Todd revolutionized the industry by developing purity testing processes. The company is headquartered in **Kalamazoo**.

Toledo War

The **Northwest Ordinance** of 1787 called for establishment of "one or two States in … territory which lies north of an east and west line drawn through the southerly bend or extreme of Lake Michigan." Later surveyors discovered that the "southerly bend" of the lake actually was farther south than was previously thought and included a 468-square-mile chunk of land claimed by Ohio.

Both Michigan and Ohio saw Toledo's potential as a great commercial port city, and neither was willing to give it up. In 1817, U.S. Surveyor General Edward Tiffin, a former Ohio governor, ordered a survey that gave the so-called Toledo Strip to Ohio. Michigan Territorial Governor **Lewis Cass** protested to President James Monroe, who ordered another survey. Although Ohio still claimed to own the Toledo Strip, it did nothing as Michigan assumed control of the area.

The controversy cooled until December 11, 1833, when Michigan sought statehood. Ohio,

Toledo Strip
Western Part of Upper Peninsula

already a state, successfully lobbied Congress to block Michigan's admission to the union until it gave up the Toledo Strip. Ohio refused to budge, so Michigan's territorial council passed the Pains and Penalties Act, a resolution that set a heavy fine for anyone other than Michigan or federal officials who exerted authority over the area. Ohio Governor Robert Lucas countered by creating a county in the disputed area, which he named for himself. The Michigan contingent had had enough so, in April 1835, Territorial Governor **Stevens T. Mason** formed a posse and headed for Ohio.

The war involved more one-upmanship than gunfire. The Ohio legislature appropriated $300,000 for its military, so Michigan appropriated $315,000. The Michigan force fired a few shots into the air and arrested a handful of Ohio surveyors and imprisoned them in Tecumseh. An Ohioan stabbed Joseph

During the Toledo War, Gov. Stevens Mason led his army into a swamp near Perrysburg, Ohio. Although the Toledo contingent also was in the swamp, the two armies couldn't find each other and thus avoided bloodshed.

At the end of the Toledo War, Ohio was in possession of the Toledo Strip and Michigan had the Upper Peninsula.

Wood, a Michigan deputy sheriff. The injury, which occurred during a bar brawl, was minor, and Wood recovered. He was the war's only casualty.

Mason returned from his saber-rattling excursion to find he had been fired from the territorial governorship by President Andrew Jackson, who had installed a new governor more favorable to Ohio's claim. The citizens of Michigan, notwithstanding Jackson's choice of territorial governor, set up their own state government with Mason as its governor. Meanwhile, Ohio conducted a new survey that, not surprisingly, included the Toledo Strip within its borders.

It was another year before, on January 26, 1836, Michigan became the 26th state of the union. Congress insisted that Michigan give up claim to the Toledo Strip in exchange for statehood. As consolation, Michigan received 9,000 square miles of wilderness in the western **Upper Peninsula**. Although no one knew it at the time, the "booby prize" was a vast source of mineral riches. Michigan inadvertently struck a great deal. The city of Toledo remains in Lucas County, Ohio.

Travelers Club International Restaurant and Tuba Museum

The walls are lined with more than 30 tubas, most in playing condition. Included is the only known example of a double-E flat Helicon tuba inscribed "The Majestic Monster." Made in Austria *c.* 1915, it played for many years in the Community Band of Iron Mountain. The Tuba Museum, at 2138 Hamilton Road, Okemos, opens every day at 8 a.m.

Traverse City

Visitors who fly into Traverse City alight at Cherry Capital Airport. For cherry lovers, this part of the state is heaven. Michigan produces 70 to 75 percent of the tart cherries in the United States, and most of those, upward of 228.5 million pounds' worth, are grown in the area around Traverse City.

The first cherry trees were grown in 1852 by the area's first European settler, Peter Dougherty, a Presbyterian missionary. People thought he was crazy to plant a cherry orchard in the sandy soil of what is now Grand Traverse County. Luckily he ignored them. More than 150 years later, cherries still thrive in this unlikely environment, aided by the lake

The brick storefronts on Traverse City's Front Street date back 100 years. Also on Front Street is the 1,200-seat City Opera House, built in 1891.

View on Front Street, Traverse City, Mich.

FRONT STREET LOOKING WEST, TRAVERSE CITY, MICH.—2

© O. W. PECK

TRAVERSE CITY, MICH.

5A-H547

T

The anti-slavery campaigner Sojourner Truth was "commanded in a vision" to take her name, which described her vocation as a traveling preacher.

effects of nearby Lake Michigan, which tempers both the frigid winter wind and the scorching summer air.

In the early part of the 19th century, the area was home to Ottawa, Chippewa, and Potowatomi Indians, called the Three Brothers because of their close social relations. The **Native Americans** were driven away by settlers, arriving in the 1840s, who saw the forested areas in close proximity to Lake Michigan and realized the potential to create a **logging** industry. The first lumber mill was opened by

William Boardman near the mouth of a river that leads into Grand Traverse Bay; the river is named for him. Boardman sold his mill to Perry Hannah, a businessman from Chicago who is considered the founding father of Traverse City for his influence on the developing town. Hannah built docks to the bay and bridges over the river.

Lumbering created a boomtown. Houses, schools, and churches sprang up. There were libraries and opera houses. Traverse City came to be known as the Queen City of the North. But by the early 1900s, the forests had been decimated. The lumber industry faded and the industrial focus shifted to agriculture. The Queen City gave way to the Cherry Capital of the World.

In recent years tourism has given the cherry industry a run for its money. The Grand Traverse Bay region is an alluring playground for winter sports enthusiasts. The area has bunny hills, more advanced slopes, and miles of trails for cross-country skiing and snowshoeing. Summer vacationers too are attracted to the area, with more than 180 miles of sandy shoreline and 149 clear lakes. Among the more popular summer activities is diving for shipwrecks in Manitou Passage, a treacherous stretch of water that has pulled many ships down; scuba shops offer training classes. And every July Traverse City celebrates its fruit-growing prowess with the **National Cherry Festival**. Area attractions include the **City Opera House**, built during the lumbering boom, **Grand Traverse Lighthouse**, one of the oldest on the lakes, and, not far from Traverse City, **Sleeping Bear Dunes National Lakeshore**, a 35-mile stretch of coastal dunes, some rising nearly 500 feet.

Truth, Sojourner (1797–1883)

Abolitionist. Born into slavery as Isabella Baumfree, she changed her name in 1843, believing it to be God's will, and became what her name implied: a traveling preacher.

Although she never learned to read or write, she was a fiery speaker. She stood nearly six feet tall; when asked if she was a man in disguise, she bared her breasts for the audience.

By the time she was freed by the New York State Anti-Slavery Act of 1828, she had already run away from her master in Ulster County. When she found out that one of her sons had been sold from New York to Alabama, she sued on the basis of New York law and won his return.

She was the first person in the country to link slaves' oppression with women's oppression. She did not believe in traditional roles for women.

She lived in several religious communities, including one in Michigan, which became her home. In 1881, when the state legislature was considering a bill to institute capital punishment, she spoke to the legislators about God's love. The bill was dropped.

During the **Civil War**, she gathered food and clothing for black regiments and visited President Abraham Lincoln in the White House. For a short time after the war, she advocated for a "Negro state" in the West. She continued to speak on issues such as women's rights, religion, and temperance until 1875, when the grandson who accompanied her became ill.

Tucker, Preston (1903–1956)

Automobile designer. He created a car ahead of its time, with independent four-wheel suspension, a swiveling center headlight, and safety features such as a padded dashboard and pop-out windshield. Although his design was widely acclaimed, he couldn't compete with the Big Three automakers, which put him out of business after a single model year.

Of the 51 Tuckers built, most still survive. One is on display at the Napa Valley winery owned by **Francis Ford Coppola**, who directed the 1988 film *Tucker: The Man and His Dream*.

U

STOCKHOLDERS
OF THE UNDERGROUND
R. R. COMPANY
Hold on to Your Stock!!

The market has an upward tendency.   By the express train which arrived this morning at 3 o'clock, fifteen thousand dollars worth of human merchandise, consisting of twenty-nine able-bodied men and women, fresh and sound, from the Carolina and Kentucky plantations, have arrived safe at the depot on the other side, where all our sympathising colonization friends may have an opportunity of expressing their sympathy by bringing forward donations of ploughs, &c., farming utensils, pick axes and hoes, and not old clothes; as these emigrants all can till the soil.   N. B.—Stockholders don't forget the meeting to-day at 2 o'clock at the ferry on the Canada side.   All persons desiring to take stock in this prosperous company, be sure to be on hand.   **By Order of the**

Detroit, April 19, **1853.**   **BOARD OF DIRECTORS.**

An advertisement to "Stockholders of the Underground R.R. Company" was a thinly disguised message that runaway slaves had arrived safely in Canada.

Underground Railroad

With its antislavery sentiments and lengthy international border, Michigan was a haven for runaway slaves from the 1830s until the **Civil War** started in 1861. Runaways who managed to cross the Ohio River were conducted by "stationmasters" from station to station along informal, secret routes to Canada.

Although stations were no more than 10 to 15 miles apart, stationmasters knew only the next stop along the route, never the preceding one, so if they were caught they couldn't break the chain. "Fares" generally took one of two primary lines to **Detroit**, the last stop on the U.S. side. They caught the Central Michigan line at Cassopolis, near the Indiana boarder, and traveled through Schoolcraft and Climax to **Battle Creek**, then along a route similar to today's Interstate 94: Marshall, Albion, Parma, Jackson, Michigan Centre, Dexter, **Ann Arbor**, Ypsilanti, Plymouth, and finally Detroit, known as Midnight in the underground code. The Southern line began either at Morenci, on the Ohio border, or a bit farther north, at Hillsdale, and went through Adrian and Tecumseh to Ann Arbor, where it continued along the same route to Detroit.

Travelers were hidden during the day and sent on their way at night by foot, horse, carriage, or occasionally by train. They might be disguised or secreted in wagons with false compartments or in caskets or boxes. Some of the conductors were themselves fugitives but had stopped running long enough to help others.

It was a dangerous business. Escapees who were caught might be beaten or whipped and taken back to their masters in chains. Entering a "free" state didn't necessarily make a slave free. In one well-publicized case, a family named Crosswhite, who had escaped to Marshall and settled, were pursued by slave catchers from Kentucky. The Crosswhites had arranged a signal, the firing of a single shot, in case they were caught. On a January morning in 1847, neighbors heard the

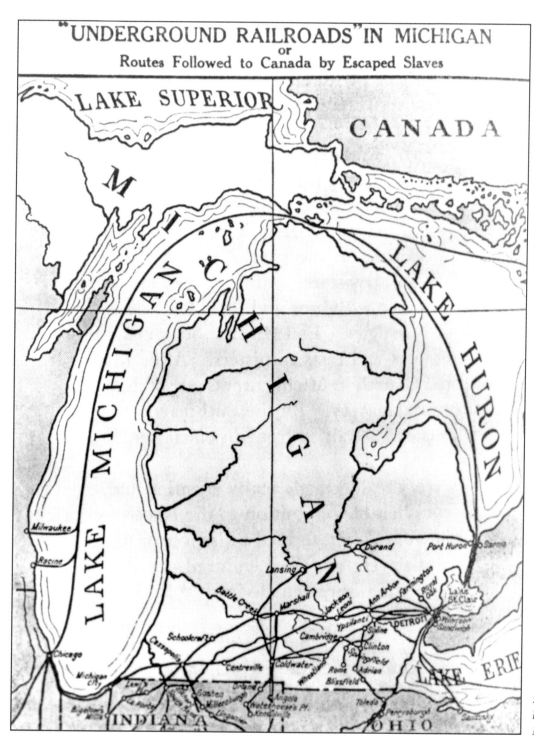

Several Underground Railroad lines ran across southern Michigan.

signal and nearly a hundred people ran to the Crosswhites' assistance. Chased away, the Kentuckians sued and won. The citizens of Marshall were fined the amount the family would have sold for on the auction block. But by the time the trial was over, the Crosswhites had been safely smuggled into Canada.

Robert Cromwell, who had escaped from Missouri in 1840, was located by his owner in Detroit in 1847 and dragged to the courthouse by the owner's agent, to be reclaimed. His shouts attracted abolitionist leaders, who organized a crowd to go after the Missouri agent, as they themselves spirited Cromwell

U

across the Canadian border. The agent, who had been beaten by the crowd, was charged with kidnapping. He was acquitted, but the six months he spent in jail awaiting trial served as a warning to other slave catchers.

Quakers were in the forefront of the Underground Railroad movement. **Laura Haviland**, an Adrian abolitionist, was so effective, Southern slave owners put a $3,000 price on her head. **Erastus Hussey**, who served in both houses of Michigan's legislature, had a station in his **Battle Creek** home.

Estimates are that anywhere from 20,000 to 100,000 fugitive slaves "rode" the Underground Railroad into Canada.

United Auto Workers

The UAW was founded in May 1935 through a merger of federal labor unions originally set up by the AFL. The new union broke away from the AFL in 1936, and **Homer S. Martin** was elected president. Automobile workers joined in rapidly increasing numbers, and by late fall of 1936 the UAW had 300,000 members. The union prepared to demand recognition from the giants of the industry—General Motors, Chrysler Corporation, and Ford Motor Company. When Martin asked the officers of General Motors for a conference of collective bargaining, he was told that the workers should take up grievances with local plant managers.

Before the national UAW could respond, a group of union militants in **Flint** took matters into their own hands. The **Flint Sit-Down Strike**, which began December 30, 1936, paralyzed the General Motors empire and affected

National Council of the United Auto Workers, in Washington, D.C.

112,000 of the company's 150,000 workers. The workers occupied the plant and stopped production for six weeks, until General Motors agreed to recognize the UAW as the bargaining agents for auto workers and not to discriminate against union members.

Chrysler presently followed suit, but Ford held out. The company used in-house spies and a squad of thugs to root out anyone associated with the union. On May 26, 1937, in what came to be known as the **Battle of the Overpass**, UAW organizers including **Walter Reuther** were openly brutalized outside the **Ford River Rouge** plant, and the public began to turn against Ford. In 1941, Ford became the last of the Big Three to recognize the UAW by signing a union-shop agreement, the first in the auto industry.

Reuther, Martin's successor as the union's president, served from 1946 until his death in 1970. He held enormous economic power; during his tenure UAW members became one of the best-paid groups of industrial workers in the country.

The UAW was one of the first major unions to organize African-American workers. In the 1940s, the union began collective bargaining in the area of gender inequity. Women historically comprised only a small proportion of the labor force in the automotive and aerospace industries—about 15 percent of UAW membership, except during **World War II**. In 1944, **Millie Jeffrey** signed on as director of the newly formed UAW Women's Bureau. She organized the first UAW women's conference to protest the massive postwar layoffs of women production workers. She ran the union's radio station and its community relations and consumer affairs departments. Years later, two UAW leaders were founders of the National Organization for Women and Olga Madar, the UAW's first female vice president, served as the first president of the Coalition of Labor Union Women.

Under Jeffrey's influence, the UAW strongly supported federal legislation to eliminate sex discrimination in employment. In 1970, the

UAW became the first U.S. union to endorse the Equal Rights Amendment. The greater presence of women in the UAW also has prompted union attention to the issues of sexual harassment and comparable worth.

In the 1990s, the UAW began to focus on new areas of organizing, both geographically and in terms of occupations. Today, this largest labor union in North America has more than 700,000 members and is organized into approximately 950 local unions.

University of Michigan

The University of Michigan has long been among the most prestigious universities in the nation. Located in **Ann Arbor** since 1837, the university is at the center of the action in the city of 250,000 residents and 40,000 students.

Burton Memorial Tower, a University of Michigan landmark, houses the 55-bell Charles Baird Carillon.

U

The University of Michigan was founded in Detroit in 1817 via a legislative act. The Rev. **John Monteith** was the first president of the Catholepistemiad, or University of Michigania, as it was then called. The first graduating class, in 1845, consisted of 11 men.

The 1850s were a big decade for the UOM. Although it did not become official until 1915, the medical school, first of the university's three top-tier professional schools—the others are business and law—began to teach classes. Courses in engineering, the first observatory, the first student newspaper, the law school, and cricket, the first organized sport on campus, all came to the university during that period. The famous maize and blue colors were adopted by the 1867 class, and in 1912 the regents applied them to the entire university.

In 1868 Gabriel Franklin Hargo became the first black student to attend the UOM. He graduated two years later, the same year the first woman, **Madelon Stockwell**, was admitted; the first female dorm on campus, still in use, was named for her. In 1873, the University Football Association was founded, leading to the famous Michigan football that fans nationwide continue to enjoy. In 1875 came the Homeopathic Medical College, College of Dental Surgery, School of Pharmacy, and School of Mines, which would become one of the most competitive architecture programs in the country.

In 1876 the university had another first with the admission of its first black female student, Mary Henrietta Graham. In 1879 UOM won its first intercollegiate football game. The following year, the music program was established.

The *Michigan Daily*, still the main student-run campus newspaper, commenced publication in 1890. The yearbook, *Michiganensian*, began publication in 1887. And a year later, in 1888, the famous school theme song, "The Victors," was written by Louis Elbel.

As the country moved into the 20th century, the university updated itself by creating a

building for male students, faculty, and staff in 1904. The Michigan Union opened to all students in 1920 and remains a center of student activity today. In 1913, the famous **Hill Auditorium**, a "monument to perfect acoustics," was dedicated. And two years later, the first two residence halls—Martha Cook and Helen Newberry—were opened; those two buildings are still currently in operation, providing housing as women-only dorms. In 1924 the Business Administration school was added, completing the triangle of professional schools. The University of Michigan continues to update its policies, programs, and buildings.

University of Michigan Medical Center

Since it opened in 1850, the medical center has consistently ranked among the top medical institutions in the country. In 2003, it was placed ninth on the *U.S. News & World Report* magazine honor roll, with excellent rankings in 11 of 17 "best hospitals" specialties.

UOM researchers developed the EKG machine in 1913 and, in 1940, created the nation's first human genetics program. Other breakthroughs include discovery of the two classes of diabetes, discovery of the genes that cause cystic fibrosis and Huntington's disease, and the world's first gene therapy protocol for AIDS.

The medical school, considered one of the nation's best, graduates about 170 physicians a year.

Upjohn, William (1853–1932)

Founder of the Upjohn Company. William Upjohn was one of 12 children, four of whom became doctors. He invented a pill that could be crushed easily, making it likely the ingredients would be used more effectively by the body. His patent of the pill in 1885 was the genesis of his company.

Upjohn established the commission-manager form of government in **Kalamazoo**. He was subsequently elected mayor.

The philanthropic Upjohn established the Kalamazoo Community Foundation. He also donated the city's Civic Auditorium. Upjohn earned the title Kalamazoo's First Citizen and, after he died, all businesses and schools in the city were closed during the hour of his funeral.

Upper Peninsula

When Michigan became a state in 1837, its Upper Peninsula was a great mystery. It was a vast land that barely hinted at its potential. Beyond the French explorers and *voyageurs*, few white men had ventured into this forested wilderness. Early settlers had been living and working in the **fur trade** at Sault Ste. Marie since the 1600s. And there were the long-heard Jesuit missionary tales of untapped mineral wealth.

Michigan had grudgingly accepted the Upper Peninsula, or U.P., as part of an unpopular compromise that gave Michigan its statehood. The concession came after the bitterly contested **Toledo War** (actually a war of words, not bullets). In the end, in exchange for becoming a state, Michigan got the Upper Peninsula and Ohio took control over the strip of territory, including Toledo, along the Michigan-Ohio border.

In terms of natural resources, what some thought would be a raw deal turned out to be a steal. Just as Michigan was becoming a state, the U.P.'s fabulous deposits of pure copper were being uncovered, based on late 1830s discoveries by surveyor **Douglass Houghton**. Soon afterward iron ore deposits were also unearthed. A **mining** boom followed, bringing

Above left: William Upjohn, mayor of Kalamazoo.

Above right: Opera House, Fayette State Park, Upper Peninsula.

Below: The 73,000-acre Pictured Rocks National Lakeshore provides year-round fun in the Upper Peninsula.

U

prosperity and waves of **immigrants**, many of them from Finland and England's Cornwall. New communities such as Iron Mountain and Copper Harbor were created. Moving the copper and iron to market would result in the construction of the **Soo Locks**, with the first locks opening in 1855. While mining would continue into the mid-20th century, the glory days were long gone.

Today tourism is the mainstay of many Upper Peninsula communities. The growth of the tourist trade was particularly aided by the 1957 opening of the **Mackinac Bridge**, which connects the Upper and Lower peninsulas and makes the U.P. easily accessible by car. Just across the bridge is **St. Ignace**, a gateway to the U.P. and to **Mackinac Island**, a popular resort community.

Outdoor lovers flock to this four-season destination. U.P. activities range from boating, fishing, and hunting to Alpine and cross-country skiing and snowmobiling. The Ottawa and **Hiawatha** National forests cover much of the land, with **Isle Royale National Park** and **Pictured Rocks National Lakeshore** preserving some of the peninsula's most scenic and impressive terrain. Aspen, birch, fir, maple, and spruce shelter black bears, timber wolves, deer, and moose. Roaring waterfalls, like those found at Tahquamenon Falls State Park near

Waterfalls are a common sight in the Upper Peninsula.

Paradise, are scattered across the countryside. In the Ottawa National Forest, near Ironwood in the western U.P., more than 35 forest waterfalls are accessible by woodland hiking trails. The 11-mile Black River National Forest Scenic Byway at Bessemer follows waterfalls on a winding path to Lake Superior.

Preserved examples of Michigan's mining heritage may be seen at the **Calumet Historic District** in Calumet and the **Quincy Mining Company Historic District** in Hancock. The **Michigan Iron Industry Museum** in Negaunee overlooks the site of the first iron forge in the Lake Superior region. At the **Great Lakes Shipwreck Museum** in Whitefish Point ship disasters—including the wreck of the *Edmund Fitzgerald* ore carrier—are recalled.

Popular annual events in the U.P. include the **International 500 Snowmobile Race**, Sault Ste. Marie, early February; **National Lilac Festival**, **Mackinac Island**, mid-June; **Upper Peninsula Championship Rodeo**, Iron River, mid-July; **Upper Peninsula State Fair**, Escanaba, mid-August; and **Michinemackinong PowWow**, St. Ignace, early September.

Upper Peninsula Championship Rodeo

West is best—the Western **Upper Peninsula**, that is—for professional rodeo performances in Iron River in mid-July. Calf-roping, bronco- and bull-riding, and barrel-racing are just some of the events. A chuckwagon breakfast and Wild West parade are also featured.

Upper Peninsula State Fair

The **Upper Peninsula** stages its own state fair each year in Escanaba, in mid-August. Midway rides, livestock shows, crafts, and food judgings fill the days. And then there's fair food… .

U.S. National Ski Hall of Fame and Museum

The museum follows the growth and development of the sport of skiing and honors hundreds of extraordinary skiers. There are over 100 displays, including the story of the 10th Mountain Division, the first mountain skiing regiment in the U.S. Army. The museum, at 610 Palms Avenue, Ishpeming, is open Monday through Saturday, 10 a.m. to 5 p.m.

U.S. Olympic Education Center

In February 1985, Northern Michigan University in Marquette caught up with Lake Placid, New York, and Colorado Springs, Colorado, to become the third U.S. Olympic Training Center. Four years later, in February 1989, NMU left the field behind and was named the only U.S. Olympic Education Center.

The USOEC's primary program enables world-class student athletes to attend high school or college while training for the Olympics. The resident program accepts athletes ranked among the top 10 in their sport, subject to approval by the sport's governing board, NMU, and the USOEC. Students receive in-state tuition and other benefits including coaching, free use of training facilities, and free sports medicine services. To stay in the program, they must maintain a minimum grade point average.

Training programs are available in boxing, short track speedskating, weightlifting, biathlon, cross-country skiing, luge, and Greco-Roman wrestling.

Training facilities on and around the NMU campus include the only natural luge track in the country, 50- and 70-meter ski jumps, and hundreds of miles of cross-country ski trails.

USOEC also offers training camps, competitions, clinics for coaches and officials, and an educational program for athletes retired from U.S. Olympic and Pan American to transition from sports to the business world.

USS *Silversides*

This famous **World War II** Gato submarine is docked in Muskegon at the **Great Lakes** Naval Memorial and Museum. It was commissioned into the U.S. Navy shortly after the attack on Pearl Harbor on December 15, 1941. Its mission during the course of the war was to stop raw materials such as oil, coal, and food from being delivered to Japan. It sank 30 ships and damaged 14; it is the only remaining submarine from World War II that holds a most-ships-sunk title. The historical naval memorial is open for tours. Hours vary.

USS Silversides *was commissioned into the U.S. Navy shortly after the attack on Pearl Harbor.*

Van Allsburg, Chris (1949–)

Children's author, illustrator. The **Grand Rapids** native is well known for his mysterious stories and eerie, dreamlike images. He has won two Caldecott Medals, for *Jumanji* (1982) and *Polar Express* (1986); both have been made into movies.

Vandenberg, Arthur (1884–1951)

Senator. The Republican Vandenberg served as United States Senator for Michigan from 1928 to 1951, becoming Senate minority leader in 1935. Early in his career, he was known as an isolationist, but the attack on Pearl Harbor began his conversion to a position of internationalism in foreign policy.

In 1947, Vandenberg became chairman of the Senate Foreign Relations Committee. He became known as a master of bi-partisanship, helping the Truman Administration bring about such programs as the Marshall Plan, which he described as "the final product of eight months of more intensive study by more devoted minds than I have ever known to concentrate upon any one objective in all my twenty years in Congress."

Van Hoosen, Bertha (1863–1952)

Physician. Born in Rochester, she was an early **University of Michigan** Medical School graduate and co-founder and first national president of the American Medical Women's Association. She was a world-renowned surgeon and teacher of surgery and was instrumental in developing the use of twilight sleep for women in childbirth. She wrote *Petticoat Surgeon* (1947), a narrative of the life of a pioneer physician in the Midwest.

Van Raalte, Albertus (1811–1876)

Minister. Leader of a persecuted secessionist Christian in the Netherlands, he took his followers to Michigan and founded Holland. He also founded schools, including Hope College. He opposed slavery and urged his followers to vote for Abraham Lincoln.

Vernors Ginger Ale

In 1858, **Detroit** pharmacist James Vernor began to experiment with a ginger ale recipe. When he was called up to fight in the **Civil War**, he placed his brew into an oaken cask. On his return from the war, he opened the cask and found that it had transformed into a delicious drink, rich with ginger flavor. Demand for the drink grew, and Vernor and his son blended, bottled, and sold the beverage to other pharmacies, at first locally and then in other cities. Later, the Vernor's Company opened a bottling plant in downtown Detroit. In 1966, the Vernor family sold the company.

Arthur Vandenberg was Senator of Michigan from 1928 to 1951.

Walbridge, David S. (1802–1868)

Statesman. He moved to **Kalamazoo** from Vermont in the 1840s and soon became one of the city's leading businessmen. A committed Whig, he was named permanent chair of the 1854 convention in Jackson, where the **Republican Party** was born. He served in Congress from 1855 to 1858.

Walker Tavern

For more than 160 years, the intersection known as Cambridge Junction played a role in the development of the state of Michigan. The location, which was significant to **Native Americans** long before roads were developed, became economically vital soon after the first settlers arrived.

Walker Tavern was a stopping-off place for stagecoaches and pioneer wagons. James Fenimore Cooper stayed there, as did Daniel Webster.

Restored as a museum in 1921, the tavern chronicles early stagecoach travel. It's a part of Cambridge Junction Historic State Park and is open May through October.

Walk-in-the-Water

Built for passenger service between Black Rock, New York, and **Detroit** and making stops at Cleveland and Erie, *Walk-in-the-Water* was the first steamboat on the upper **Great Lakes**. Named for a Wyandotte Indian chief, the steamboat entered service in the summer of 1818. When full it carried about 150 passengers, though it carried 200 passengers to **Mackinac Island** and Green Bay on its first trip into Lake Michigan, in August 1821.

The ship's first season was also its last. Encountering a stiff gale after leaving Black Rock, on October 31 the ship fetched up on the shore and was a total loss.

Wallace, Sippie (1898–1986)

Blues/jazz singer. Born Beulah Thomas, she was known as the Texas Nightingale. She moved to **Detroit** in 1929 and performed in black cabarets and clubs. She appeared at the **Ann Arbor Blues and Jazz Festival** in 1972. Despite suffering a stroke, she continued her career and was inducted into the **Michigan Women's Hall of Fame** in 1993.

Wallenberg, Raoul (1912–?)

Diplomat. He studied architecture at the **University of Michigan** in **Ann Arbor** beginning in 1931. In 1944 he was sent to Hungary to rescue Jews from being deported to concentration camps. Credited with saving 100,000 Jews, he was eventually arrested and was never seen again.

War of 1812

Rumors of unrest among the **Native Americans** were often heard during the early years in Michigan. In 1811, Shawnee leader Tecumseh and his brother, known as the Prophet, were making hostile threats as they attempted to unite the tribes of Ohio, Indiana, and Michigan in opposition to further white settlement. In the late fall of 1811, Indiana Governor William Henry Harrison

Lieutenant Oliver Hazard Perry (standing) commanded the American fleet against British squadrons at Lake Erie on September 10, 1813.

would defeat the Indians at the Battle of Tippecanoe.

But remote frontier outposts such as **Detroit** continued to fear attacks. The American belief that the British were helping the Indians was a major cause of support for the June 12, 1812, declaration of war against Great Britain. Michigan Territory Governor **William Hull**, a Revolutionary War veteran, was given command of the Army of the Northwest under orders to invade Canada. Hull, who had brought in troops from Ohio and Indiana, crossed the **Detroit River** on July 12. Rather than capture Fort Malden, a nearby British fort, Hull waited for artillery that was unable to get through Ohio and Michigan countryside controlled by British forces and their Indian allies. An overcautious Hull eventually pulled his men back across the river into the fort at Detroit on August 8. When British General Sir Isaac Brock arrived a week later and advanced toward the town, Hull surrendered Detroit without a fight. At about the same time, the British surprised and overtook a small American garrison at **Fort Mackinac** without a shot being fired. Brock and British forces would go on to seize control of the entire upper **Great Lakes**.

In January 1813, American troops were sent on an ill-fated move north from Ohio to Frenchtown (now Monroe) on the Raisin River in southeastern Michigan. Although the Americans initially drove off the Canadian militia and Indians who were guarding the town, they could not sustain the heavier fighting that ensued on January 22 when the town's defenders returned with reinforcements. The American force surrendered and the prisoners were taken to Fort Malden. The next morning Indians swept down, killing the wounded American soldiers who had been left behind. "Remember the Raisin!" became a battle cry.

The U.S. government finally realized control of the lakes would be necessary to defeat the British. In September 1813, a small American fleet, with Lieutenant Oliver Hazard Perry in command, routed the British in the Battle of Lake Erie, leading them to abandon Detroit. Harrison, who had succeeded Hull as the American commander, defeated the British and Indian allies in October at the Battle of the Thames near Toronto, Canada. Although the Americans regained Detroit, most of Michigan was still controlled by the British at Fort Mackinac. But when the Treaty of Ghent was signed on Christmas Eve 1814, ending the war, it reaffirmed the prewar boundaries between the United States and Canada along the Great Lakes.

Wayne County Courthouse

Once described as the "most sumptuous building in Michigan," the four-story Beaux-Arts courthouse is one of **Detroit**'s landmark structures. Built in 1897 by John Scott, it was an architectural masterpiece. By 1970, it had deteriorated so much that the county considered demolishing it. Through private and historic preservation funds, the courthouse was restored and reopened in 1987.

Wayne County Courthouse, Detroit, was restored and reopened in 1987.

Wheelock, Julia (1833–1900)

Civil War heroine. She left her home in Ionia to nurse her wounded, dying brother and served in hospitals until the end of the war. Called the Florence Nightingale of Michigan, she spent 12-hour days feeding and offering moral support to soldiers, then baked pies to take to the hospitals the next day. She worked to improve the unsanitary conditions of what she saw less as healing places than as repositories for the dying. She described her experiences in a journal, later published as *Boys in White: The Experiences of a Hospital Agent in and Around Washington*. She was posthumously inducted into the **Michigan Women's Hall of Fame** in 2002.

White, Byron (1917–2002)

U.S. Supreme Court Justice. A Rhodes Scholar, he played running back with the **Detroit Lions** in 1940, leading the league in rushing before retiring in 1941. He was named to the Supreme Court by President Kennedy in 1962 and served until 1993. He entered the National Football Hall of Fame in 1954.

Charline Rainey White was the first African American woman in the Michigan House of Representatives.

White, Charline Rainey (n.d.)

Legislator. The first African American woman in the Michigan House of Representatives, the **Detroit** native was elected in 1950.

Whiting, Margaret (1924–)

Singer. Margaret Whiting was one of the top pop/jazz singers of the 1940s and '50s; she recorded more than 500 songs and received 12 gold records. Her hits included "Now is the Hour," "A Tree in the Meadow," "Far Away Places," and "Slippin' Around."

In 1977, Whiting began touring with Rosemary Clooney, Rose Marie, and Helen O'Connell in 4 Girls 4. The tour lasted five years and was a sell-out throughout its duration.

Whiting is now president of the board of directors of the Johnny Mercer Foundation, which supports a wide array of charitable causes and events.

Whooping Cough Vaccine

In 1939, two Michigan Department of Health researchers, Pearl Kendrick and Grace Eldering, developed a vaccine for the dreaded disease. Although the organism that caused whooping cough had been discovered 30 years before, there had been no effective treatment and each year 6,000 Americans, 95 percent of them children under five, had died of the disease. Following distribution of the vaccine in Michigan in 1940, the highly contagious disease was nearly wiped out.

Kendrick (1890–1980) and Eldering (1900–1988) also developed the DPT shot, which combines vaccines for diphtheria, whooping cough, and tetanus.

Both are enshrined in the **Michigan Women's Hall of Fame**.

Willow Run

In February 1941, **Henry Ford** purchased additional land next to acreage he already owned near Ypsilanti. It was in a sleepy village called Willow Run. In April ground was broken for the construction of a **World War II** airplane

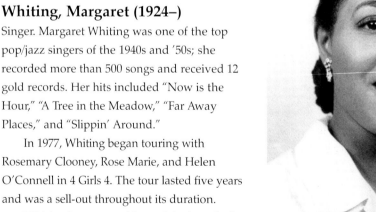

plant that would become the largest factory in the world. **Detroit** architect **Albert Kahn** designed the 3.5 million-square-foot building.

During 1944, its year of peak production, Willow Run produced a B-24 bomber an hour. As many as 44,000 worked at the plant. By the time the Willow Run facility closed in 1945, it had produced more than 8,600 B-24s, more wartime aircraft than any other U.S. factory.

Women's Air Force Service Pilots (WASP)

With a shortage of male pilots during **World War II**, the Army Air Force reluctantly turned to women. Commanding General Henry H. Arnold, who had rejected the idea more than once, agreed to the recruitment of female pilots for noncombat missions.

The Women's Auxiliary Ferrying Squadron (WAFS), directed by Houghton native **Nancy Harkness Love**, was created in September 1942. To qualify, women were required to be high school graduates and have at least 500 hours of flying time. Still, they were restricted to ferrying small trainer and liaison planes, while men, with requirements of only three years of high school and 200 hours of flying, did the heavy lifting. And though male civilians were commissioned after 90 days of training, women continued as civilians.

As Love was organizing WAFS, famed aviatrix Jacqueline Cochran was training female pilots as director of the Women's Flying Training Detachment. Unlike their male counterparts, women in the program received neither aerial gunnery nor formation flying training.

The two groups were combined in August 1943 as the Women's Air Force Service Pilots, with Cochran as director. They proved so skillful, they were commonly requested by commanding officers. Still, as the need to supplement ranks declined, the unit was disbanded in December 1944.

Ferrying and towing was dangerous business, and some of the women were injured or killed. Yet the survivors, as civil service employees, were ineligible for veterans benefits. That changed on November 23, 1977, when President Jimmy Carter signed legislation granting them veteran status. Coincidentally, the Air Force graduated its first class of female pilots the same year. In 1979, WASP veterans received discharge certificates. In 1984 they were awarded **World War II** Victory Medals.

Wonder, Stevie (1950–)

Musician. Blind from birth, Wonder was hailed as a prodigy by the age of 12. His first hit single, "Fingertips," was written before he became a teenager. During his teen years, he churned out hit after hit for **Motown** Records, and when he was 21, he produced two of his own albums, which he used to bargain with Motown for greater creative control. He received it, and during the following five years, he produced four additional albums that are considered to represent his artistic peak.

He is the winner of 19 Grammys and a Grammy Lifetime Achievement Award. He

Stevie Wonder, whose hits include "My Cherie Amour" (1973) and "Master Blaster (Jammin')" (1980).

W

campaigned effectively to have Martin Luther King's birthday declared a national holiday.

Woodcock, Leonard (1911–2000)

Union leader, statesman. The Rhode Island native moved to **Detroit** as a teenager. During the Depression he worked at Borg-Warner Corporation's Detroit Gear and Machine Division. The poor working conditions, low pay, and undignified treatment of workers he found there directed the rest of his life.

In the late 1930s Woodcock conducted classes on union organizing and associated himself with **Walter Reuther**, who, upon taking the helm of the United Auto Workers, made Woodcock his administrative assistant. Woodcock rose through UAW ranks, eventually becoming vice president and director of the union's Aerospace and Aircraft Department. He succeeded Reuther as president in 1970. Reuther had died in a plane crash during contract negotiations with the Big Three automakers. Woodcock stepped in and led the union through its longest nationwide strike.

While still with the UAW, Woodcock played a pivotal role in the establishment of Wayne State University in 1956. Three years later, he was elected president of the university's first board of governors. He served as chair for five of his 11 years on the board. Later, he taught at the **University of Michigan**.

After retiring from the UAW in 1977, he was appointed to head a U.S. mission to Beijing. He was instrumental in negotiating

Leonard Woodcock was America's first ambassador to the People's Republic of China.

U.S.-China diplomatic relations and served for two years as American's first ambassador to the People's Republic of China.

Woodward, Augustus B. (n.d.)

Philosopher and judge. Authorized by President Thomas Jefferson to help rebuild **Detroit** after a fire destroyed the city in 1805, he created a street plan based on the layout of Washington, D.C. Broad boulevards were to run east-west and north-south, with streets intersecting diagonally like the spokes of a wagon. Only a part of the reconstruction utilized his plan. Grand Circus Park and the surrounding streets date back to his plan.

He created an educational outline that ran from primary grades through college and, with **Father Gabriel Richard**, was instrumental in establishing the **University of Michigan**.

The design of Grand Circus Park hearkens back to Augustus B. Woodward's street plan for Detroit.

Works Progress Administration

A great deal of art was produced in Michigan during the New Deal period. Over 40 murals and sculptures, most of them created by the WPA, were installed in U.S. post offices. The **Lansing City Market**, a Walter Speck mural, and several murals at Grosse Pointe High School are among projects that remain today.

World's Largest Bedding Plant Cooperative

The **Kalamazoo** Valley Plant Growers Co-Op began in November 1967 with 18 greenhouse operators who wanted to standardize pricing, packaging, and labeling of their plant products. It grew into the largest co-op of its kind. In addition to growing hundreds of thousands of plants each year, the co-op funds scientific research to improve production.

Murals painted by the Works Progress Administration in the 1940s often reflected the history and politics of the city or town they were designed for.

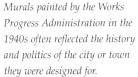

World's Largest Cement Plant

Huron Portland Cement Company opened the Alpena plant in 1908 because of the vast supplies of limestone, gypsum, and shale in the area. Within two years, the company had produced 900,000 barrels. Then, as now, cement was shipped throughout the **Great Lakes** region from Thunder Bay.

World's Largest Cherry Pie

Baked in 1976 on the grounds of a **Traverse City** cement company, the pie measured 14 feet in diameter, weighed seven tons, and contained 4,950 pounds of cherries. Just north of Traverse City, Charlevoix also claims the world's largest cherry pie.

World's Largest Limestone Quarry

Limestone from Michigan comes primarily

World's largest limestone quarry,
at the Michigan Limestone and
Chemical Company

Valley Plant Growers Co-Op
services dealers all over the
country.

W from three major quarries, all on Lake Huron. The Michigan Limestone and Chemical Company, founded in 1910, runs supposedly the world's largest quarry. It supplies limestone to industrial ports throughout the **Great Lakes**.

World War II

The most devastating war in human history, in terms of lost lives and material destruction, it began in 1939 as a conflict between Germany and an Anglo-French coalition and eventually widened to include most of the nations of the world. It resulted from the rise of totalitarian, militaristic regimes in Germany, Italy, and Japan. When it ended in 1945, a new world order dominated by the United States and the USSR had emerged.

More than any previous war, this one blurred the distinction between combatant and noncombatant, expanded the battlefield to include all of the enemy's territory, and established industrial capacity and personnel as the most important elements for winning.

To gain the support of business leaders, the U.S. federal government suspended competitive bidding, offered cost-plus contracts, guaranteed low-cost loans for retooling, and paid huge subsidies for plant construction and equipment. Lured by huge profits, the American **auto industry** made the switch to military production. In 1940, 6,000 planes rolled off **Detroit**'s assembly lines. Production jumped to 47,000 in 1942, and by the end of the war it exceeded 100,000.

World War I set the stage for World War II, leaving Germany highly dissatisfied with territorial losses and reparations payments imposed by the Treaty of Versailles. Frustrated Germany,

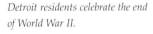
Detroit residents celebrate the end of World War II.

Uncle Sam army recruiting poster

disappointed Italy, and ambitious Japan all adopted forms of dictatorship that made the state supreme and called for expansion at the expense of neighboring countries.

Adolf Hitler first launched aggression with his expansionist drive to annex Austria in March 1938. Benito Mussolini in Italy supported Hitler, and the British and French accepted Hitler's claim that this was an internal German affair. In 1939, Germany occupied all of Czechoslovakia and Italy seized Albania. Germany signed a full military alliance with Italy and a non-aggression pact with the Soviet Union, then invaded Poland on September 1. On September 3, Britain and France declared war on Germany. Soon German troops occupied Belgium and Holland, and by June Germany controlled northern France and the Atlantic Coast. The United States entered the

Draftees say their last goodbyes as civilians during World War II.

News headline proclaiming the end of World War II

war after the Japanese attacked Pearl Harbor on December 7, 1941. The war continued another three and a half years, until Germany surrendered on May 2, 1945, and Japan, devastated by the atom bombs dropped at Hiroshima and Nagasaki, surrendered on August 14.

Among Michigan's war heroes was Joseph Beyrle, a paratrooper with the famed 101st Airborne Division. Beyrle was the first American paratrooper to land in Normandy. Jumping with his regiment on the night before D-Day, he landed on the roof of a church. He was captured two days later, escaped, and was recaptured by the Nazis. They gave his dog tag to a German soldier who was subsequently killed attempting to enter the American lines. Beyrle's parents were notified of his death, and funeral services were held in Muskegon. Later, after more escapes, captures, and a brush

with execution by the Gestapo, Beyrle ended up with a Russian unit commanded by a female officer on the Eastern front. He was the only soldier in the war to fight for both the United States and the Soviet Union.

Wright Museum of African American History, Charles H.

Founded in 1965, the museum offers educational exhibits and programming about African American history and culture. Hours at the museum, 315 E. Warren Avenue, **Detroit**, are Wednesday through Saturday, 9:30 a.m. to 5 p.m., Sunday, 1 to 5 p.m.

WWJ

The first regularly scheduled radio program in the nation was broadcast on August 31 1920, by WWJ, a radio station owned by the *Detroit News*. The station later became WJR.

Yamasaki, Minoru (1912–1986)

Architect. In 1945, he went to **Detroit** as chief of design for a local firm. His design for the McGregor Center, on the Wayne State University campus, won the first honor award of the American Institute of Architects in 1959. He also designed the World Trade Center.

Young, Coleman (1918–1997)

Mayor of Detroit. A shrewd, pugnacious, and frequently controversial politician who made history in 1973 as the first African American to be elected mayor of **Detroit**. His subsequent popularity led him to be re-elected to terms that spanned two decades.

Young, politically liberal but fiscally conservative, he helped Detroit steer clear of bankruptcy in 1981. He worked with the business community to rebuild the downtown and revitalize the city's riverfront with the $500 million **Renaissance Center**, the nation's first privately financed urban development project. He is credited with bringing the city's black population into political power and integrating the municipal work force. But critics saw in him a man who was sometimes profane and rarely apologetic, who often alienated the business community and presided over Detroit's economic decline during the 1970s and 1980s.

Young was born in Tuscaloosa, Alabama. When he was five, his family moved to Detroit, and settled in the ethnically and racially mixed Black Bottom neighborhood. Drafted at the beginning of **World War II**, Young served with the Tuskegee Airmen. After the war, Young returned to Detroit, where he became a union organizer.

Young won his first political race in 1961 when he was elected as a delegate to the state convention that rewrote the Michigan Constitution. In November 1964, he was elected to the Michigan Senate. Re-elected in 1966, Young was voted by Senate Democrats to the position of floor leader. He

Minoru Yamasaki designed One Woodward in Detroit as headquarters for Michigan Consolidated Gas.

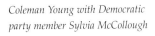
Coleman Young with Democratic party member Sylvia McCollough

was highly regarded as a legislator, both for his service to constituents and his ability to forge coalitions.

Zingerman's Delicatessen

It started in a little house at the edge of **Ann Arbor**'s business district. Twenty years later, it's in the same little house, but it has a big international reputation. From imported olive oils to traditional pastrami on rye, Zingerman's is the place to satisfy that deli craving. Zingerman's was one of only two U.S. venues to be listed in *Food & Wine* magazine's "25 best food markets in the world" in 2004.